STRESS-FREE
ACT®

A Step-by-Step Beginner's Guide to ACT Preparation

The Staff of The Princeton Review

PrincetonReview.com

Penguin
Random
House

The Princeton Review
110 East 42nd Street, 7th Floor
New York, NY 10017

E-mail: editorialsupport@review.com

Published in the United States by Penguin Random House
LLC, New York, and in Canada by Random House of Canada, a
division of Penguin Random
House Ltd., Toronto.

Terms of Service: The Princeton Review Online Companion
Tools ("Student Tools") for retail books are available for only the
two most recent editions of that book. Student Tools may be
activated only once per eligible book purchased for a total of 24
months of access. Activation of Student Tools more than once
per book is in direct violation of these Terms of Service and may
result in discontinuation of access to Student Tools Services.

ISBN: 978-0-525-57151-3
eBook ISBN: 978-0-525-57189-6
ISSN: 2766-9521

ACT is a registered trademark of ACT, Inc, which is not affiliated
with, and does not endorse, this product.

The Princeton Review is not affiliated with Princeton University.

Permission has been granted to reprint portions of the following:

Editor: Orion McBean
Production Editors: Kathy Carter and Sarah Litt
Production Artist: Jason Ullmeyer

Printed in the United States of America.

10 9 8 7 6 5 4 3 2 1

EDITORIAL

Rob Franek, Editor-in-Chief
David Soto, Director of Content Development
Stephen Koch, Student Survey Manager
Deborah Weber, Director of Production
Gabriel Berlin, Production Design Manager
Selena Coppock, Director of Editorial
Aaron Riccio, Senior Editor
Meave Shelton, Senior Editor
Chris Chimera, Editor
Anna Goodlett, Editor
Eleanor Green, Editor
Orion McBean, Editor
Patricia Murphy, Editorial Assistant

RANDOM HOUSE PUBLISHING TEAM

Tom Russell, VP, Publisher
Alison Stoltzfus, Publishing Director
Brett Wright, Senior Editor
Amanda Yee, Associate Managing Editor
Ellen Reed, Production Manager
Suzanne Lee, Designer

For customer service, please
contact editorialsupport@review.
com, and be sure to include:

• full title of the book

• ISBN

• page number

Acknowledgments

Special thanks to Sara Kuperstein, Amy Minster, Cynthia Ward, and Cat Healey for their expert review and contributions to the content of this book.

Thanks also to Anne Goldberg-Baldwin, Aleksei Alferiev, Emily Baumbach, Gabby Budzon, Nicole Cosme, Stacey Cowap, Elizabeth Evangelista, Spencer LeDoux, Jomil London, Scott O'Neal, Danielle Perrini, Sara Soriano, Benjamin Tallon, Jess Thomas, and Jimmy Williams for their contributions to this book.

The Princeton Review would also like to thank Jason Ullmeyer, Kathy Carter, and Sarah Litt for their time and attention to each page.

Special thanks to Adam Robinson, who conceived of and perfected the Joe Bloggs approach to standardized tests, and many other techniques in this book.

Contents

Get More **(Free)** Content
at **PrincetonReview.com/prep**

As easy as **1·2·3**

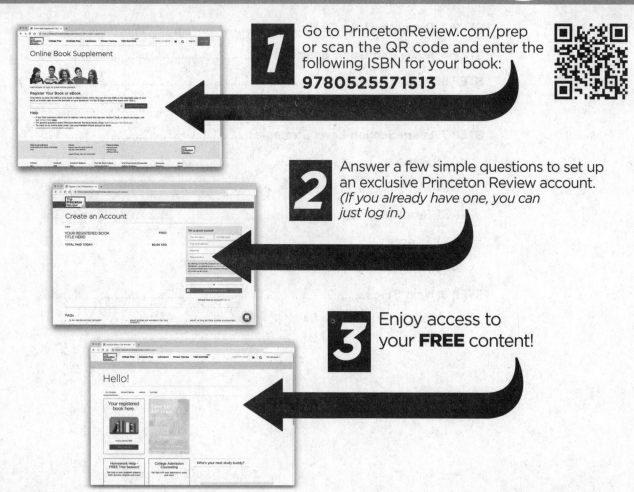

1 Go to PrincetonReview.com/prep or scan the QR code and enter the following ISBN for your book: **9780525571513**

2 Answer a few simple questions to set up an exclusive Princeton Review account. *(If you already have one, you can just log in.)*

3 Enjoy access to your **FREE** content!

Once you've registered, you can...

- Get our take on any recent or pending updates to the ACT

- Take a full-length practice ACT

- Get valuable advice about the college application process, including tips for writing a great essay and where to apply for financial aid

- If you're still choosing between colleges, use our searchable rankings of *The Best 387 Colleges* to find out more information about your dream school.

Need to report a potential **content** issue?

Contact **EditorialSupport@review.com** and include:

- full title of the book
- ISBN
- page number

Need to report a **technical** issue?

Contact **TPRStudentTech@review.com** and provide:

- your full name
- email address used to register the book
- full book title and ISBN
- Operating system (Mac/PC) and browser (Firefox, Safari, etc.)

INTRODUCTION

What is the ACT?
Do I need to take it?
How do I sign up?
How long is the test?
WHAT AM I GOING TO DO???

If the above freak-out sounds familiar, relax! We're here to help. You probably have a lot of questions about the ACT, most or all of which are answered in this book. The ACT can be an intimidating test, and there's a lot to know about it, but let's take it one step at a time. This book will help you break your ACT prep into eight easy-to-manage steps and put it into the context of your own personal college application journey. Let's start with the most basic question:

Do I need to take the ACT, and what is it for?

The ACT and the SAT are two different tests used to determine admission to colleges and universities in the United States (and some schools internationally). These days, any school that requires a standardized test will allow you to take either the SAT or the ACT, so which one you take comes down to your preference. Since you've picked up this book, we'll assume that you have chosen the ACT. That being said, if you take a practice test and find you really hate the ACT, consider trying a practice SAT to see whether you like the SAT any better.

Although not all schools require you to take the SAT or ACT, enough of them do. Therefore, if you are planning to apply to college, you will most likely need to take one of them. Even when schools do not require one of these tests, a great ACT score can still help you get in and earn scholarships.

> If you decide to switch to the SAT, check out *Stress-Free SAT* or *SAT Prep*.

What does the ACT mean for me?

An ACT score in and of itself is meaningless. It isn't an indication of your intelligence, your worth as a human being, or even your academic skills. If you don't score as high as you'd like on the ACT, it does not mean that you aren't smart or capable. The ACT tests one thing: your ability to take the ACT. If you are very good at the skills that are tested on the ACT, then you will do very well on the test. If you haven't yet mastered the ACT skills, you may have trouble with the test, even if you have great academic skills. Let's take a look at some of the items that are tested on the ACT and some that are not.

Tested on the ACT	Not Tested on the ACT
Choosing the correct answer from 4 or 5 options	Your intelligence
Answering many questions in a short amount of time	Your creativity, passion, attitude, and self-worth
Knowing a handful of grammar and punctuation rules	How well you will do, academically, in college
Using a little of the math you've learning in school, and maybe some you haven't	How much effort you put into your schoolwork
Answering questions about a reading passage	The depth of your understanding of various topics and your ability to explain yourself on those topics
Answering questions about science-related charts and texts	Your abilities in subjects that don't appear on the ACT
Writing a 40-minute opinion essay	Most of what you've learned in school about english, math, reading, science, and writing

Look again at what is tested on the ACT. Are those the same things you learned in school? Unless you went to ACT school (then why are you reading this book?), the answer is "NO!" That's why you shouldn't compare the ACT to how well you do in school. You've learned much more in school than what is tested on the ACT, and some of the skills you need for the ACT simply aren't taught in school at all.

So, what are you to do? Learn the skills you need for the ACT. It all starts with a change to your mindset. We aren't going to teach you everything there is to know about writing, math, literature, and science. To get a great ACT score, you only need to master the topics that actually appear on the test and the strategies needed to approach them.

What is a great ACT score?

Well, it all depends on where you plan to apply to college. A great score at one school might not be a great score at another school. There is no such thing as a "passing" score on the ACT, but there is such thing as an "average" score. For example, the incoming freshman class at every college has an average ACT score that you can use to determine how your own ACT score compares. We'll go into the ACT structure and scoring in Step 3. For now, just keep in mind that the ACT is scored from 4 to 36, and the main score is an average of four multiple-choice sections. For reference, the national average ACT score is about 21.

With that said, let's get begin with Step 1, Researching Schools. As we said above, you'll need to compare your starting ACT score with the score you need for the schools you personally plan to apply to. So, how do you figure out what score you need? Read on to find out!

STEP 1: Research Schools

Throughout your ACT prep, remember your ultimate goal: to gain admission into the college *of your choice*. Every student needs a target score to aim for, but it's impossible to know what you are aiming for until you find out what score you need for the schools you plan to apply to.

Let's start by understanding why people go to college. There are several different degrees you can earn at a college or university. The first type of degree, after a high school diploma, is an **Associate's degree**, which typically takes two years of full-time study to earn, often at a community college or technical school. Some jobs that may require only an Associate's degree are physical therapist assistant, dental hygienist, paralegal, and veterinary technician. The next type of degree is a four-year **Bachelor's degree**, which is most often referred to as a "college diploma." You don't need to earn an Associate's degree first in order to earn a Bachelor's degree, although some four-year programs will award you one after the first two years. After earning a Bachelor's degree, you may choose to attend graduate school if you are pursuing a career that requires an advanced degree, such as a **Master's degree** or a **Ph.D**.

In addition to the different types of degrees, there are also different types of higher education institutions.

Community College/Junior College

These schools are generally open to everyone. They are often the least expensive college option, especially if you're a local resident. Some offer Bachelor's degrees, and all offer Associate's degrees. You don't need an ACT or a SAT score to get in, but your standardized test score can help with placement into higher-level courses.

Technical/Trade/Vocational School

These schools are designed to prepare you for a job in a certain field. Instead of a degree, students typically earn a certificate in a trade (such as cosmetology or emergency medical response). Programs focus students' time on the skills they need for a future career in their chosen trade. Like community colleges, most are open enrollment, so test scores generally aren't required.

College

In the U.S., the word "college" is commonly used for just about any level of study after high school. When *College* is part of the name of a school, though, it generally means that the school is smaller than a university, has more limited courses, and offers Bachelor's degrees but not many graduate degrees. A liberal arts college allows or requires students to study a wide variety of subjects, not just one. Most colleges require ACT or SAT scores.

University

A university is typically a larger school, and it may contain multiple colleges (such as the College of Engineering or the College of Medicine). Universities typically offer graduate programs in addition to Bachelor's, and sometimes Associate's, degrees. These schools offer the broadest range of classes and generally require ACT or SAT scores.

Public? Private? For-profit?

Public colleges and universities are partially funded by states, so they tend to be less expensive, especially if you live in that state. Private schools are more expensive but may offer more services to students, and their costs typically don't vary based on where you are from. For-profit institutions are run like businesses. This does not necessarily mean they can't provide a quality education, but not all are accredited, which means they may not be able to offer you a real degree for your money. Check to make sure any institution you're interested in is accredited to offer the degree you're seeking.

One great way to save money is to attend a local community or junior college for two years and take the general required courses such as English and Math. Then, transfer to a college or university for classes in your desired major to earn your Bachelor's degree. Speak with a counselor first to ensure that your credits will transfer.

As you can see, if you want to go to trade school or a community college, you can stop here because you won't need to worry about the ACT. If you plan to apply to a four-year college or university, however, let's take a look at how to research which ones to apply to.

Start by considering what you are looking for in a college. For instance, do you want to attend a school near where you currently live or in a different state or region? What career do you hope to pursue, and what kind of degree is required? How much can you afford to pay for college?

You may have an idea about some things you are looking for and not others. That's okay! For example, it's completely fine if you're not sure yet what you would like to study in college. Here are a few ways to find information about schools that might be a good fit.

- Both the Princeton Review https://www.princetonreview.com/college-search and the College Board https://www.bigfuture.collegeboard.org/college-search have College Search tools on their websites that allow you to identify the criteria you're looking for. Then you'll be shown profiles of schools that match your preferences.

- *The Best 387 Colleges* is a Princeton Review book with college profiles and rankings by category, including quotes from actual students.

- Talk to a college counselor. If you have a school counselor, schedule a meeting to discuss schools that might be a good fit for you. You can also find a private college counselor at the Princeton Review here: https://www.princetonreview.com/college-admissions/college-counseling

What's the best college?

You will often see lists that claim to broadly rank colleges against each other, but these lists don't mean much. Every college has its pros and cons. Generally, the colleges that are considered to be the strongest academically naturally tend to be the most selective schools (those that accept the lowest percentage of applicants). However, you should never compare one school to another based on an arbitrary ranking. One school could be superior in one program, while another could have a different program that is stronger. Above all, what matters is whether the school is a good fit for you. The fact that someone might tell you, "This is the best school!" does *not* mean it is the best school for you. For instance, if you hate sports, a school where most students love to participate in athletic events is probably not going to be the best fit, no matter how great its academics are. Likewise, if you are hoping to join a fraternity or sorority, a school that doesn't offer those organizations isn't for you.

What should I look for when I view college profiles?

Start to think about your personality and learning style as well as what you hope to do while in college. Here are just some considerations:

- What programs does the school offer?

- Where is it located, and what is the town or city like?

- How much does it cost? How much financial aid is offered?

- What do students do for fun—sports, Greek life, arts events, parties, student organizations?

- Do most students live on campus or in off-campus apartments? Do many students commute from home?

- How big is the school? How big are classes?

- What is the typical student like? Would I fit in?

If you like what you see from the college profile, there are lots of ways to get more information. Here are a few:

- Look at the information provided on the school's website.

- Request a brochure or other information to be sent to you through the mail.

- Check out the school's social media pages.

- Read blogs or forums written by students.

- Reach out to someone you may know who attends the school.

- Check the admissions office's website for events near you.

- Schedule a campus visit.

Should I visit campus, and if so, what should I look for?

You may be surprised to hear that visiting campus isn't just about seeing what the buildings look like. After all, you can get that from a brochure! If possible, it's best to visit when school is in session rather than during spring or summer break. This will give you a better idea of what the campus is actually like for students.

During your visit, try to determine how you would fit in on campus. In addition to tours, some colleges offer overnights with students or opportunities to sit in on classes. Those are great ways to get a sense of what the students are like and how the school fits with your preferences. Are students socializing and having fun, or are they keeping to themselves? Do they seem passionate about academics, or are they more focused on extracurricular activities? Try to get a feel for the campus community, since that is what you'll be surrounded by as a student. A campus visit can also be a good opportunity to introduce yourself to the admissions office if you are strongly interested in the school—consider signing up for an interview.

The College Application Process

We've established that ACT scores are one component of your college applications, but luckily, they are far from the only thing colleges look at. Let's take a look at the typical parts of a college application.

The #1 thing you should know about applying to college is that every school is different. Unfortunately, we can't provide detailed universal advice because each school has its own admissions requirements. Use the following information as a general guideline, but be sure to check the admissions website for each individual school to see what is required.

Application

It might seem obvious, but all colleges have some sort of application you need to fill out with information such as your name, address, high school, parent and sibling information, and extracurricular activities. Many colleges these days use what's called the Common Application, which is a website that allows you to fill out your information one time and have it sent to any participating colleges you apply to. The Common App is typically available to applicants on August 1, so you'll have plenty of time to gather your information and work on it. Most likely, you'll need to sit down with a parent or guardian since you'll need some information from them. For schools that don't use the Common App, the admissions website will provide information on how to access the application.

High school transcript

Your transcript is an official document from your high school that is like a report card for your entire high school career. It shows all of the classes you took and your final grade in each one. It may also include your grade point average (GPA) and class ranking. To make arrangements for submitting your transcript, you will generally contact your school counselor or college counselor and let that person know which colleges you are applying to. Your school will then send the transcripts either electronically or by mail to the colleges. Alternatively, the school might provide a sealed transcript in an envelope for you to send yourself. Either way, you most likely won't see the actual transcript.

If you are home-schooled, go to high school outside the United States, or attend a school without traditional classes and grades, check each college's admissions website to see what it says about those special circumstances. If you can't find the information you need, just call or email the admissions office.

Essay

You have probably heard of a "college essay." The good news is that you can typically write just one essay to send to every college—it is usually not specific to each school. The essay is your opportunity to showcase your writing skills but also to show the admissions officers your personality and what is important to you. The Common App provides several different broad essay topics (such as "Describe a problem you've solved or would like to solve" or "Reflect on a time when you questioned or challenged a belief or idea"), and there is also an option to write on the topic of your choice.

Test scores

The organization that handles the ACT will send your scores directly to the colleges you provide. If you take the ACT multiple times, you'll have the option to send the scores from all the dates or just some of them. Many colleges offer a "superscore," which means if you send the scores from multiple dates, they will take your highest overall English score, highest overall Math score, and so on to create the highest total composite score. If you do single-section retesting when it becomes available (more on that in Step 3), ACT will provide this superscore. Other colleges require you to send all of your scores or just those from one date of your choosing, so check each school's website for what it requires. Some schools don't require test scores, but they'll still accept them—and great scores can boost your chances of being accepted. Better yet, some schools offer significant scholarships just for certain ACT scores, which can be a great reason to spend some time working on your ACT skills. Much more on ACT scores in Step 3!

Recommendations

Most colleges require you to send two or three recommendations from adults who aren't related to you. Some schools also specify that a certain number of the recommendations must be from teachers. Other than teachers, you may be able to ask for a recommendation from a coach, an employer, or any other adult who knows you and your abilities. Again, check each school for its process, but the person writing you a recommendation may do it through the Common App or the school's website, or they may simply write the recommendation and give it to you or your school counselor to send to the school.

> Some of the components you see here may be recommended, but not required, by some schools. In general, it's best to include any parts of the application that are recommended, in order to give yourself the best possible chance at being admitted.

Other materials

Those are the most universal requirements, but here are a few more that may be required, recommended, or just possible to include in your application.

- Portfolio or audition if you're applying for a program in the arts

- Graded paper from a high school class—so it's worth holding on to those well-written papers

- SAT Subject Test scores

- Interview, either with the admissions office or with a graduate of the school

- Grades from the first semester of senior year. If you have a great semester, you can have your school send those grades separately if they are released after the admissions deadline.

- Supplemental essays or short-answer questions that are specific to the individual school

- Résumé—if you have one and feel it better highlights your work or volunteer experiences than the space available on the application does

Most college applications are due in January, but if you're set on one top choice, you may be able to apply Early Decision or Early Action, which usually has a November or December deadline. Some schools offer rolling admissions, which means you can apply at any time of the year.

Where does the ACT score fit in?

Some schools place more importance on the ACT score than others do. In general, a large state school looks at your ACT score and GPA first and foremost. Smaller schools also care about those numbers, but compared to bigger schools, they typically place more of an emphasis on your essay, recommendations, and other materials that show who you are as a person. It's also worth noting that while colleges generally focus on your composite or overall ACT score, some programs may have more specific requirements. For instance, if you're applying to an Engineering program, you may have to hit a minimum ACT Math score. Do your research!

Determining Your Target Score

Once you have started researching schools that might be a good fit for you, start to think about your target score—that is, a score that you would be happy sending to those schools. The first step is finding the average ACT score of the recently admitted freshman class for each school. Look on the school's admissions website for this info or give them a call and ask. Then, consider the strength of the rest of your application. If you know you have taken challenging classes, have excellent grades, and expect to have strong recommendations, you might decide that it's okay if your ACT score is a little lower than the school's average. On the other hand, if the other parts of your application aren't very strong, you might decide you need to push for an above-average ACT score to balance them out. In Steps 3 and 4, we'll talk about how to make your goals more specific. For now, make sure you have an idea of what composite score you're aiming for, and then take a practice test to help you figure out how much work you need to put in.

Paying for College

How much does college cost?

We mentioned earlier that local public community colleges are typically the cheapest option: on average, they cost about $3,000 to $5,000 per year (but remember, most don't offer Bachelor's degrees). Likewise, in-state public schools tend to be relatively inexpensive, as they are partially funded by their states; such schools on average charge approximately $10,000 per year in tuition. You'll pay about double that for an out-of-state public college. Private colleges cost the most, with an average annual tuition of just over $35,000 and some schools charging $50,000 or more per year. By the way, that price does *not* include the cost of room and board (housing and meals), healthcare, or textbooks!

Those numbers may sound unbelievable, but it's worth recognizing that most students receive some form of financial aid. This means they aren't on the hook for the full tuition amount. In fact, schools with higher tuition rates may even have more financial aid options available because those who can afford to pay the sticker price help subsidize the costs for those who can't. To make more sense of this, let's take a look at financial aid.

What is financial aid?

Financial aid, which helps you pay for college, has nothing to do with your grades or any other merits (in the next section we'll look at how your hard work can get you money for college via scholarships). Financial aid is based on how much money your family has and how much your college charges for tuition. Your family must complete a U.S. Department of Education form called the FAFSA (Free Application for Federal Student Aid), which will determine your family's Expected Family Contribution (EFC). This is the amount of money the government thinks your family can pay for your college in a given year, based on income, savings, and other financial information. The colleges you apply to will determine your annual Cost of Attendance (COA), which includes tuition, fees, and room and board if you'll be living on campus. Then, the colleges will use the difference between your EFC and COA to award financial aid. Let's take a look at an example.

Let's say your family fills out the FAFSA, and the government decides your parents can afford to pay $15,000 this year for your college. Here are the schools you get accepted to:

Local Public University (LPU), COA $12,000—You aren't awarded any financial aid, because the government thinks your parents can afford at least $12,000 per year.

Out-of-State Public University (OSPU), COA $25,000—This school may award you up to $10,000 in financial aid, because the government thinks your parents can afford only $15,000 per year, and the school costs $25,000.

Private College (PC), COA $55,000—This school may award you up to $40,000 in financial aid, as that is the difference between your EFC and the COA.

You may notice we use the word *may* above. A college or university does not have to award financial aid to you, unless it has made a commitment to meet 100% of demonstrated need. Colleges with this attribute promise to award you the full difference between your EFC and the COA. When you view college profiles, you can look to see whether each school meets 100% of demonstrated need.

Types of Financial Aid

Before you get too excited about all the money coming your way, you should know that financial aid may have stipulations. If you qualify, you'll receive an offer along with your college acceptance letter. That offer will detail how the money will be awarded to you, and it may come in any combination of grants, loans, and work-study. Let's take a look at what those are.

GRANTS

Grants are the best kind of financial aid—you receive money toward your tuition and other expenses with no strings attached. These funds never need to be paid back—it's free money. Grants can come from various levels of government or from the college or university.

FEDERAL LOANS

You probably have a sense of what federal loans are: you receive money toward college, but you'll have to pay back the loans starting six months after you graduate. There are also two key types of loans, which have to do this the way in which they accrue interest. (That is, you'll ultimately pay back more than you borrowed.) With subsidized loans, the government pays the interest on your loans until the six-month grace period ends, at which point you become responsible for making payments. For unsubsidized loans, interest accrues while you are attending school, so you'll be starting out your payments with a larger balance than the amount you borrowed.

Clearly, subsidized loans are better, but they have a maximum limit, so some students may need to take out both types of loans. It's worth noting that subsidized loans are available only for students with demonstrated need. However, some students don't qualify for financial aid and others need to make up a gap between the Cost of Attendance and the amount of financial aid they receive. Such students are still able to take out unsubsidized loans.

FEDERAL WORK-STUDY

As the name implies, work-study is a type of financial aid that you have to work for. This program qualifies you for a certain amount of money that you can earn through part-time employment, either on campus (such as in the library or dining hall) or in the community (often for a nonprofit or community organization). Of course, you can also find your own job and make money unrelated to the work-study award. However, some programs may be available only to students who qualify for Federal Work-Study, and other jobs may prioritize those students. Like any other job, you'll earn an hourly wage, and you can apply your paycheck to your tuition or simply keep the money for daily expenses.

What if...

There are a couple of big concerns you might have here. First off, what if the government decides your family can afford a certain amount, but your family can't or doesn't want to pay that amount? Or what if a college doesn't meet 100% of your demonstrated need? For instance, let's say OSPU (from page 12) offers you only $5,000 of the $10,000 gap between your EFC and the school's COA. In either of these cases, you may decide to choose a more affordable school, or you may have to come up with another way to pay for college. Perhaps you can save money from a job before college starts—or even take a gap year to earn more before you begin school. It's also possible to take out private loans, rather than government ones, but this can be risky because private loans typically have higher interest rates and aren't as flexible when it comes to repayment.

Merit Aid

Another way to help cover the gap is by applying for and winning a scholarship. Whereas financial aid doesn't take into consideration your grades or any personal attributes—it's related only to your ability to pay—scholarships do. There are many sources of scholarships, and they generally relate to your merit, which could include your grades, test scores, community involvement, leadership, and other areas of excellence, such as athletics. And while some scholarships may take your financial need into account, some don't. For instance, in our example from earlier, even though you don't qualify for financial aid from LPU, that school could still offer you a scholarship if the admissions officers really want you to attend because of all of your great attributes.

You may receive a scholarship from a college you have been accepted to, or you may apply for a scholarship from an outside organization. You may also have to meet certain criteria for a scholarship, such as living in a certain region, having a certain ethnic background, or pursuing a career in a particular field. To apply for a scholarship, you will typically have to fill out an application, and some scholarships also require you to write an essay or complete a project such as a video. A scholarship could be as low as $50 (every little bit helps!) or as high as what's commonly called a full ride (your entire tuition along with room and board). Some scholarships give you money only once, while others are for all four years—assuming you continue to meet the conditions of the scholarship.

HOW DO I FIND OUT ABOUT SCHOLARSHIPS?

During the college admissions process, you'll either automatically qualify for a scholarship, based on a school's preset criteria, or you may be manually selected for a scholarship if the school wants to offer you an additional incentive to attend. When you're researching colleges, you should be able to find information about scholarships on each school's website. For instance, some schools automatically offer scholarships based on an applicant's SAT or ACT scores and/or GPA (the average of your grades from high school). It's worth looking into that because a few months of test prep could pay off big time in the form of a significant reduction to your college costs. The PSAT in 11th grade can also qualify you for a National Merit Scholarship if you score in the top 1% of students in your state.

For scholarships outside a college or university, start by asking your school counselor, who may be aware of local scholarships that you may be eligible for. You can also find websites with lists of thousands of different scholarships, and you can filter them to find the ones you qualify for.

You can apply for as many scholarships as you want. Just remember that there are many other students applying for them, so you may be best off focusing your time on the scholarships for which you feel your background makes you especially well suited.

A Few Words of Advice

Be careful not to mortgage your future on your present-day desires. Think about how much debt each offer on the table would leave you with, and measure that against how much you're likely to be making from your chosen career. On average, college graduates make about $50,000 a year and owe about $30,000. With interest, that loan can take a considerable amount of time to pay off, especially if you also have to pay for rent and other necessities. (This also assumes you'll immediately land a job.) There are millions of successful people who graduated from state universities and other non-brand-name schools, so finding an affordable good-fit school may be more prudent than attending one that will leave you drowning in debt.

When you get your acceptance letters and financial aid offers, really consider what makes the most financial sense. Working hard in college and taking advantage of every opportunity that's available to you will often do far more to set you up for future success than name recognition of a particular college.

STEP 2: Take a Practice Test

Now that you have some idea of where you may want to apply for college and what kind of ACT score you will need, it's time to get more familiar with the ACT. Namely, it's time to find out what your starting score is: the score that you'd get if you took the ACT right now. Knowing your starting score will help you determine how much work you need to put in to achieve the score you need when you take the official ACT. You might find that you are already scoring within the range that you need, and you don't need to prep at all. On the other hand, you might find that you will need to put in a fair amount of effort to achieve the score you need. Either way, it is extremely helpful to know your starting score.

In this chapter, you will find a sample of each type of question you can expect to see on the ACT. If you have not yet taken a full practice ACT, you can try out these sample passages and questions to get a sense of what topics are tested and how comfortable you are with them. Alternatively, Steps 6 and 7 of this book provide you with some great ACT strategies, so you may also choose not to try the sample passages and questions until after you have learned our strategies. The choice is yours!

Regardless of whether you try the samples now or later, it's a good idea to take a full-length practice test now. It's the only way to determine your starting score. You can find a free practice test on the official ACT website, www.act.org. If you want to save printer ink, check with your school counselor's office—some offices have a registration booklet that contains the practice test from ACT's website. Alternatively, if you register this book online following the instructions under *Get More (Free) Content* on page vi, you can access our free ACT practice test.

Sometimes students feel intimidated to take a practice test or feel they need to do some preparation first. Keep in mind that a practice test is just that—practice. There are no stakes whatsoever. No one will ever see your practice test score, and if you bomb it, who cares? It's also not necessary to prep before taking your first practice ACT. When you take the practice test, you will find out the question types and topics that were easy for you, as well as those that were hard for you. If you know what aspects of the test you find easy or hard, you can focus your time around your *own* strengths and weaknesses and maximize your ability to get the score you need. If you prep before determining what those easy and hard things are, you might not use your time as efficiently. Steps 4 and 5 of this book will help you determine how best to prep based on your practice test scores.

You can check out the following mini test to get an idea of a real ACT. However, to get the most from this book, you should take a full-length practice test before moving on to Steps 3 through 5.

Mini Practice Test

Remember!

The following mini test of sample questions are set up like a real ACT test. The sections are reflective of the type of content you will see on the test but with fewer questions. To help you become familiar with each section, we've included the actual instructions you will see on test day. Make sure to read them now so you don't have to waste time when taking the real test.

ENGLISH TEST

DIRECTIONS: In the five passages that follow, certain words and phrases are underlined and numbered. In the right-hand column, you will find alternatives for the underlined part. In most cases, you are to choose the one that correctly expresses the idea, makes the statement appropriate for standard written English, or is worded most consistently with the style and tone of the passage as a whole. If you think the original version is correct, choose "NO CHANGE." In some cases, you will find in the right-hand column a question about the underlined part. You are to choose the correct answer to the question.

You will also find questions about a section of the passage, or about the passage as a whole. These questions do not refer to an underlined portion of the passage, but rather are identified by a number or numbers in a box.

For each question, choose the alternative you consider correct and fill in the corresponding oval on your answer document. Read each passage through once before you begin to answer the questions that accompany it. For many of the questions, you must read several sentences beyond the question to determine the answer. Be sure that you have read far enough ahead each time you choose an alternative.

PASSAGE I

Axolotl Salamanders

Lake Xochimilco in southern Mexico City is one in the only places left of the world where an unusual creature nicknamed the "walking fish" lives.

1. **A.** NO CHANGE
   B. of the only places left in
   C. of the only places left of
   D. in the only places left in

The amphibian, a salamander called the axolotl—looks like a fish with small legs. Rarely seen in the

2. **F.** NO CHANGE
   G. amphibian—a salamander called the axolotl
   H. amphibian a salamander called the axolotl—
   J. amphibian—a salamander called the axolotl—

3 .

GO ON TO THE NEXT PAGE.

wild, axolotls have been found in Mexico for nearly [3] 10,000 years.

One of the most remarkable characteristics of the axolotl is its lack of metamorphosis. Most salamanders undergo metamorphic changes, such as growing limbs, developing teeth, and losing gills, that allow them to live on land. In fact, the ability to metamorphose is commonly found in amphibian species that begin life in the water but eventually move to land. Axolotls are unusual; remaining [4] aquatic throughout their entire lives. They maintain their juvenile, aquatic features due to a lack of thyroid-stimulating hormone, which, in humans, contributes to how quickly people metabolize food. [5] Without this hormone, metamorphosis does not happen.

3. A. NO CHANGE
   B. wild. Axolotls
   C. wild, and axolotls
   D. wild and axolotls

4. F. NO CHANGE
   G. unusual, remaining
   H. unusual. Remaining
   J. unusual and remaining

5. The writer is considering deleting the following clause from the preceding sentence (adjusting the punctuation as needed):

   > which, in humans, contributes to how quickly people metabolize food

   Given that the information is accurate, should the writer make this deletion?

   A. Yes, because the information is largely unrelated to the paragraph's main idea.
   B. Yes, because the information can be inferred from information stated in the previous paragraph.
   C. No, because the information explains why axolotls do not produce thyroid stimulating hormone.
   D. No, because the information explains why axolotls are able to spend their entire lives in freshwater lakes.

GO ON TO THE NEXT PAGE.

Avoiding metamorphosis may allow axolotls to survive in a wider range of environments, particularly those with low levels of iodine. Juvenile salamanders, in general, can live on a lower quantity and quality of food than metamorphosed adults can. By <u>boycotting</u>
6
metamorphosis, axolotls can ensure maintenance

of <u>its'</u> juvenile traits and live in environments
7

<u>of nutrients</u> with lower levels and little competition from
8
other salamander species.

<u>While axolotls are not nearly as long as other</u>
9
<u>salamanders,</u> many scientists seem most excited about the
9
axolotl's regeneration abilities. After sustaining an

6. F. NO CHANGE
G. isolating
H. ignoring
J. avoiding

7. A. NO CHANGE
B. its
C. their
D. it's

8. The best placement for the underlined portion would be:
F. where it is now.
G. after the word *live*.
H. after the word *levels*.
J. after the word *species* (and before the period).

9. Given that all the choices are accurate, which one most effectively leads the reader from the preceding paragraph to the new paragraph?
A. NO CHANGE
B. While scientists are working to develop conservation plans for these salamanders,
C. Although these salamanders are only found in two freshwater lakes in Mexico City,
D. Although research on axolotls' lack of metamorphosis is of great interest to the scientific community,

GO ON TO THE NEXT PAGE.

injury, they can regenerate limbs and return to life as
normal. Axolotls can restore lost appendages in just a few
weeks, and eyes, heart tissue, and nervous systems can
redevelop over a few months. Because this rare ability
might be useful for medical research, scientists have
carefully reviewed these critically endangered amphibians.

    In addition to their regeneration abilities, axolotls are
over 1,000 times more resistant to cancer than mammals
are and avoid many diseases that challenge humanity.
Besides, there's a reason these salamanders are well

suited of scientific research. Unfortunately, the axolotl

population in the wild is declining rapidly their main
threats are pollution and the introduction of invasive
species. Researchers are

10. **F.** NO CHANGE
    G. regrow limbs to build new body parts and return
    H. regrow limbs through regeneration to return
    J. regenerate to full form once more, returning

11. **A.** NO CHANGE
    B. studied
    C. deliberated
    D. measured

12. **F.** NO CHANGE
    G. For example,
    H. Clearly,
    J. With this in mind,

13. **A.** NO CHANGE
    B. for
    C. in
    D. with

14. **F.** NO CHANGE
    G. rapidly; their main threats are pollution
    H. rapidly, their main threats are pollution
    J. rapidly, their main threats are pollution,

GO ON TO THE NEXT PAGE.

casually considering building rock "shelters" to help
protect this special amphibian.
₁₅

15. The writer wants to emphasize that conservationists are
concerned about the declining axolotl population and are
taking immediate steps to preserve them. Which choice
best accomplishes that goal?

A. NO CHANGE
B. sporadically thinking about
C. working urgently to build
D. slowly developing

PASSAGE II

Exploring the High Line Park

In the mid-1930s, elevated trains on Manhattan's West
Side Elevated Railroad were a staple of New York
commerce, carrying essential items like produce and meat
to local businesses. By the 1980s, however, traffic had
ceased completely on the West Side Line. With tracks and
footing, remaining intact from the line the seemingly
₁₆
unusable elevated structure became an urban eyesore for

16. F. NO CHANGE
G. footing—remaining intact from the line—
H. footing (remaining intact from the line)
J. footing remaining intact from the line,

GO ON TO THE NEXT PAGE.

nearby residents. [17] The elevated track has since been transformed into a park called the High Line. History lovers may enjoy connecting the park's functional past to its innovative present, as they imagine riding a train along the now-repurposed track that lies beneath their feet.

The park is also frequented by urban nature enthusiasts, people seeking a unique outdoor experience in the middle of a metropolitan city.
[18]

[1] At the south end of the park is an overlook, visitors get a one-of-a-kind view of Manhattan's busy Meatpacking District. [2] The High Line stretches lengthwise for 1.45 miles and is filled with hundreds of species of carefully curated plants. [3] Positioned above Manhattan's urban streets, therefore, the elevated park provides visitors with both a bird's-eye view of NYC life and a chance to connect with nature. [4] Accordingly, the

17. Which of the following true statements, if added here, would provide the best transition between the story of the park's history and the description of its present purpose?

   A. The features of the elevated track today are incredible; the track is simultaneously a man-made and an environmental marvel.

   B. Those not wishing to visit the park on top of the track may still gaze in awe at the structure from the streets below.

   C. The structure remained untouched for years, and by the late 1990s, wild plants had grown over it, creating a pop of greenery in a concrete jungle.

   D. Before the West Side Line opened, trains in the area ran on the street and had caused 540 collisions with pedestrians by 1910.

18. F. NO CHANGE
   G. are to seek
   H. who were to seek
   J. who sought

19. A. NO CHANGE
   B. overlook, from which
   C. overlook, there
   D. overlook; from which

20. F. NO CHANGE
   G. as a result,
   H. contrastingly,
   J. DELETE the underlined portion.

GO ON TO THE NEXT PAGE.

views from within the park are exciting and diverse.
21

[5] Next to the overlook, a quiet woodland area eliminates
22

its visitors from the bustle below. 23

Plants and trees span the length of the park and
24
intertwine, with scenic overlooks, seating areas,
24

and art exhibits; shops and eateries are found at each end
25
of the High Line. Visitors can walk down the

lengthy boardwalk lined with lush greenery and then
26
browse sustainable food options. From below, pedestrians

21. **A.** NO CHANGE
    B. this park that spans almost two miles
    C. this elevated, plant-filled park
    D. the park that is in Manhattan

22. **F.** NO CHANGE
    G. quarantines
    H. shelters
    J. covers

23. For the sake of logic and coherence of this paragraph, Sentence 1 should be placed:

    A. where it is now.
    B. after Sentence 2.
    C. after Sentence 4.
    D. after Sentence 5.

24. **F.** NO CHANGE
    G. park, and intertwine,
    H. park and intertwine
    J. park, and intertwine

25. Which of the following alternatives to the underlined portion would NOT be acceptable?

    A. exhibits. Shops
    B. exhibits, shops
    C. exhibits, and shops
    D. exhibits; in addition, shops

26. Which choice emphasizes the length of the boardwalk with the clearest and most specific reference to scale?

    F. NO CHANGE
    G. impressive
    H. three-block-long
    J. north-to-south

GO ON TO THE NEXT PAGE.

get a glimpse of train tracks, stable footings, and other

remnants from that time.
                27

Today, the tranquil greenery of the High Line provides

what looks as an urban oasis.
     28

New York native Pauline Frommer has described it as the
               29
city's "coolest park." People across the globe continue

to visit the New York City High Line to experience a park
                                     30
with truly unique origins.

27. **A.** NO CHANGE
    B. when it was industrial.
    C. the park's industrial past.
    D. the park's ownership.

28. **F.** NO CHANGE
    G. can be seen as
    H. is seen as it were as
    J. occasionally is understood as kind of

29. Given that all the choices are accurate, which one provides the clearest and most relevant information at this point in the essay?

    A. NO CHANGE
    B. Co-owner of a prominent company
    C. A well-known person named
    D. Travel guide publisher

30. **F.** NO CHANGE
    G. that experiences
    H. as it experiences
    J. continue experiencing

GO ON TO THE NEXT PAGE.

PASSAGE III

A Day in the Life

After being invited to the University of California, Irvine's Center for the Neurobiology of Learning and Memory, Jill Price <u>astounded</u> scientists with her
₃₁
exceptional memory, including her capacity to remember with great detail almost every day of her life. This

<u>ability, remembering detailed accounts of autobiographical</u>
₃₂
<u>events</u> is called Highly Superior Autobiographical
₃₂
Memory (HSAM). People with HSAM can also recall information about particular events that occurred during their lifetimes.

HSAM is extremely rare, with fewer than 100 individuals diagnosed throughout history. This uniqueness makes HSAM <u>even more appealing</u> to memory
₃₃
researchers. Studying HSAM could reveal more about

how memories are <u>created, scientists</u> think there may be a
₃₄
physical explanation for HSAM. Neurobiologist Aurora LePort and her colleagues found subtle differences in the size and structure of certain brain areas in people with HSAM.

31. Which choice most clearly indicates the scientists' response to Price's memory abilities?
- **A.** NO CHANGE
- **B.** came up to
- **C.** desired to please
- **D.** approached

32. F. NO CHANGE
- **G.** ability—remembering detailed accounts of autobiographical events,
- **H.** ability—remembering detailed accounts of autobiographical events—
- **J.** ability, remembering detailed accounts of autobiographical events—

33. A. NO CHANGE
- **B.** absolutely neat
- **C.** completely awesome
- **D.** a complicated occurrence that introduces an interesting puzzle

34. F. NO CHANGE
- **G.** created and scientists
- **H.** created and those scientists
- **J.** created. Scientists

GO ON TO THE NEXT PAGE.

However, psychologist Lawrence Patihis, who believes that thinking patterns and habits are behind the ³⁵ development of HSAM in certain individuals. Research

indicates, that people memorizing impersonal information ³⁶ use various memorization tools, which include rehearsal techniques, mnemonic devices, and mind palaces. People with HSAM don't use any memorization techniques or tools. However, they do not perform better on standard ³⁷ memory tasks focused on impersonal information than other individuals do. They only have superior memory when it comes to events they personally experienced or heard about.

Patihis's research exposed that people with HSAM ³⁸ score high on measures of absorption and fantasy proneness. Absorption is the ability to fully immerse oneself in an activity. When people experience events during which they pay close attention, people can create ³⁹

35.
A. NO CHANGE
B. Patihis. He believes
C. Patihis believes
D. Patihis, in believing

36.
F. NO CHANGE
G. indicates that people, memorizing impersonal information,
H. indicates, that people memorizing impersonal information,
J. indicates that people memorizing impersonal information

37.
A. NO CHANGE
B. Similarly,
C. Accordingly,
D. In reality,

38.
F. NO CHANGE
G. found
H. relayed
J. flaunted

39.
A. NO CHANGE
B. to
C. which may
D. DELETE the underlined portion.

GO ON TO THE NEXT PAGE.

memories with more details. ☐40 Fantasy proneness is one's tendency to daydream or imagine. Using one's imagination to relive past moments can strengthen those memories. Together the two thought

samples affect how strong and detailed memories are.
41
Patihis believes that people with HSAM create detailed memories that they relive often; therefore, they have

stronger memories of their lives. As for achieving HSAM
42
without effort, the likelihood is

small science says that strengthening memories of any
43
kind takes work. It may not be a goal worth pursuing, as

40. At this point, the writer is considering dividing the paragraph into two. Should the writer begin or not begin a new paragraph here, and why?

F. Begin a new paragraph, because it would separate the ideas about absorption and fantasy proneness from the essay's conclusion.

G. Begin a new paragraph, because the essay changes at this point from concentrating on people with HSAM to concentrating on people without HSAM.

H. DO NOT begin a new paragraph, because doing so would disrupt the link between how people think and HSAM.

J. DO NOT begin a new paragraph, because doing so would make a connection between fantasy proneness and HSAM.

41. A. NO CHANGE
B. patterns affect
C. designs effect
D. types effect

42. F. NO CHANGE
G. a person easily attaining HSAM
H. attaining HSAM so that it is something you have achieved
J. the slight probability of attaining HSAM

43. A. NO CHANGE
B. small,
C. small; and
D. small:

GO ON TO THE NEXT PAGE.

people with HSAM consider it a <u>unique talent.</u>
₄₄

44. Given that all the choices are accurate, which one most clearly indicates that people with HSAM have mixed feelings about HSAM?

    F. NO CHANGE
    G. complicated ability.
    H. rare condition.
    J. wondrous skill.

Question 45 asks about the preceding passage as a whole.

---

45. Suppose the writer's purpose had been to equally examine LePort's and Patihis's theories about the development of HSAM in certain people. Would this essay accomplish that purpose?

    A. Yes, because it plainly details the reasons why LePort's theory is more accurate.
    B. Yes, because it examines both of the theories with equal weight.
    C. No, because it shows a preference for LePort's theory, preventing an unbiased examination.
    D. No, because it presents Patihis's theory with more detail than it does LePort's.

END OF TEST 1

STOP! DO NOT TURN THE PAGE UNTIL TOLD TO DO SO.

MATHEMATICS TEST

DIRECTIONS: Solve each problem, choose the correct answer, and then darken the corresponding oval on your answer sheet.

Do not linger over problems that take too much time. Solve as many as you can; then return to the others in the time you have left for this test.

You are permitted to use a calculator on this test. You may use your calculator for any problems you choose, but some of the problems may best be done without using a calculator.

Note: Unless otherwise stated, all of the following should be assumed:

1. Illustrative figures are NOT necessarily drawn to scale.
2. Geometric figures lie in a plane.
3. The word *line* indicates a straight line.
4. The word *average* indicates arithmetic mean.

---

2. What is the result of subtracting complex number $6 - 8i$ from $7 + 2i$?

   F. 11
   G. 58
   H. $1 + 10i$
   J. $10 + i$
   K. $42 - 16i$

DO YOUR FIGURING HERE.

GO ON TO THE NEXT PAGE.

4. Line segments $\overline{LM}$, $\overline{NO}$, and $\overline{PQ}$ intersect to form the figure below, with angles of 135°, 80°, and $a°$. What is the value of a ?

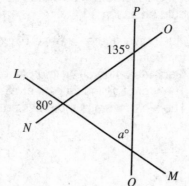

F. 45
G. 50
H. 55
J. 60
K. 65

6. Which of the following equations represents $7 = 6x + y - 3$ in slope-intercept form?

F. $y = -6x - 10$
G. $y = -6x + 10$
H. $y = 6x - 10$
J. $y = 6x + 10$
K. $y = 10x - 6$

GO ON TO THE NEXT PAGE.

8. Which of the following is the solution set to the inequality
$18 \le 3y - 9$?

    F. $y \le -9$
    G. $y \le 3$
    H. $y \ge 3$
    J. $y \le 9$
    K. $y \ge 9$

DO YOUR FIGURING HERE.

10. What is the value of $g(-2)$ if $g(x) = -4x^2 - 5x + 11$?

    F. -15
    G. -5
    H. 5
    J. 25
    K. 85

12. A farmer has 180 apple trees that he needs to plant. The field is arranged such that if the farmer plants 8 apple trees in the first row, he can plant 3 more apple trees in each succeeding row. How many rows will the farmer need to plant all the apple trees?

    F. 32
    G. 13
    H. 10
    J. 9
    K. 8

GO ON TO THE NEXT PAGE.

Use the following information to answer questions 14–16.

A local newspaper is collecting statistics on annual subscriptions in 6 neighborhoods. The table below shows, for each neighborhood, the number of annual subscriptions sold and the total dollar amount collected from subscription sales.

Neighborhood	Number of annual subscriptions	Total sales
Cedarvale	25	$2,225
Riverview	70	$6,650
Parkside	55	$5,075
Westmount	80	$7,400
Glendale	60	$5,700
Elmhurst	70	$6,250

14. The newspaper offers two types of annual subscriptions: print-only for $85 or digital-and-print for $105. How many digital-and-print subscriptions were sold in Westmount?

    F. 30
    G. 39
    H. 40
    J. 50
    K. 67

GO ON TO THE NEXT PAGE.

15. The delivery company that delivers newspapers in Elmhurst charged the newspaper a flat fee of $250 to deliver the newspapers. The delivery company also received 20% of the total sales of the newspapers as payment. How much money did the delivery company make delivering newspapers in Elmhurst?

A. $1,500.00
B. $1,250.00
C. $500.00
D. $250.00
E. $200.00

16. What is the sum of the mode and the mean number of subscriptions sold in the 6 neighborhoods?

F. 140
G. 130
H. 75
J. 50
K. 45

18. The average of a certain set of 8 numbers is 18. If that set of numbers is represented as {17, 9, 15, 20, 17, 4, 23, x}, then what is the value of x ?

F. 14
G. 15
H. 17
J. 38
K. 39

DO YOUR FIGURING HERE.

GO ON TO THE NEXT PAGE.

20. What is the area, in square inches, of the figure below, if the side lengths are given in inches and all angles are right angles?

DO YOUR FIGURING HERE.

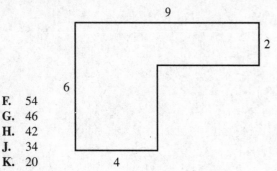

F. 54
G. 46
H. 42
J. 34
K. 20

22. Two trucks work to remove snow from a highway. One blows snow into an empty dump truck that drives beside it. The dump truck can hold a total of 12 cubic meters of snow. The blower deposits snow into the dump truck at a rate of 3 cubic meters per hour. If the two trucks travel together at a constant rate of 0.5 kilometer per minute, how many kilometers will they cover before the dump truck is full?

F. 4.0
G. 15.5
H. 24.0
J. 41.7
K. 120.0

GO ON TO THE NEXT PAGE.

24. For $\triangle WXY$ shown below, $WX = 24$ inches and $WY = 26$ inches. If $\overline{WZ}$ intersects $\overline{XY}$ at the midpoint, what is the length, in inches, of $\overline{WZ}$?

DO YOUR FIGURING HERE.

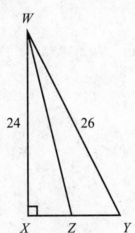

F. $\sqrt{700}$
G. $\sqrt{651}$
H. $\sqrt{626}$
J. $\sqrt{601}$
K. $\sqrt{551}$

26. A certain geometric sequence can be written as follows: $x_1, x_2, x_3, 2, -\dfrac{2}{3}$. What is the value of x_1 ?

F. -162
G. -54
H. -18
J. 18
K. 54

GO ON TO THE NEXT PAGE.

28. Which of the following best describes the roots of the equation $x^2 - 3x + 6 = 0$?

    F.   Two irrational roots
    G. Two rational roots
    H. One irrational root
    J.   One rational root
    K. Zero real roots

DO YOUR FIGURING HERE.

32. The right triangle $\triangle LMN$ is shown below, where LN is 16 inches. If $\tan M = \dfrac{8}{7}$, what is the value of x, in inches?

    F.   2
    G. 8
    H. 14
    J.   20
    K. $2\sqrt{113}$

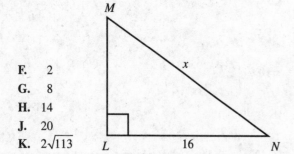

GO ON TO THE NEXT PAGE.

Use the following information to answer questions 35–37.

A plant breeder is giving a tour of an arboretum to interns and guests during a summer convention. The arboretum charges a fee of $15 to enter and $5 for lunch. While on the tour, one intern records the following data on her pedometer: the tour took 0.56 hours, and the group traveled at an average walking pace of 106.8 feet per minute. The distance from the arboretum's visitor center, in meters, with respect to the time into the tour, in minutes, is displayed in the graph below.

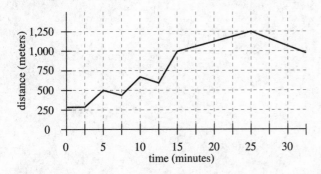

35. Which of the following is closest to the total distance walked during one tour, in feet?

A. 1,794.2
B. 2,134.6
C. 3,588.5
D. 5,321.2
E. 11,442.9

GO ON TO THE NEXT PAGE.

36. During each complete tour, the group spends a total of 13 minutes at a distance at least 1,100 meters from the visitor center. Which of the following is closest to the percent of the time during a complete tour that the group is at least 1,100 meters from the visitor center?

F.　4%
G.　12%
H.　22%
J.　40%
K.　56%

37. Which of the following values is closest to the average slope, in meters per minute, of the graph on the interval between 15 minutes and 25 minutes?

A.　$\dfrac{1}{25}$

B.　$\dfrac{5}{3}$

C.　10

D.　25

E.　50

38. When $a = 10$, the value of the expression $a^6(0.0003a^3 - 0.065a + 0.7)$ is between which of the following numbers?

F.　3×10^5 and 4×10^5
G.　6×10^5 and 7×10^5
H.　3×10^7 and 4×10^7
J.　6×10^7 and 7×10^7
K.　1×10^9 and 1×10^{10}

DO YOUR FIGURING HERE.

GO ON TO THE NEXT PAGE.

40. Marcos plans to paint a frame holding a circular mirror. The frame is a triangle with three equal sides with a semicircle removed and is shown shaded in the figure below. The lengths of the sides and the approximate height of the frame are given in inches. To determine how much paint Marcos needs, he needs to determine the area of the frame. Which of the following is the area of the frame to the nearest square inch?

DO YOUR FIGURING HERE.

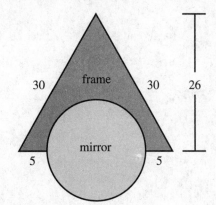

F. 71
G. 157
H. 233
J. 253
K. 294

42. What is the value of $k(h(x))$ for the functions $h(x) = x^3$ and $k(x) = \dfrac{5}{x+2}$?

F. $\dfrac{5x^3}{x^3 + 2}$

G. $\dfrac{5}{x^3 + 2}$

H. $\dfrac{5}{(x+2)^3}$

J. $\dfrac{5}{x^3 + 8}$

K. $\dfrac{5x^3}{x+2}$

GO ON TO THE NEXT PAGE.

44. The coordinates of the y-intercept of the graph of the function $g(x)$ are (0,4) when g is graphed in the standard (x,y) coordinate plane. Which of the following are the coordinates of the y-intercept of the graph of the function $g(x) + 7$?

   F. (0, −3)
   G. (0, 4)
   H. (0, 7)
   J. (0, 11)
   K. (0, 28)

DO YOUR FIGURING HERE.

46. The value of $\dfrac{1}{t-2} + 4$ most closely approaches which of the following as t continuously decreases in value without bound?

   F. 0

   G. $\dfrac{7}{2}$

   H. $\dfrac{9}{2}$

   J. 4

   K. ∞

GO ON TO THE NEXT PAGE.

48. For what value of f is the expression $\dfrac{3f + 4g}{f + \dfrac{1}{3}g}$ undefined?

F. $-3g$

G. $-\dfrac{1}{3}g$

H. 0

J. $\dfrac{1}{3}g$

K. $3g$

DO YOUR FIGURING HERE.

51. An ellipse with the equation $\dfrac{(x-4)^2}{100} + \dfrac{(y-1)^2}{64} = 1$ is shown in the standard (x,y) coordinate plane below.

The foci of the ellipse are represented by which of the following ordered pairs?

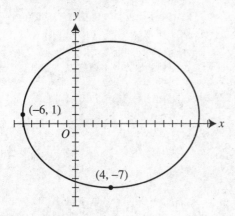

A. $(-6, 1)$ and $(10, 1)$
B. $(-6, 1)$ and $(14, 1)$
C. $(-2, 1)$ and $(10, 1)$
D. $(4, -7)$ and $(4, 1)$
E. $(4, 1)$ and $(4, 9)$

GO ON TO THE NEXT PAGE.

53. The given side lengths of $\triangle DEF$ are in centimeters in the figure below. What is the area of $\triangle DEF$ in square centimeters?

DO YOUR FIGURING HERE.

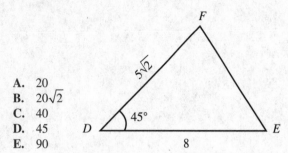

A. 20
B. $20\sqrt{2}$
C. 40
D. 45
E. 90

55. In the diagram below, $\overline{SU} \perp \overline{TV}$, and T is on line $\overline{WX}$, U is on line TV, and V is on line YZ. The area of rectangle WXYZ is 4 times the area of rectangle SUVZ. What percent of the area of WXYZ does the shaded portion represent?

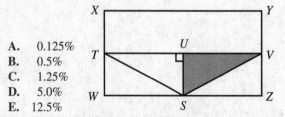

A. 0.125%
B. 0.5%
C. 1.25%
D. 5.0%
E. 12.5%

GO ON TO THE NEXT PAGE.

56. The number with the least value in a data set of 7 distinct values is removed to form a new data set. Which of the following statements is true about the values of the median and mean for the new data set when compared to the original data set?

   F. The median and mean will both increase.
   G. The median and mean will both stay the same.
   H. The median will decrease; the mean will stay the same.
   J. The median will stay the same; the mean will decrease.
   K. Based on the given information, the medians and means of the 2 data sets cannot be compared.

57. Sean is a personal trainer who has individual appointments with two clients on Tuesday. Each session consists of sets of squats for 6 minutes per set and sets of deadlifts for 4 minutes per set. The first client performs 4 sets of squats and 3 sets of deadlifts, and the second client performs 7 sets of squats and 5 sets of deadlifts. The total time, in minutes, for Sean to lead the two clients through all the sets can be represented by which of the following matrix products?

   A. $\begin{bmatrix} 6 \\ 4 \end{bmatrix}\begin{bmatrix} 4 & 7 \\ 3 & 5 \end{bmatrix}$

   B. $\begin{bmatrix} 6 \\ 4 \end{bmatrix}\begin{bmatrix} 4 & 3 \\ 7 & 5 \end{bmatrix}$

   C. $\begin{bmatrix} 6 & 4 \end{bmatrix}\begin{bmatrix} 4 & 3 \\ 5 & 7 \end{bmatrix}$

   D. $\begin{bmatrix} 6 & 4 \end{bmatrix}\begin{bmatrix} 4 & 3 \\ 7 & 5 \end{bmatrix}$

   E. $\begin{bmatrix} 6 & 4 \end{bmatrix}\begin{bmatrix} 4 & 7 \\ 3 & 5 \end{bmatrix}$

DO YOUR FIGURING HERE.

END OF TEST 2

STOP! DO NOT TURN THE PAGE UNTIL TOLD TO DO SO.

READING TEST

DIRECTIONS: There are four passages in this test. Each passage is followed by several questions. After reading a passage, choose the correct answer to each question and fill in the corresponding oval on your answer document. You may refer to the passages as often as necessary.

Passage III

HUMANITIES: Passage A is adapted from "Dancing in Death's House" by Laura Shapiro. (©1994 by *Newsweek*). Passage B is adapted from "Bill T. Jones' experimental storytelling: Exciting and profound" by Ian Anstee. (©2015 by Ian Antsee).

Passage A by Laura Shapiro

Since November 1992, Jones has traveled to 11 cities around the country to conduct and videotape what he calls survival workshops—four-hour sessions with groups of people, ages 11 to 75, who have life-threatening illnesses.
5 "This isn't therapy," he says. "It's about creativity." The words and gestures of the workshop participants became the raw material for Jones's new, evening-length dance, "Still/Here." Jones, 42, long recognized as a choreographer who thrives on risk, here grapples with material that's almost
10 unfairly powerful. A bright student with lung disease. . . A mother hoping her children won't have to watch her die . . . Jones himself, whose HIV status is as well-known as his superb dancing. . . How much skill does it take to get an audience to dab its eyes over subjects like these? Not
15 much, but this isn't a piece about people sadly wasting away. It's about living—about how to live in the same house as death, when the house is your body.

Life has given Jones a great deal to say. At the state university in Binghamton, N.Y., he became a dancer,
20 and he also fell in love with Arnie Zane. Over time they assembled a dance company in their own image: different sizes, shapes and races, men and women happy to hoist one another without regard to gender. In 1988, Zane died of AIDS. The company kept going; it's still called the Bill
25 T. Jones/Arnie Zane Dance Company.

Diagnosed HIV-positive 10 years ago, Jones is in excellent health; he does 90 minutes of calisthenics every morning and continues to dance, direct and choreograph. "When I tell someone I'm HIV-positive I can see in their
30 eyes that they feel sorry for me, that I'm already dead," he says. "And that makes me mad. When did I cross over?"

"Still" opens with the company reciting and demonstrating the movement vignettes created by the workshop participants, "I like to hit the inside pitch," says a dancer,
35 doing a quick swing of an imaginary bat. "Engulfing the whole universe," says another, with a sweep of her arms. Dozens of these gestures appear and reappear throughout the dance. The participants' faces appear, too, on the video screens. Later the video imagery turns into a visual
40 scream, an explosion of teeth, eyes, bones and body parts. By the end of "Still," the video images have turned to triumph—a boy whirling in karate, a woman lifting her arms like wings—and while some dancers have started to fall, others support them and keep going.

GO ON TO THE NEXT PAGE.

Passage B by Ian Anstee

45　　0:01, 0:02, 0:03. The bold, green numbers ticked upward on the black, rectangular clock behind Bill T. Jones as he began his 40th performance of "Story/Time" last Friday. A multidisciplinary work incorporating storytelling and choreography, "Story/Time" is the telling
50　of 70, one-minute vignettes written and narrated by Jones. Through these stories, Jones and the Bill T. Jones/Arnie Zane Dance Company tested the boundaries of what qualifies as dance and theater at Memorial Auditorium.

　　Bill T. Jones and Arnie Zane founded the Bill T.
55　Jones/Arnie Zane Dance Company together in 1983. They dreamed of challenging notions about what kind of bodies belong on stage and how dancing should look. Drawing from both John Cage's "Indeterminacy" and contact improvisation—a postmodern style of dance focused on bodily
60　awareness and the point of physical contact between two dancers—Jones and Zane gained international renown for their experimental theater-dance hybrid.

　　As the narrator, Jones played an integral role in "Story/Time." Smooth and deep like molasses, Jones'
65　voice reverberated through the auditorium as he recounted 70 different stories, each exactly one minute long. Jones' appreciation for silence augmented the narration of these vignettes. Most storytellers shy away from silence because they think that it will interrupt their flow; however, Jones
70　embraces it, modeling his storytelling technique after that of John Cage, a composer who esteemed silence to be equal with sound. Oddly enough, the most poignant moments in Jones' narration were the ones in which he said nothing.

　　Orbiting the cool, self-assured Jones, nine dancers
75　echoed his narrations with distinctively fluid and intercon-nected movements. Lunging, sweeping their arms about and rolling over one another gracefully, the dancers, who seemed more concerned with letting their bodies speak than with conveying any particular message, captivated
80　the audience's attention.

　　As the clock approached 70 minutes, I realized that I had registered very little of what Jones had said; I had been listening, but I had been so distracted by the aesthetic of it all that I had forgotten to process what his words meant.
85　To a certain extent, I feel like this may have been Jones' intention. Finally, the clock struck 70 minutes; Jones and company took their final bow. I left the theater without a clear idea of what I had just witnessed, but felt satisfied nonetheless.

Questions 21–24 ask about Passage A.

---

21. In Passage A, the first paragraph (lines 1–17) functions mainly to emphasize the:

A. number of people Jones interviewed in survival workshops to create "Still/Here."

B. type of stories Jones collected from survival workshops to create "Still/Here."

C. personal relationships Jones formed with the people interviewed in the survival workshops for "Still/Here."

D. organizational skills Jones showcased in traveling to multiple cities to host the workshops for "Still/Here."

GO ON TO THE NEXT PAGE.

22. Which of the following performance pieces would be most conceptually similar to Jones's performance piece discussed in the fourth paragraph of Passage A (lines 32–44)?

F. A traditional folk tale told through dance
G. A multimedia performance inspired by accounts of life-changing accidents
H. An overlapping series of words, gestures, and images chosen by chance
J. A multimedia performance based on the actors' own experiences

23. As it is used in line 7, *raw* most nearly means:

A. unfinished.
B. sore.
C. organic.
D. unpleasant.

24. It can most reasonably be inferred from Passage A that the main reason Jones interviewed real people to create "Still/Here" is that he wanted the stories to expand upon his examination of the:

F. connection between therapy and dance.
G. similarities between postmodern and traditional dance.
H. interplay between theater and dance.
J. complexities of living with death.

Questions 25–27 ask about Passage B.

25. The author of Passage B was least engaged with which aspect of Jones's piece "Story/Time"?

A. Aesthetics of the performance
B. Dancers' movements
C. Video imagery
D. Words in the narration

26. In Passage B, the author most likely references John Cage's "Indeterminacy" and contact improvisation in order to emphasize that Jones's dance company is:

F. innovative.
G. balanced.
H. engaging.
J. traditional.

27. As it is used in line 86, *struck* most nearly means:

A. attacked.
B. signaled.
C. found.
D. impressed.

GO ON TO THE NEXT PAGE.

Questions 28–30 ask about both passages.

28. Which of the following statements best captures a difference in the purposes of the passages?

  F. Passage A provides a history of Jones's evolution as a dancer, while Passage B provides an analysis of one of Jones's dance pieces.
  G. Passage A provides a contrast between Jones's earlier and later works, while Passage B provides a story about Jones's exploration of Cage's work.
  H. Passage A provides a look at Jones's personal connection to one of his dance pieces, while Passage B provides a review of his dance piece "Story/Time."
  J. Passage A provides a review of how Jones constructs his dance pieces, while Passage B provides a contrast between Jones and other experimental choreographers.

29. Compared to Passage B, Passage A provides more information regarding how Jones:

  A. includes contact improvisation in his dance pieces.
  B. responds to creative analyses of his choreography.
  C. feels about John Cage's work.
  D. uses people's stories to create dance pieces.

30. The authors of Passage A and Passage B both remark on Jones's use of:

  F. material from survival workshops.
  G. silence during his narration.
  H. separate vignettes combined in one performance.
  J. traditional dance methods and techniques.

GO ON TO THE NEXT PAGE.

Passage IV

NATURAL SCIENCE: This passage is adapted from the article "Platypus Genome Reveals Secrets of Mammal Evolution" by Scott Norris (©2008 by *National Geographic*).

The genome of the platypus—our most distant mammal relative—has been decoded and analyzed, researchers reported today. The duck-billed mammal has a genetic affinity with both reptiles and birds, according to
5   a new study. Decoding the platypus genome has long been an important goal for biologists seeking to understand the origins of mammal evolution.

The study, appearing in today's edition of the journal *Nature,* gives scientists a new window into the
10 genetic architecture of the earliest mammals. "The platypus genome, like the animal itself, is an amazing amalgam of reptile-like and mammal-like features," said project co-leader Jennifer Graves, of the Australian National University in Canberra. The analysis confirms that the
15 platypus was the earliest offshoot of the mammalian family tree, Graves noted. The group of animals called monotremes—which includes the platypus and the closely related echidna—is thought to have split from other mammals at least 166 million years ago. That early
20 divergence means platypus genes carry information from a transitional point on the evolutionary timeline leading from reptiles to mammals, said project leader Wesley Warren of Washington University in St. Louis, Missouri. "The platypus is critical to helping us understand what genes
25 were present in the ancestral reptilian lineage and how mammals evolved their particular traits," Warren said.

Aquatic animals native to eastern Australia, platypuses have long perplexed biologists. Although classified as mammals, they retain a number of primitive characteris-
30 tics—including egg-laying—that are thought to have been passed down from mammal-like reptiles that lived over 300 million years ago.

As part of the new study, researchers compared the platypus's genetic makeup with other fully sequenced ge-
35 nomes, including those of chickens, mice, and humans. A central goal was to determine which platypus features may have been inherited from ancient reptilian ancestors and which evolved independently in the monotreme lineage. As expected, platypus DNA was found to include a number
40 of genes not found in other mammals. For example, the researchers identified genes for egg yolk proteins shared only with reptiles and fish. "The new genomic data makes a water-tight case for [platypus] egg-laying truly being a primitive retention from reptilian ancestors," said Matt
45 Phillips, an Australian National University scientist who was not involved in the genome project.

On the other hand, the set of mammalian genes responsible for lactation—or milk production—was also found in the platypus genome. While milk production and
50 giving birth to live young would seem to go hand in hand, the platypus genome shows that the two common mammalian traits evolved at very different points in evolutionary time. "The presence of the full repertoire of milk genes confirms that lactation evolved at least 166 million years
55 ago, way before live-bearing," Graves said.

The genomic analysis also uncovered new information about the platypus's basic biology and the origin of some of its particularly unusual features. One big surprise was the discovery of a number of specialized genes associated
60 with odor detection, said lead author Warren. The finding suggests that, in addition to electroreceptors in their bills, platypuses also rely on chemical cues when navigating and locating prey underwater.

Scientists also identified a set of genes associated with
65 platypus venom production. Male platypuses produce a pain-inducing, snake-like venom, composed of at least 19 different substances, which is delivered to enemies or rival males through spurs on the males' hind legs. Previ-

GO ON TO THE NEXT PAGE.

ous studies of venomous snakes had found that poison
70 production is the result of evolutionary modifications to
genes that once served other functions. Some of the same
genes appear to have modified in the platypus, but in a
process entirely separate from the evolution of venom in
snakes, according to the new study.

75   Elliott Margulies, a scientist at the National Human
Genome Research Institute in Bethesda, Maryland, said the
significance of the platypus genome extends well beyond
the field of early animal evolution. "In the human genome,
we're always trying to find sequences that are functional
80 and doing something important, but it's a very tedious and
difficult process," Margulies said. Comparing the human
and platypus genomes, he said, will enable researchers to
locate functional DNA sequences more easily. "Because
the platypus has evolved independently for such a long
85 period of time, any sequences it still has in common with
humans are probably important," Margulies said.

31. One main purpose of the passage is to:

A. discuss a recent genomic finding that may help
scientists better understand how mammals have
evolved.

B. give facts showing that the platypus has not undergone significant evolutionary changes since it split
from mammals 300 million years ago.

C. contrast two prominent hypotheses about the genetic bases for the platypus's unique traits, given recent
genomic evidence.

D. explain why the modern platypus's egg-laying and
lactation properties are of great interest to scientists.

32. Which of the following statements best summarizes the
author's claim about the relationship between the platypus
genome and mammal evolution?

F. When the platypus split from other mammals, it
developed an entirely new genome, retaining none
of its reptilian features.

G. The platypus genome helps scientists to understand
mammal evolution because it is related to the echidna genome.

H. The platypus genome does not hold much relevant
information for the modern study of mammal evolution.

J. Studying the platypus genome helps scientists to
identify which genetic features are inherited from
reptiles and which came about through mammalian
evolution.

33. It can be reasonably inferred from the passage that the
phrase "early divergence" (lines 19–20) refers to:

A. a time of rapid genomic change for all mammals.

B. the point when aquatic animals shifted from
egg-laying to live birthing.

C. the time at which monotremes split genetically from
other mammals.

D. the period when the platypus began to inhabit its
modern habitat.

GO ON TO THE NEXT PAGE.

34. According to the passage, a little less than 166 million years ago, what was true of the platypus's genes for lactation and its genes for live-bearing?

F. The platypus had genes for neither live-bearing nor lactation.

G. The platypus had genes for both lactation and live-bearing.

H. The platypus had genes for lactation but not for live-bearing.

J. The platypus had genes for live-bearing but not for lactation.

35. In the passage, the author concludes that sequencing the platypus genome is broadly important for scientists because it will help them to:

A. determine which genetic sequences are most important to humans.

B. locate functional DNA sequences in the human genome.

C. understand the echidna's genetic split from other mammals.

D. analyze the platypus's genetic affinity with reptiles and birds.

36. According to the passage, which of the following genetic processes is thought to have given snakes the ability to produce venom?

F. A series of evolutionary modifications to genes that once had other purposes

G. The development of a delivery system utilizing spurs

H. Partial gene repurposing, through the same evolutionary process as that of the platypus

J. The evolved ability to synthesize 19 different substances into one compound

37. The passage indicates that the platypus's genes for lactation and live-bearing are evolved traits characteristic of:

A. snakes.

B. other monotremes.

C. ancient reptiles.

D. mammals.

38. Based on the passage, which of the following genetic traits discovered in the study best indicated to scientists that the platypus inherited some of its genome from reptilian ancestors?

F. Odor detection

G. Egg-laying

H. Lactation

J. Venom production

39. As it is used in line 71, the word *served* most nearly means:

A. attended.

B. fulfilled.

C. produced.

D. initiated.

40. The passage most strongly suggests that scientists were surprised to learn that, in order to locate prey underwater, platypuses developed:

F. a system of echolocation similar to that used by other aquatic animals.

G. sharp eyesight that allows them to distinguish plants from prey.

H. specialized genes that allow them to detect chemical cues in their surroundings.

J. the ability to sustain long dives without oxygen.

END OF TEST 3
STOP! DO NOT TURN THE PAGE UNTIL TOLD TO DO SO.

SCIENCE TEST

DIRECTIONS: There are six passages in this test. Each passage is followed by several questions. After reading a passage, choose the correct answer to each question and fill in the corresponding oval on your answer document. You may refer to the passages as often as necessary.

You are NOT permitted to use a calculator on this test.

Passage I

The *resistance* of a material is a measure of the material's opposition to the flow of charged particles through it.

Table 1 shows how the resistance, in ohms, in wires made of 6 copper alloys (Alloys A–F), varies with length of the wire, in meters (m), at a cross-sectional area of 1.00 square millimeters (mm²).

Table 2 shows how the resistance in wires made of each of the 6 copper alloys varies with cross-sectional area at a length of 16 m.

Table 1						
Length (m)	Resistance (ohms) at cross-sectional area of 1.00 mm² of:					
	Alloy A	Alloy B	Alloy C	Alloy D	Alloy E	Alloy F
2	0.0345	0.0342	0.0348	0.0344	0.0356	0.0352
4	0.0690	0.0684	0.0696	0.0688	0.0712	0.0704
16	0.2758	0.2736	0.2784	0.2752	0.2848	0.2816
32	0.5517	0.5472	0.5568	0.5504	0.5696	0.5632
128	2.2067	2.1888	2.2272	2.2016	2.2784	2.2528
256	4.4134	4.3776	4.4544	4.4032	4.5568	4.5056

Table 2						
Cross-sectional area (mm²)	Resistance (ohms) at length of 16 m of:					
	Alloy A	Alloy B	Alloy C	Alloy D	Alloy E	Alloy F
0.25	1.1034	1.0944	1.1136	1.1008	1.1392	1.1264
0.50	0.5517	0.5472	0.5568	0.5504	0.5696	0.5632
0.75	0.3678	0.3648	0.3712	0.3669	0.3797	0.3755
1.50	0.1839	0.1824	0.1856	0.1835	0.1899	0.1877
2.00	0.1379	0.1368	0.1392	0.1376	0.1424	0.1408

GO ON TO THE NEXT PAGE.

1. Based on Table 2, for a wire of Alloy B with a length of 16 m, the absolute value of the difference between the resistance at a cross-sectional area of 0.25 mm^2 and the resistance at a cross-sectional area of 0.50 mm^2 is closest to:

   A. 0.18 ohms.
   B. 0.25 ohms.
   C. 0.55 ohms.
   D. 1.10 ohms.

2. Consider the resistances of wires made of Alloys B, D, E, and F listed in Table 1 at 32 m. What is the order of these alloys from the alloy having the largest resistance to the alloy having the smallest resistance?

   F. Alloy B, Alloy D, Alloy F, Alloy E
   G. Alloy B, Alloy F, Alloy D, Alloy E
   H. Alloy E, Alloy D, Alloy F, Alloy B
   J. Alloy E, Alloy F, Alloy D, Alloy B

3. Based on Tables 1 and 2, at any given length and cross-sectional area, the resistance of which other alloy is most similar to the resistance of Alloy A ?

   A. Alloy B
   B. Alloy C
   C. Alloy D
   D. Alloy E

4. A certain project requires a wire with a cross-sectional area of 0.75 mm^2, a length of 16 m, and a resistance of at least 0.3650 ohms. At 0.75 mm^2 and 16 m, how many of the alloys listed in Table 2 have a *smaller* resistance than is suitable for this project?

   F. 0
   G. 1
   H. 5
   J. 6

5. The *electric current* of a wire is the rate of flow of charged particles through the wire. The amount of electric current passing through a wire decreases as the resistance of the wire increases. Based on Table 1, the electric current would be *greatest* for a wire with a cross-sectional area of 1.00 mm^2 at which length?

   A. Alloy B at 2 m
   B. Alloy E at 2 m
   C. Alloy B at 256 m
   D. Alloy E at 256 m

6. Consider two separate wires made of Alloy D, each with a cross-sectional area of 1.00 mm^2. One wire has a resistance of approximately 0.03 ohms, and the other has a resistance of approximately 4.40 ohms. Based on Table 1, the transmission time for a signal to pass through the wire is likely less in which wire?

   F. The wire with resistance of 0.03 ohms, because it has a longer length.
   G. The wire with resistance of 0.03 ohms, because it has a shorter length.
   H. The wire with resistance of 4.40 ohms, because it has a longer length.
   J. The wire with resistance of 4.40 ohms, because it has a shorter length.

GO ON TO THE NEXT PAGE.

Passage V

Two students debated the evolution of respiration in *chelicerates*, a group of animals that includes *eurypterids* (extinct giant sea scorpions) as well as modern spiders and horseshoe crabs. They classified the chelicerates in each group based on their *gas exchange rate* (the rate at which gas is absorbed into the body during respiration), and whether their respiratory structures were gills or *book lungs* (internal respiratory organs made of many very thin plates).

Student 1

Eurypterids and horseshoe crabs are descended from a common ancestor that had gills and a low gas exchange rate. Horseshoe crabs retained these traits while eurypterids evolved book lungs and a high gas exchange rate. The ancestors of spiders were closely related to eurypterids and inherited these traits, and both of these traits are present in modern spiders.

The respiratory structures of eurypterids were internal, contained many blood vessels, and were highly *convoluted* (characterized by a high ratio of surface area to volume). Convoluted respiratory structures, which are also seen in modern spiders, are evidence of an efficient respiratory system and a high gas exchange rate. An efficient respiratory system can absorb oxygen effectively from air. Therefore, eurypterids had book lungs and could survive on land for extended periods of time.

Student 2

Eurypterids and horseshoe crabs are descended from a common ancestor that had gills and a low gas exchange rate. Horseshoe crabs retained these traits. Eurypterids also had gills and a low gas exchange rate. Conversely, the ancestors of spiders evolved a high gas exchange rate as they diverged from the closely related eurypterids. Modern spiders evolved book lungs after eurypterids became extinct.

The respiratory structures of eurypterids were external and contained few blood vessels. Each of these features indicates a low gas exchange rate and can be found in horseshoe crabs. Eurypterid respiratory structures also were not extensively convoluted, suggesting an inefficient respiratory system that would not have been able to absorb oxygen effectively from air. Therefore, eurypterids had gills and could not survive on land.

27. Both students would likely agree that modern spiders:

    A. have always had a low gas exchange rate.
    B. have always had respiratory structures with few blood vessels.
    C. evolved from horseshoe crabs.
    D. evolved from species closely related to eurypterids.

28. Would Student 2 more likely expect to find respiratory structures with few blood vessels in a horseshoe crab or a modern spider?

    F. Horseshoe crab; Student 2 suggested that respiratory structures with few blood vessels indicate a low gas exchange rate.
    G. Horseshoe crab; Student 2 suggested that respiratory structures with few blood vessels indicate a high gas exchange rate.
    H. Modern spider; Student 2 suggested that respiratory structures with few blood vessels indicate a low gas exchange rate.
    J. Modern spider; Student 2 suggested that respiratory structures with few blood vessels indicate a high gas exchange rate.

GO ON TO THE NEXT PAGE.

29. In which of the three groups of chelicerates would Student 1 most likely expect to find convoluted respiratory structures?

    A. Eurypterids only
    B. Horseshoe crabs only
    C. Eurypterids and modern spiders only
    D. Horseshoe crabs and modern spiders only

31. Suppose it was discovered that the common ancestor of eurypterids and horseshoe crabs had a low gas exchange rate. This discovery would be consistent with the viewpoint(s) of which of the students, if either?

    A. Student 1 only
    B. Student 2 only
    C. Both Student 1 and Student 2
    D. Neither Student 1 nor Student 2

32. Student 2 characterized the chelicerates in which of the 3 groups as having gills?

    F. Horseshoe crabs only
    G. Modern spiders only
    H. Eurypterids and horseshoe crabs
    J. Eurypterids and modern spiders

30. Consider a horseshoe crab and a modern spider, each having the same body mass. Based on Student 1's discussion, which animal would likely produce less energy through cellular respiration: the horseshoe crab or the modern spider?

    F. Horseshoe crab; Student 1 argues that modern spiders have a low gas exchange rate and horseshoe crabs have a high gas exchange rate.
    G. Horseshoe crab; Student 1 argues that modern spiders have a high gas exchange rate and horseshoe crabs have a low gas exchange rate.
    H. Modern spider; Student 1 argues that modern spiders have a low gas exchange rate and horseshoe crabs have a high gas exchange rate.
    J. Modern spider; Student 1 argues that modern spiders have a high gas exchange rate and horseshoe crabs have a low gas exchange rate.

33. Consider a rock formation that is known to have formed from fossilized mud that was above sea level at the time of deposition and was confirmed to date from the time that eurypterids were alive. Suppose the rock was discovered to contain fossil trackways that were made by eurypterids. This finding would support the viewpoint(s) of which of the students, if either?

    A. Student 1 only
    B. Student 2 only
    C. Both Student 1 and Student 2
    D. Neither Student 1 nor Student 2

GO ON TO THE NEXT PAGE.

Passage VI

Hemoglobin is a protein found in red blood cells that contains the ferrous ion, Fe^{2+}, in its active state and is responsible for binding oxygen and transporting it throughout the body. Three experiments were done to study factors that affect the *saturation* (oxygen binding) of hemoglobin. In each trial in each experiment, the following steps were performed:

1. 50 mL of a 3 mg/L hemoglobin solution was placed into a sealed container at a particular temperature. The container was purged of oxygen to return the hemoglobin to the active state containing Fe^{2+}.

2. A particular amount of carbon dioxide and acetic acid was added to the container.

3. Pure oxygen gas was slowly pumped from a tank into the container. As the partial pressure of oxygen inside the container increased, samples were removed and analyzed to determine the percentage of the hemoglobin saturated with oxygen.

Experiment 1

In each of Trials 1–4, a hemoglobin solution with 10 mg added acetic acid was tested at a temperature of 20° C. The concentration of carbon dioxide was varied from trial to trial. The results are shown in Figure 1.

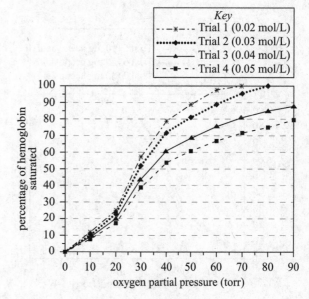

Figure 1

GO ON TO THE NEXT PAGE.

Experiment 2

In each of Trials 5–7, a hemoglobin solution with a carbon dioxide concentration of 0.02 mol/L was tested at a temperature of 20° C. The amount of acetic acid added to the container was varied from trial to trial. The results are shown in Figure 2.

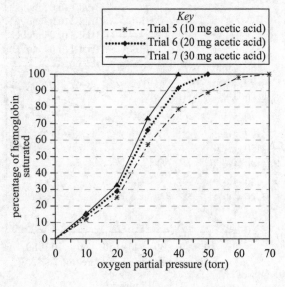

Figure 2

Experiment 3

In each of Trials 8–11, a hemoglobin solution with 10 mg added acetic acid and a carbon dioxide concentration of 0.02 mol/L was tested. The temperature was varied from trial to trial. The results are shown in Figure 3.

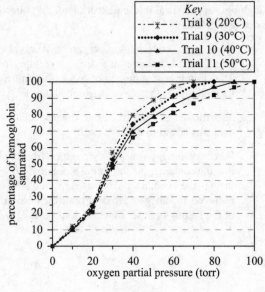

Figure 3

GO ON TO THE NEXT PAGE.

34. According to the results of Experiment 2, as the amount of acetic acid increased from 10 mg to 30 mg from trial to trial, the oxygen partial pressure needed to saturate all of the hemoglobin:

    F. increased only.
    G. decreased only.
    H. increased and then decreased.
    J. decreased and then increased.

35. Based on Figure 1, if a sample from Trial 4 had been analyzed at an oxygen partial pressure of 100 torr, the percentage of hemoglobin saturated would most likely have been:

    A. less than 70%.
    B. between 70% and 75%.
    C. between 75% and 80%.
    D. greater than 80%.

36. According to the results of Experiment 1, as the concentration of carbon dioxide increased from trial to trial, the oxygen partial pressure at which 20% of the hemoglobin remained unsaturated:

    F. decreased only.
    G. increased only.
    H. decreased and then increased.
    J. increased and then decreased.

37. In how many trials in Experiments 1–3 did the percentage of hemoglobin saturated reach 100% at an oxygen partial pressure of less than 60 torr ?

    A. 2
    B. 3
    C. 8
    D. 9

38. The binding of hemoglobin to oxygen requires a one-time transfer of an electron from the iron present in the active state of hemoglobin to the oxygen molecule. Based on the information in the passage, the resulting charge of each hemoglobin iron ion after it loses an electron is:

    F. 1+, because electrons have negative charge.
    G. 1+, because electrons have positive charge.
    H. 3+, because electrons have negative charge.
    J. 3+, because electrons have positive charge.

39. The hemoglobin solution used in Step 1 of each experiment was measured to have a pH of 7.0. In Experiment 2, how many of the trials were performed at a pH of higher than 7.0 ?

    A. Zero, because the addition of acid decreases the pH of a solution.
    B. Zero, because the addition of acid increases the pH of a solution.
    C. Three, because the addition of acid decreases the pH of a solution.
    D. Three, because the addition of acid increases the pH of a solution.

40. Based on Figure 3, which of the following expressions best approximates the *mass* of the *unsaturated* hemoglobin remaining in the 40° C solution at 80 torr ?

    F. $50 \text{ mL} \times \dfrac{1 \text{ L}}{1{,}000 \text{ mL}} \times \dfrac{3 \text{ mg}}{1 \text{ L}} \times 5\%$

    G. $50 \text{ mL} \times \dfrac{1{,}000 \text{ mL}}{1 \text{ L}} \times \dfrac{3 \text{ mg}}{1 \text{ L}} \times 5\%$

    H. $50 \text{ mL} \times \dfrac{1 \text{ L}}{1{,}000 \text{ mL}} \times \dfrac{3 \text{ mg}}{1 \text{ L}} \times 40\%$

    J. $50 \text{ mL} \times \dfrac{1{,}000 \text{ mL}}{1 \text{ L}} \times \dfrac{3 \text{ mg}}{1 \text{ L}} \times 40\%$

END OF TEST

Mini Practice Test: Answers and Explanations

Mini Practice Test: Answers and Explanations

English

1. **B** Words are changing in the answer choices, so the question is testing consistency. Notice that only the first and last words of the answers change, so consider where each of the two words falls in the sentence. The first word is part of the phrase, *one…the only places*. Since *Lake Xochimilco* is just one out of many places, the first word should be *of*, creating the common phrase *one of the many places*. Eliminate (A) and (D) because neither uses the word *of* first. Now consider the second word, which is part of the phrase *places left…the world*. Since places are discussed as being "in" *the world*, the second word should be *in*. Eliminate (C) because it does not use the word *in* last. The correct answer is (B).

2. **J** Punctuation is changing in the answer choices, so the question is testing punctuation rules. The phrase *a salamander called the axolotl* provides information that is not absolutely essential to the sentence's main meaning, so it needs matching commas or dashes before and after the phrase. Eliminate (F) because it mixes a comma with a dash, and the punctuation needs to match. Eliminate (G) because it lacks a dash after the phrase. Eliminate (H) because it lacks a dash before the phrase. Keep (J) because it contains a dash both before and after the phrase. The correct answer is (J).

3. **A** Punctuation and words are changing in the answer choices, so the question is testing punctuation rules. Consider the two parts of the sentence. The first part of the sentence, *Rarely seen in the wild*, is a describing phrase that is not a complete idea. The second part of the sentence, *axolotls have been found in Mexico for nearly 10,000 years*, is a complete idea. Keep (A) because a comma can be used after a describing phrase. Eliminate (B) because a period can go only at the end of a sentence, and the first phrase isn't a complete sentence. A comma followed by *and* works the same way a period does (it can come only after a complete idea), so eliminate (C). Eliminate (D) because the beginning phrase describes the *axolotls*, so the word *and* should not separate the description from the subject. The correct answer is (A).

4. **G** Punctuation and words are changing in the answer choices, so the question is testing punctuation rules. Consider the two parts of the sentence. The first part of the sentence, *Axolotls are unusual*, is a complete idea. The second part of the sentence, *remaining aquatic throughout their entire lives*, is a phrase that describes the *axolotls* and is not a complete idea. Eliminate (F) because a semicolon works in the same way a period does—both ideas need to be complete

in order to have a semicolon between them. Keep (G) because a comma can be used before a describing phrase. Eliminate (H) for the same reason (F) was eliminated: *remaining aquatic throughout their entire lives* is not a complete sentence. Eliminate (J) because the two verbs *are* and *remaining* are not in the same form, so they cannot be connected with the word *and*. The correct answer is (G).

5. **A** Note the question! The question asks whether the clause should be deleted, so it's testing consistency. If the content of the clause is consistent with the ideas surrounding it, then it should be kept. The paragraph discusses a unique characteristic about the *axolotl*, which is that it does not undergo *metamorphosis*. The clause in question discusses the purpose of a hormone in *humans*, so it is not consistent with the ideas in the text; the clause should not be kept. Eliminate (C) and (D). Keep (A) because it correctly states that the clause is irrelevant. Eliminate (B) because the information is not provided in the *previous paragraph*. The correct answer is (A).

6. **J** Vocabulary is changing in the answers, so the question is testing word choice. Determine what meaning of the underlined portion would be consistent with the sentence. The underlined portion should mean something like "preventing." Eliminate (F) because *boycotting* means "refusing to support." Eliminate (G) because *isolating* means "separating." Eliminate (H) because *ignoring* means "not paying attention to." Keep (J) because *avoiding* matches "preventing." The correct answer is (J).

7. **C** Pronouns are changing in the answer choices, so the question is testing consistency of pronouns. A pronoun must be consistent in number with the noun it is replacing. The pronoun refers to the noun *axolotls*, which is plural. To be consistent, the pronoun in the answer choice must also be plural. Eliminate (A), (B), and (D) because none of these is plural. Keep (C) because *their* is plural. The correct answer is (C).

8. **H** Note the question! The question asks where the underlined portion should be placed, so it's testing consistency. Look for a clue in the sentence to determine what word or idea it needs to come before or after. The underlined portion says *of nutrients*, so it must come after something in which nutrients can be measured. Eliminate (F) because the idea that *axolotls* can live in *environments* made *of nutrients* isn't clear. Eliminate (G) because the phrase *live of nutrients* isn't clear. Keep (H) because the *axolotls* could live in *environments* that have *lower levels of nutrients*. Eliminate (J) because the phrase *salamander species of nutrients* isn't clear. The correct answer is (H).

9. **D** Note the question! The question asks which option would lead the reader *from the preceding paragraph to the new paragraph*. The preceding paragraph discusses how *axolotls* might be able to *survive in a wider range of environments*, and the new paragraph discusses the

regeneration abilities of axolotls, which are of interest to *scientists*. Check each answer choice to see whether it is consistent with the ideas in both paragraphs. Eliminate (A) because it does not mention a lack of metamorphosis or abilities that interest scientists. Eliminate (B) because, though it mentions *scientists*, it does not mention what interests them or the axolotl's lack of metamorphosis. Eliminate (C) because it does not mention a lack of metamorphosis or abilities that interest scientists. Keep (D) because it mentions the interests of the *scientific community* and *the axolotl's lack of metamorphosis*. The correct answer is (D).

10. **F**   The length of the phrase is changing in the answer choices, so the question could be testing concision. Each choice has the same meaning in context, so determine which choice is both most concise and most precise. *Regrow limbs, build new body parts, regenerate*, and *regenerate to full form* all mean the same thing in context because they all describe what happens when an animal undergoes regeneration. There is no need to use two items from this list in the same sentence, so eliminate answer choices that are redundant. Eliminate (G), (H), and (J) because each of these is redundant. Keep (F) because it is the most concise and the meaning of the sentence is clear. The correct answer is (F).

11. **B**   Vocabulary is changing in the answer choices, so the question is testing word choice. Determine what meaning of the underlined portion would be consistent with the sentence. The underlined portion should mean something like "watched" or "analyzed." Eliminate (A) because *reviewed* means "read again." Keep (B) because *studied* means "analyzed." Eliminate (C) because *deliberated* means "thought about." Eliminate (D) because *measured* means "calculated." The correct answer is (B).

12. **H**   Transitions are changing in the answer choices, so the question is testing consistency with transitions. Look at the previous sentence to determine how the two ideas are related. The previous sentence gives a fact about axolotls (they avoid some of humanity's worst diseases), and this sentence gives a conclusion that follows from the fact in the preceding sentence (axolotls are of interest to scientists). Eliminate (F) because *Besides* implies that the second idea will be another fact apart from the first idea, which isn't true. Eliminate (G) because the second idea is not an example of the first idea. Keep (H) because *Clearly* implies that the second idea will be a conclusion easily gained from the first idea. Eliminate (J) because *With this in mind* implies that a person in the second sentence will be acting while keeping in mind the information from the first sentence, but the second sentence doesn't describe any person taking an action. The correct answer is (H).

13. **B**   Words are changing in the answer choices, so the question is testing consistency. The part of the sentence without the underlined portion says that *these salamanders are well suited...scientific research*. The correct phrasing is that someone or something is *well suited* "to" or "for" something else, so eliminate (A), (C), and (D). The correct answer is (B).

14. **G** Punctuation and words are changing in the answer choices, so the question is testing punctuation rules. Consider the two parts of the sentence. The first part of the sentence, *Unfortunately, the axolotl population in the wild is declining rapidly*, is a complete idea. The second part of the sentence, *their main threats are pollution and the introduction of invasive species*, is also a complete idea. Eliminate (F) because it creates a run-on sentence by not using any punctuation to separate the complete ideas. Keep (G) because a semicolon works in the same way a period does—both ideas need to be complete in order to have a semicolon between them. Eliminate (H) and (J) because putting a comma between two complete ideas creates a run-on sentence. The correct answer is (G).

15. **C** Note the question! The question asks which option would indicate the conservationists' concern *about the declining axolotl population* and the fact that they *are taking immediate steps to preserve them*. Check each answer choice to see whether it has to do with the conservationists being concerned and acting quickly. Eliminate (A), (B), and (D) because *casually considering*, *sporadically thinking about*, and *slowly developing* don't convey that the conservationists are acting quickly. Keep (C) because *working urgently* matches the idea that conservationists are *taking immediate steps* and are concerned. The correct answer is (C).

16. **J** Punctuation is changing in the answer choices, so the question is testing punctuation rules. The phrase *With tracks and footing remaining intact from the line* is one idea, so there is no reason to put any punctuation within the phrase. Eliminate (F), (G), and (H) because they all contain punctuation within that phrase. The correct answer is (J).

17. **C** Note the question! The question asks which statement *would provide the best transition between the story of the park's history and the description of its present purpose*. The previous sentence says the West Side Line *became an urban eyesore*, and the next sentence says it *has since been transformed into a park*. Check each answer choice to see whether it connects *the park's history* and *its present purpose*. Eliminate (A) and (B) because they both mention only the park, which is the *present purpose*, and don't mention the *history* of the West Side Line. Keep (C) because it mentions the history of *being untouched for years* and the growth of *wild plants*, which connects to it becoming a park. Eliminate (D) because it's not about the *West Side Line* but about trains in general. The correct answer is (C).

18. **F** Verbs are changing in the answer choices, so the question is testing consistency of verbs. The answer choices are in different tenses, so look for a clue in the sentence or surrounding sentences to identify the appropriate tense. The beginning of the sentence says *is also frequented*, which is in present tense, so the underlined portion needs to be in present tense to be consistent. Eliminate (H) and (J) because they are both in past tense. Keep (F) because it is in present tense. Although (G) is in present tense, it is not as concise as (F) and lacks the word *who*, so eliminate (G). The correct answer is (F).

19. **B** Punctuation is changing in the answer choices, so the question is testing punctuation rules. Consider the two parts of the sentence. The first part of the sentence, *At the south end of the park is an overlook*, is a complete idea. The second part of the sentence, *visitors get a one-of-a-kind view of Manhattan's busy Meatpacking District*, is a complete idea. Eliminate (A) because the comma creates a run-on sentence. Likewise, eliminate (C) because the second idea is still complete with *there* added, so it also creates a run-on sentence. Adding *from which* changes the second idea so that it is no longer complete. A comma is the correct punctuation to use when the second idea starts with *from which*, so keep (B). Eliminate (D) because a semicolon works exactly like a period, and *from which* makes the second idea not complete, so a period or a semicolon could not be used. The correct answer is (B).

20. **J** Transitions are changing in the answer choices, so the question is testing consistency with transitions. There is also the option to DELETE; consider this choice carefully as it's often the correct answer. Look at the previous phrase to determine how the two ideas are related. The previous phrase, *Positioned above Manhattan's urban streets*, is a description, and the second phrase, *the elevated park provides visitors with both a bird's-eye view of NYC life and a chance to connect with nature*, is what is being described. Since the first phrase describes the second, there is no reason to put a transition word between them. Eliminate (F), (G), and (H). The correct answer is (J).

21. **A** The phrase around *park* is changing in the answer choices, so the question could be testing concision. First determine whether the phrase is necessary. The paragraph already states that the park is *1.45 miles* long, so eliminate (B). The paragraph states that the park is *elevated* and contains *plants*, so eliminate (C). The paragraph states that the park is in *Manhattan*, so eliminate (D). The correct answer is (A).

22. **H** Vocabulary is changing in the answers, so the question is testing word choice. Determine what meaning of the underlined portion would be consistent with the sentence. The underlined portion should mean something like "protects." Eliminate (F) because *eliminates* means "gets rid of." Eliminate (G) because *quarantines* means "isolates." Keep (H) because *shelters* means "protects." Eliminate (J) because *covers* means "puts something over." The correct answer is (H).

23. **C** Note the question! The question asks where Sentence 1 should be placed, so it's testing consistency. Look for a clue in the sentence to determine what idea it needs to come before or after. Sentence 1 says that *At the south end of the park is an overlook*. Sentence 5 starts with the phrase *Next to the overlook*. Therefore, Sentence 1 should come before Sentence 5 and after Sentence 4. The correct answer is (C).

24. **H** Commas are changing in the answer choices, so the question is testing comma rules. A comma shouldn't be placed after *intertwine* because it separates the verb, *intertwine*, from what the plants are intertwining with, so eliminate (F) and (G). There is no reason to put a comma after *park*, so eliminate (J). The correct answer is (H).

25. **B** Note the question! The question asks what alternatives *would NOT be acceptable*. Cross out the word *NOT* and mark each answer with a Yes or No. Punctuation is changing, so the question is testing punctuation rules. The first part of the sentence, *Plants and trees span the length of the park and intertwine with scenic overlooks, seating areas, and art exhibits*, is a complete idea. A period can go at the end of a complete idea, so mark (A) as Yes. The second part of the sentence, *shops and eateries are found at each end of the High Line*, is a complete idea. The comma in (B) creates a run-on sentence, so mark (B) as No. The word *and* can link the ideas, and there should be a comma when both ideas could be separate sentences, so mark (C) as Yes. A semicolon works the same as a period and can be used to connect two complete ideas in one sentence, so mark (D) as Yes. Choice (B) is the odd one out. The correct answer is (B).

26. **H** Note the question! The question asks which choice *emphasizes the length of the boardwalk with the clearest and most specific reference to scale*. Check each answer choice to see whether it gives a specific *length of the boardwalk*. Eliminate (F) because *lengthy* is not specific. Eliminate (G) because *impressive* is not specific. Keep (H) because *three-block-long* is specific. Eliminate (J) because *north-to-south* is about direction, not *length*. The correct answer is (H).

27. **C** Pronouns and nouns are changing in the answer choices, so the question is testing clarity with pronouns. Determine who or what the pronoun refers to, and choose an answer that makes the meaning 100% clear. There's nothing in the sentence that makes it clear what *that time* refers to, so eliminate (A). There's nothing in the sentence that makes it clear what *it* refers to, so eliminate (B). Between (C) and (D), *industrial past* more clearly connects to *train tracks, stable footings, and other remnants*. Eliminate (D). The correct answer is (C).

28. **G** The length of the phrase is changing in the answer choices, so the question is testing clarity and concision. Look for an answer choice that makes the meaning of the sentence clear. For (F), the correct phrase is "looks like," not *looks as*. Eliminate (F). Keep (G) because it is clear and concise. Eliminate (H) and (J) because neither is as concise as (G). The correct answer is (G).

29. **D** Note the question! The question asks which choice *provides the clearest and most relevant information*. The paragraph is about *High Line Park* providing an *urban oasis* in Manhattan, and the sentence says, *Pauline Frommer has described it as the city's "coolest park."* Check each answer choice to see whether it has to do with *Pauline Frommer* and the *High Line Park*. Eliminate (A), (B), and (C) because being *a New York native*, *co-owner of a prominent company*, or *a well-known person* doesn't describe *Pauline Frommer* in a way that explains why she is being

mentioned. Being a *travel guide publisher* implies that *Pauline Frommer* knows more about the city and that her opinion about the *High Line Park* is important. The correct answer is (D).

30. **F**   Verbs are changing in the answer choices, so the question is testing consistency of verbs. Choice (F) makes the meaning of the sentence clear, so keep it. Choice (G) uses the word *that* to imply that the High Line *experiences a park*, which is not the correct meaning, so eliminate (G). Choice (H) uses the word *it* to also imply that the park is experiencing the park, so eliminate (H). Eliminate (J) because the sentence includes *continue* in the non-underlined part, and *continue experiencing* is redundant. The correct answer is (F).

31. **A**   Note the question! The question asks which option *most clearly indicates the scientists' response to Price's memory abilities*. Check each answer choice to see whether it has to do with the *scientists' response* to Price's *exceptional memory*. Keep (A) because *astounded* means the scientists were pleasantly surprised by Price's unique abilities. Eliminate (B) and (D) because they don't indicate how the scientists *responded* to her abilities, merely that they became aware. Eliminate (C) because it describes Price's feelings, not the *scientists' response*. The correct answer is (A).

32. **H**   Punctuation is changing in the answer choices, so the question is testing punctuation rules. The phrase *remembering detailed accounts of autobiographical events* is not necessary for the meaning of the sentence, so it needs matching commas or dashes before and after the phrase. Eliminate (F) because it lacks a comma after the phrase. Eliminate (G) and (J) because they both mix dashes and commas. Keep (H) because it contains dashes before and after the phrase, which work like a set of parentheses for information that is not absolutely essential in the sentence. The correct answer is (H).

33. **A**   The phrase after *HSAM* is changing in the answer choices, so the question is testing word choice. Choices (B) and (C) both use overly casual language, *neat* and *awesome*, which are not consistent with the passage's tone. Eliminate (B) and (C). Choices (A) and (D) both mean essentially the same thing in context, but (A) is more concise. Eliminate (D). The correct answer is (A).

34. **J**   Punctuation and words are changing in the answer choices, so the question is testing punctuation rules. Consider the two parts of the sentence. The first part of the sentence, *Studying HSAM could reveal more about how memories are created*, is a complete idea. The second part of the sentence, *scientists think there may be a physical explanation for HSAM*, is also a complete idea. Eliminate (F) because putting a comma between two complete ideas creates a run-on sentence. When two complete thoughts are connected with the word *and*, there must be a comma in between them. Eliminate (G) and (H) because they do not contain commas. The correct answer is (J).

35. **C** Punctuation and words are changing in the answer choices, so the question is testing punctuation rules. Consider the two parts of the sentence. The first part of the sentence, *However, psychologist Lawrence Patihis*, is not a complete idea. Eliminate (B) because a period can only go at the end of a sentence, and the first phrase isn't a complete sentence. Eliminate (A) and (D) because the words *who* and *in* make the sentence not complete. Keep (C) because the word *believes* makes the sentence complete. The correct answer is (C).

36. **J** Punctuation is changing in the answer choices, so the question is testing punctuation rules. There is no reason to put a comma after the word *indicates, people,* or *information*, so eliminate (F), (G), and (H). Keep (J) because it does not contain any commas. The correct answer is (J).

37. **C** Transitions are changing in the answer choices, so the question is testing consistency with transitions. Look at the previous sentences to determine how the ideas are related. The second sentence of the paragraph indicates that *people memorizing impersonal information use various memorization tools*, and the next sentence states that *People with HSAM don't use any memorization techniques*. This sentence provides the logical outcome of these statements—that people with HSAM aren't better at memorizing *impersonal information*. Since these ideas agree, eliminate any answer choices that include opposite-direction transitions. Eliminate (A) because *however* indicates a contrast, and the two facts do not have a contrast. Although (B) is an agreeing transition, *similarly* can be used only when two separate, but somehow *similar*, situations are being discussed. Since the second sentence here provides more information about the same group of people and not a separate group, *similarly* is not appropriate. Eliminate (B). Keep (C) because *accordingly* implies the second fact is a consequence or logical conclusion of the first one. Eliminate (D) because *in reality* implies that the first fact is false, but both facts are true. The correct answer is (C).

38. **G** Vocabulary is changing in the answers, so the question is testing word choice. The underlined portion should mean something like "discovered." Keep (F) because *exposed* could mean "discovered." Keep (G) because *found* could mean "discovered." Eliminate (H) because *relayed* means "passed on." Eliminate (J) because *flaunted* means "showed off." Compare the remaining answer choices. The phrase *found that* is more appropriate than *exposed that* and the word *exposed* has an additional implication of secrecy that is not supported here. Eliminate (F). The correct answer is (G).

39. **A** Vocabulary is changing in the answer choices, so this question is testing word choice. There is also the option to DELETE; consider this choice carefully as it's often the correct answer. Consider the two parts of the sentence. The first part of the sentence, *When people experience events during which they pay close attention*, is not a complete idea. The second part of the sentence, *people can create memories with more details*, is a complete idea. Choices (B), (C), and (D) all make the sentence incomplete because they do not contain a subject. In other words, even though *people* is mentioned earlier in the sentence, it is not clear who creates *memories with more details* if *people* isn't mentioned again after the comma. The correct answer is (A).

40. **H** Note the question! The question asks whether the paragraph should be divided in two at this point, so it's testing consistency. If the content of the second portion is consistent with the content of the first portion, then the paragraph should not be divided. The first part of the paragraph discusses how *people with HSAM* perform on *measures of absorption and fantasy proneness* and goes on to describe *absorption* in more detail. The second portion describes *fantasy proneness* in more detail. Since the content of the second portion is consistent with the content of the first portion, the paragraph should not be divided in two at this point. Eliminate (F) and (G). Keep (H) because it states that dividing the paragraph would *disrupt the link between how people think and HSAM*. Eliminate (J) because it states that dividing the paragraph would *make a connection* between the two thinking patterns, which isn't true. The correct answer is (H).

41. **B** Vocabulary is changing in the answers, so the question is testing word choice. The underlined portion should mean something like "types influence." Notice that the first word is a noun and the second word is a verb. Likewise, the correct answer should also have a noun followed by a verb. Eliminate (C) and (D) because the second word, *effect*, is a noun that means "the result of a change." Compare the remaining answer choices. The word *patterns* typically refers to models or examples, while the word *samples* means "parts of something." In this case, the two ideas (*absorption* and *fantasy proneness*) aren't parts of something; they are abilities, or behavioral traits, that people repeatedly display. Therefore, *patterns* is more appropriate than *samples*. Eliminate (A). The correct answer is (B).

42. **F** The phrase after *As for* is changing in the answer choices, so the question could be testing concision. First determine whether the phrase is necessary. The sentence already says *without effort* and *the likelihood is small* in reference to the possibility of a person learning HSAM, so there is no need to repeat these ideas. Eliminate any choices that are redundant. Eliminate (G) because it repeats the idea of *without effort* with the word *easily*. Eliminate (J) because it repeats the idea that *the likelihood is small* with the words *slight probability*. Choice (H) contains both *attaining HSAM* and *it is something you have achieved*, which mean the same thing in context, so eliminate (H). Choice (F) is precise and is the most concise. The correct answer is (F).

43. **D**   Punctuation is changing in the answer choices, so the question is testing punctuation rules. Consider the two parts of the sentence. The first part of the sentence, *As for achieving HSAM without effort, the likelihood is small*, is a complete idea. The second part of the sentence, *science says that strengthening memories of any kind takes work,* is also a complete idea. Eliminate (A) and (B) because they both create a run-on sentence. Eliminate (C) because the word *and* can only follow a comma, not a semicolon. The correct answer is (D).

44. **G**   Note the question! The question asks which option *most clearly indicates that people with HSAM have mixed feelings about HSAM*. Check each answer choice to see whether it has to do with conflicting emotions about HSAM. Eliminate (F) because *unique talent* is primarily positive and does not convey any conflict. Keep (G) because *complicated ability* implies there are complex layers to having HSAM. Eliminate (H) because *rare condition* is neutral and does not convey any conflict. Eliminate (J) because *wondrous skill* is positive. The correct answer is (G).

45. **D**   Note the question! The question asks whether the essay would fulfill the purpose of *equally examining LePort's and Patihis's theories about the development of HSAM in certain people*. Consider the main idea of the passage and use Process of Elimination. The passage is about HSAM and the theoretical reasons behind why it develops. Eliminate (A) and (B) because the author mentions LePort's theory in only one sentence and spends more than half of the essay discussing Patihis's theory. Eliminate (C) because showing a preference for one scientist's theory over another's does not demonstrate an *unbiased examination*. Keep (D) because it is true that the author uses *more detail* when describing Patihis's theory than when describing *LePort's*. The correct answer is (D).

Math

2. **H** The question asks for the result of subtracting one complex number from another. This operation can be represented as $(7 + 2i) - (6 - 8i)$. Distribute through the parentheses to get $7 + 2i - 6 + 8i$ and gather like terms to get $1 + 10i$. The correct answer is (H).

4. **H** The question asks for the value of an angle on a figure. When doing geometry problems, be sure to label the figure. There are 180° in a triangle, so begin by determining the other two angles. Because opposite angles are equal, the angle directly opposite 80° will also be 80°. Label this on the figure. The angle adjacent to 135° forms a straight angle with the 135° angle, so the adjacent angle can be found by $180° - 135° = 45°$. Label this on the figure.

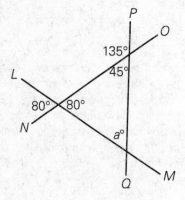

Two of the three angles of the triangle are now known. The value of a can be calculated as $a + 45° + 80° = 180°$. Simplify to $a + 125 = 180°$, and then subtract 125 from both sides to get $a = 55°$. The correct answer is (H).

6. **G** The question asks for the slope-intercept form of an equation. The slope-intercept form of a line is $y = mx + b$, so begin by rearranging the equation. Subtract $6x$ from both sides of the equation to get $7 - 6x = y - 3$. Add 3 to each side of the equation to get $10 - 6x = y$. The answer choices all have y on the left side of the equation, so rearrange the expression to get $y = -6x + 10$. The correct answer is (G).

8. **K** The question asks for the solution set to an inequality. To find this, isolate the y in the inequality. Begin by adding 9 to both sides of the inequality to get $27 \leq 3y$. Divide both sides by 3 to get $9 \leq y$. Carefully compare these to the answer choices. The correct answer is (K).

10. **H** The question asks for the value of a function. In function notation, the number inside the parentheses is the x-value that goes into the function, and the value that comes out of the function is the y-value. Plug $x = -2$ into the function g to get $g(-2) = -4(-2)^2 - 5(-2) + 11$. Simplify to $g(-2) = -4(4) - (-10) + 11$, then $g(-2) = -16 + 10 + 11$, and finally $g(-2) = 5$. The correct answer is (H).

12. **J** The question asks for the number of rows the farmer will need to plant all the apple trees. Since the question asks for a specific value and the answers contain numbers in increasing order, plug in the answers. Begin by labeling the answers as "number of rows" and start with (H), 10. If the first row contains 8 trees and the farmer *can plant 3 more apple trees in each succeeding row,* the number of trees in 10 rows can be found by adding $8 + 11 + 14 + 17 + 20 + 23 + 26 + 29 + 32 + 35$, where 8 is the number of trees in the first row, and each of the 9 remaining rows has 3 more trees than the one before it. Together, this adds up to 215 trees. This number is too large, so eliminate (H). The correct number of rows will have to be smaller than 10, so eliminate (F) and (G), which are greater than 10. Test (J), 9, by adding $8 + 11 + 14 + 17 + 20 + 23 + 26 + 29 + 32 = 180$. This matches the value in the question, so stop here. The correct answer is (J).

14. **F** The question asks for the number of digital-and-print subscription sold in a certain neighborhood. There are numbers in the answer choices, so plug in the answers. Label the answers as "digital-and-print" and start with (H), 40. According to the chart, there were 80 annual subscriptions sold in Westmount. If there were 40 digital-and-print ones sold there, then there were $80 - 40 = 40$ print-only ones sold. Use the information about prices to see if these numbers work. The 40 digital-and-print ones would account for $40(\$105) = \$4,200$ in sales, and the 40 print-only ones would account for $40(\$85) = \$3,400$ in sales. Together, this is a total sales amount of $\$4,200 + \$3,400 = \$7,600$. According to the chart, the total sales in Westmount were $\$7,400$. Eliminate (H). The total sales amount was too high, so there must be fewer of the more expensive digital-and-print subscriptions. Eliminate (J) and (K) as well. The value in (G) is only 1 less than the one in (H), so that is not likely to make enough of a difference. Try (F) next instead. For 30 digital-and-print subscriptions, the sales would be $30(\$105) = \$3,150$, and for $80 - 30 = 50$ print-only subscriptions, the sales would be $50(\$85) = \$4,250$. The total sales would be $\$3,150 + \$4,250 = \$7,400$. This matches the value in the chart, so stop here. The correct answer is (F).

15. **A** The question asks how much money a newspaper delivery company makes delivering newspapers to a certain neighborhood. Begin by ballparking to eliminate answers that are too big or too small. The question states that in addition to receiving *20% of the total sales of the newspapers*, the delivery company *charged the newspaper a flat fee of $250.* Therefore, the

correct answer must be larger than $250. Eliminate (D) and (E). According to the table, the newspaper company made $6,250 from newspaper subscriptions in Elmhurst. The 20% fee can be represented as $\dfrac{20}{100}$ or 0.20 times the total. The deliver company's fee can be calculated as $6,250 × 0.20 = $1,250. The final answer must include the $250 flat fee, so add $250 to $1,250 to get $1,500. The correct answer is (A).

16. **G** The question asks for the sum of the mode and the mean number of subscriptions. The mode is the number that occurs most frequently in a data set. According to the table, the mode of the number of annual subscriptions is 70, which is the only number that occurs more than once. Since the question asks for the sum of the mode and the mean, eliminate (J) and (K) because those values are smaller than the mode. The mean is the average of a data set, which can be calculated by adding all the values and dividing by the number of values. In this case, the mean can be calculated as $\dfrac{25+70+55+80+60+70}{6} = \dfrac{360}{6} = 60$. Add the mode to the mean to get $70 + 60 = 130$. The correct answer is (G).

18. **K** The question asks for a specific value that will result in a data set having an average of 18. Since the question asks for a specific value and the answers contain numbers in increasing order, plug in the answers. Begin by labeling the answers as "x" and start with (H), 17. The average of a data set is the total divided by the number of things. If $x = 17$, then the average of the data set can be calculated as $\dfrac{17+9+15+20+17+4+23+17}{8} = \dfrac{122}{8} = 15.25$. This does not match 18, so eliminate (H). The value of x must be larger than 17 to make the average of the whole set 18, so eliminate (F) and (G) which are too small. Next try (J) to get an average of $\dfrac{17+9+15+20+17+4+23+38}{8} = \dfrac{143}{8} = 17.875$. This does not match 18, so eliminate (J). Only (K) is left, so the correct answer is (K).

20. **J** The question asks for the area of a figure. When doing geometry problems, be sure to label the figure and write down any formulas that will be needed. When dealing with strange shapes, break them down into more familiar shapes. One way to divide the figure is as follows:

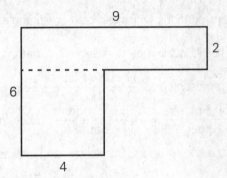

Since the figure was broken into 2 four-sided polygons, and all the angles are right angles, use the formula $A = lw$, where l is the length and w is the width. The area of the top rectangle can be calculated as $A = 9 \times 2 = 18$. To determine the area of the bottom polygon, subtract the width of the right side of the original shape from the width of its left side or $6 - 2 = 4$ to give the width of the missing side, as follows:

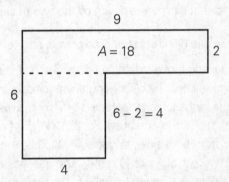

The area of the bottom polygon can be calculated as $A = 4 \times 4 = 16$. The total area of the shape is found by adding the smaller areas together to get $18 + 16 = 34$. The correct answer is (J).

22. **K** The question asks for the number of kilometers two trucks will drive before one is full. Begin by determining how long it will take before the dump truck is full. The blower fills the dump truck at a rate of 3 cubic meters per hour, which can be represented as $\dfrac{3 \text{ cubic meters}}{1 \text{ hour}}$. The dump truck will be full once it has 12 cubic meters of snow in it, but the amount of time is unknown, so the amount can be represented as $\dfrac{12 \text{ cubic meters}}{x \text{ hours}}$. Set these two proportions equal to each other to get $\dfrac{3 \text{ cubic meters}}{1 \text{ hour}} = \dfrac{12 \text{ cubic meters}}{x \text{ hours}}$. Cross-multiply to get $3x = 12$; then divide both sides by 3 to get $x = 4$ hours. This is how long it takes to fill the dump truck. Next, determine how far the two trucks will travel in 4 hours. The question states that *the two trucks travel together at a constant rate of 0.5 kilometer per minute*. To convert hours to minutes, set up a proportion such that $\dfrac{1 \text{ hour}}{60 \text{ minutes}} = \dfrac{4 \text{ hours}}{x \text{ minutes}}$. Cross-multiply to get $x = 240$ minutes. To determine the total number of kilometers driven by the two trucks, multiply 0.5 kilometers per minute by 240 minutes to get 120 kilometers. The correct answer is (K).

24. **J** The question asks for the length of a side on a figure. Since all the information from the question is labeled on the figure, begin by calculating any additional information. The length of $\overline{XY}$ can be calculated with the Pythagorean theorem, $a^2 + b^2 = c^2$, where a and b are the lengths of the legs and c is the length of the hypotenuse. For $\triangle WXY$, this becomes $a^2 + 24^2 = 26^2$ or $a^2 + 576 = 676$. Subtract 576 from both sides to get $a^2 = 100$. Take the square root of both sides to get $a = 10$. Therefore, the length of $\overline{XY}$ is 10 inches. The question states that $\overline{WZ}$ intersects $\overline{XY}$ *at the midpoint*, so the length of $\overline{XZ}$ must be half of 10 inches, or 5 inches.

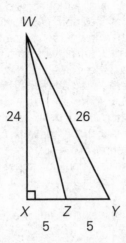

The length of $\overline{WZ}$ can then be calculated with the Pythagorean theorem again such that $5^2 + 24^2 = c^2$. Simplify to $25 + 576 = c^2$ or $601 = c^2$. Take the square root of both sides to get $c = \sqrt{601}$. The correct answer is (J).

26. **G** The question asks for a value in a geometric sequence. A geometric sequence is one in which the ratio between consecutive terms is constant. Start by using Process of Elimination. The 4th term is positive and the 5th term is negative. This means that every other term will be negative. Therefore, odd terms are negative, and x_1 will be negative. Eliminate (J) and (K). Now determine the ratio between consecutive terms. The only two consecutive terms listed are 2 and $-\dfrac{2}{3}$. If the ratio is represented by r, then $2r = -\dfrac{2}{3}$. Solve for r by dividing both sides by 2 to get $r = -\dfrac{1}{3}$. Therefore, the ratio for this geometric sequence is $-\dfrac{1}{3}$. The value of x_3 can be calculated as $x_3(r) = x_4$ or $x_3\left(-\dfrac{1}{3}\right) = 2$. Multiply both sides by -3 to get $x_3 = -6$. Use the same method to calculate the value of x_2 where $x_2\left(-\dfrac{1}{3}\right) = -6$. Multiply both sides by -3 to get $x_2 = 18$. Finally, calculate the value of x_1 as $x_1\left(-\dfrac{1}{3}\right) = 18$. Multiply both sides by -3 to get $x_1 = -54$. The correct answer is (G).

28. **K** The question asks for what is true of the roots of a given equation. The answer choices are expressed in terms of rational, irrational, and real roots. A rational number is one that can be expressed as the ratio of two other numbers, making a fraction. An irrational number is one that can be expressed as a decimal but not a fraction. Real numbers include zero, all positive and negative integers, fractions, decimals, and roots. The presence of these terms in the answer choices likely means that the quadratic is difficult to factor. In that case, the number of roots for a quadratic in the standard form, $ax^2 + bx + c = 0$, can be determined by calculating the discriminant, $D = b^2 - 4ac$. When $D > 0$, the quadratic has two real roots. When $D = 0$, the quadratic has one real root. When $D < 0$, the quadratic has no real roots. Begin by determining the discriminant for the given equation. In the given quadratic equation, $a = 1$, $b = -3$, and $c = 6$. Insert these values into the discriminant equation to get $D = (-3)^2 - 4(1)(6) = 9 - 24 = -15$. Since $D < 0$, there are no real roots. The correct answer is (K).

32. **K** The question asks for the length of a side on a figure. Begin by labeling any information from the question that is not on the figure. The tangent of an angle in a right triangle is the ratio of the opposite side length over the adjacent side length, or $\dfrac{opposite}{adjacent}$. Here, the side opposite $\angle M$ is $\overline{LN}$ and the side adjacent to $\angle M$ is $\overline{ML}$. Therefore, $\tan M = \dfrac{opposite}{adjacent} = \dfrac{LN}{ML} = \dfrac{8}{7}$. In the figure, $\overline{LN}$ is labeled as 16 inches. To find the length of $\overline{ML}$, set up the ratio $\dfrac{16}{ML} = \dfrac{8}{7}$. Cross-multiply to get $(8)(ML) = (16)(7)$ or $8ML = 112$. Divide both sides by 8 to get $ML = 14$. Label this on the figure. The length of the hypotenuse, x, can then be calculated with the Pythagorean theorem, $a^2 + b^2 = c^2$, where a and b are the lengths of the legs and c is the length of the hypotenuse. The two legs are 14 and 16, so plug those into the equation $a^2 + b^2 = c^2$ to get $14^2 + 16^2 = c^2$. Simplify to $196 + 256 = c^2$ or $452 = c^2$. Take the square root of both sides to get $\sqrt{452} = c$, which becomes $\sqrt{(4)(113)} = c$ and then $2\sqrt{113} = c$. The correct answer is (K).

35. **C** The question asks for the total distance walked during one tour based on a rate in terms of feet per minute. Begin by reading the question to find information on the walking rate. The question states that the tour took *0.56 hours* to complete. Set up a proportion to determine the

number of minutes the tour takes: $\dfrac{60 \text{ minutes}}{1 \text{ hour}} = \dfrac{x \text{ minutes}}{0.56 \text{ hours}}$. Cross-multiply to get $x = 33.6$ minutes. The question also states that *the group traveled at an average walking pace of 106.8 feet per minute*. Set up a proportion to determine how many feet will be walked in 33.6 minutes: $\dfrac{106.8 \text{ feet}}{1 \text{ minute}} = \dfrac{x \text{ feet}}{33.6 \text{ minutes}}$. Cross-multiply to get $x = 3{,}588.48$ feet. The question asks for the *closest* answer, so the correct answer is (C).

36. **J** The question asks for the percent of time that *the group is at least 1,100 meters from the starting point*. Begin by reading the question to find information on the total time of the tour. The question states that it takes *0.56 hours* to complete the tour. Set up a proportion to determine the number of minutes the tour takes: $\dfrac{60 \text{ minutes}}{1 \text{ hour}} = \dfrac{x \text{ minutes}}{0.56 \text{ hours}}$. Cross-multiply to get $x = 33.6$ minutes. The question also states that *the group spends a total of 13 minutes at a distance at least 1,100 meters from the starting point*. The percent of time is $\dfrac{\text{time at least 1,100 m away}}{\text{total time of tour}} \times 100$. Plug the two values, 13 and 33.6, into the expression to get $\dfrac{13 \text{ minutes}}{33.6 \text{ minutes}} \times 100 \approx 38.69\%$. The question asks for the *closest* answer, so the correct answer is (J).

37. **D** The question asks for the *average slope, in meters per minute*, for the *interval between 15 minutes and 25 minutes* on the graph. Use two points from the interval and the equation *slope* $= \dfrac{y_2 - y_1}{x_2 - x_1}$ to calculate the slope of the line. Use the points (15, 1,000) and (25, 1,250). The equation then becomes *slope* $= \dfrac{1{,}250 - 1{,}000}{25 - 15} = \dfrac{250}{10} = 25$ meters per minute. The correct answer is (D).

38. **F** The question asks for the value of an expression when a specific value is plugged in. Plug in $a = 10$. The expression becomes $10^6(0.0003(10)^3 - 0.065(10) + 0.7) = 10^6(0.3 - 0.65 + 0.7) = 10^6(0.35)$. The answers are all in scientific notation, so rewrite the expression as a number between 1 and 10 multiplied by a power of 10. The expression can be rewritten as 0.35×10^6. Since 0.35 is not between 1 and 10, take one power of 10 from the 10^6 to multiply it by 0.35. The 0.35 becomes 3.5 and the 10^6 becomes 10^5. The new number in scientific notation is 3.5×10^5. The question asks which numbers the value falls between, so the correct answer is (F).

40. **H** The question asks for the area of a triangular picture frame, based on a figure, *to the nearest square inch*. The question states that *the frame is a triangle with three equal sides with a semicircle removed*. Therefore, the area of the frame will be the area of the triangle minus the area of the semicircle. The figure shows that one side of the triangle is 30 inches. The figure also shows that the height is 26 inches. The formula for the area of a triangle is $A = \frac{1}{2}bh$, so plug in values from the figure to solve for the area of the triangle. The area of the triangle is $A = \frac{1}{2}(30)(26) = 390$ square inches. Now calculate the area of the semicircle and subtract this area from the total area of the triangle. The figure shows that the two edges next to the circle are each 5 inches. Since each side of the triangle is 30 inches, subtract these two edges from the length of a side to find the diameter of the circle: $30 - 2(5) = 30 - 10 = 20$ inches. The radius of a circle is half of the diameter, so $r = \frac{20}{2} = 10$ inches. The formula for the area of a circle is $A = \pi r^2$, so $A = \pi(10)^2 = 100\pi \approx 314.16$ square inches. Only half of the circle overlaps the frame, so divide this by 2 to get 157.08 square inches for the area of the semicircle. Subtract this from the area of the triangle to find the area of the picture frame: $A = 390 - 157.08 = 232.92$ square inches. The question asks for the answer *to the nearest square inch*, which is 233 square inches. The correct answer is (H).

42. **G** The question asks for the value of a compound function. In a compound function, one function is substituted into another function. When working with compound functions, work with the function on the inside first; then use the value from the inner function as the x value for the outer function. There are variables in the answer choices, so plug in. Begin with the function inside the parentheses, the function $h(x)$, and make $x = 2$. The function becomes $h(2) = (2)^3 = 8$. Because the function $h(x)$ is inside the function $k(x)$, plug $h(2) = 8$ into the function $k(x)$. The function becomes $k(8) = \dfrac{5}{8+2} = \dfrac{5}{10} = \dfrac{1}{2}$. This is the target value; circle it. Now plug $x = 2$ into the answer choices to see which one matches the target value. Choice (F) becomes $\dfrac{5(2)^3}{2^3 + 2} = \dfrac{5(8)}{8+2} = \dfrac{40}{10} = 4$. This does not match the target value, so eliminate (F). Choice (G) becomes $\dfrac{5}{2^3 + 2} = \dfrac{5}{8+2} = \dfrac{5}{10} = \dfrac{1}{2}$. This matches the target, so keep (G), but check the remaining answers just in case. Choice (H) becomes $\dfrac{5}{(2+2)^3} = \dfrac{5}{(4)^3} = \dfrac{5}{64}$. Eliminate (H). Choice (J) becomes $\dfrac{5}{2^3 + 8} = \dfrac{5}{8+8} = \dfrac{5}{16}$. Eliminate (J). Choice (K) becomes $\dfrac{5(2)^3}{2+2} = \dfrac{5(8)}{4} = \dfrac{40}{4} = 10$. Eliminate (K). Another way to approach this problem is to substitute the entire h function into the k function for x. The result is $k(x^3) = \dfrac{5}{x^3 + 2}$. Either way, the correct answer is (G).

44. **J** The question asks for the coordinates of the y-intercept for the function $g(x) + 7$ based on the y-intercept for the function $g(x)$. In function notation, the number inside the parentheses is the x-value that goes into the function, and the value that comes out of the function is the y-value or $g(x)$. The y-intercept is defined as the value of $g(x)$ when $x = 0$. The question states that the *coordinates of the y-intercept of the graph of the function g(x) are (0, 4)*. The function $g(x) + 7$ adds 7 to all the y-values of the function $g(x)$. Therefore, add 7 to the y-value of the y-intercept to get $4 + 7 = 11$. The new intercept is at (0, 11). The correct answer is (J).

46. **J**   The question asks for the value of an expression as *t* decreases in value without bound. A line that an expression approaches, but never reaches, is called an asymptote. Plug a few points into the equation and sketch a graph or graph the function on a calculator, as seen here. As *t* approaches −∞, the line approaches 4.

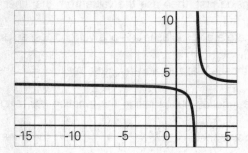

Another way to approach this is to notice that as *t* decreases in value, the expression $\frac{1}{t-2}$ also decreases to nearly zero. The expression approximately becomes $0 + 4 = 4$. Either way, the correct answer is (J).

48. **G**   The question asks for the value of *f* that makes an expression undefined. An expression is undefined if the denominator has a value of 0. Even though there are variables in the answers, plugging in will be difficult due to the number of variables in the expression. Instead, set the denominator equal to 0 and solve for *f*. This becomes $f + \frac{1}{3}g = 0$. Subtract $\frac{1}{3}g$ from both sides of the equation to get $f = -\frac{1}{3}g$. The correct answer is (G).

51. **C**   The question asks for the coordinates of the foci of the provided ellipse equation. Foci are two points inside an ellipse and are equally spaced from the center on the vertical or horizontal axis. The standard form of the ellipse equation is represented as $\frac{(x-h)^2}{a^2} + \frac{(y-k)^2}{b^2} = 1$, where (h, k) represents the center of the ellipse. The center of the ellipse is (4, 1). There are specific points in the answers, so use those points to ballpark. Eliminate (D) and (E) because they both include the center, and the center cannot be a focus. Check the location of the remaining ordered pairs

on the graph of the ellipse and look for a pair in which both coordinates fall inside the ellipse. Start with the ordered pair (–6, 1) because it shows up in multiple answers. The point (–6, 1) is part of the ellipse, not inside it, so it cannot be a focus. Eliminate (A) and (B). The correct answer is (C).

53. **A** The question asks for the area of a triangle based on a figure. The formula for the area of a triangle is $A = \frac{1}{2}bh$. Draw a vertical line perpendicular to the base to represent the height as shown below.

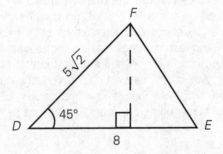

There are 180° in a triangle, so the triangle on the left is a 45°-45°-90° special triangle and the side lengths opposite each angle are x, x, and $x\sqrt{2}$, respectively. The length of the hypotenuse, or the side opposite 90°, is $5\sqrt{2}$, so the height, or one of the sides opposite 45°, is 5. Plug in values from the figure to solve for the area of the triangle. The figure shows that the base is 8, so the equation becomes $A = \frac{1}{2}(8)(5) = 20$. The correct answer is (A).

55. **E** The question asks for the percent of *the area of rectangle WXYZ* that is represented by the shaded triangle. The question states that *the area of rectangle WXYZ is 4 times the area of rectangle SUVZ*, so rectangle *SUVZ* is $\frac{1}{4}$ the total area of rectangle *WXYZ*, or 25%. The figure shows that $\overline{SV}$ divides rectangle *SUVZ* in half, so the shaded triangle represents $\frac{1}{2}$ of the area of rectangle *SUVZ*, or $\frac{25\%}{2} = 12.5\%$ of the total area of rectangle *WXYZ*. The correct answer is (E).

56. **F** The question asks how the median and mean of a data set of distinct values will change when the smallest value is removed. The median of a list of numbers is the middle number when all values are arranged in order. In lists with an even number of items, the median is the average of the middle two numbers. Since no values are given, plug in for the original list. The numbers could be 1, 2, 3, 4, 5, 6, 7. When the number with the least value is removed, the list becomes 2, 3, 4, 5, 6, 7. The median of the original list is 4 and the median on the new list is 4.5. The median increased, so eliminate (G), (H), and (J). Also eliminate (K), which indicates that the medians of the two lists cannot be compared. The correct answer is (F).

57. **E** The question asks for the matrix product that represents the total time it will take Sean to lead two clients through sets of exercises. For matrix products, the number of vertical columns in the first matrix must be equal to the number of horizontal rows in the second matrix. Choices (A) and (B) both have one column in the first matrix and two rows in the second matrix. These numbers do not match, so eliminate (A) and (B). To find the total time it takes Sean to lead the sets, the total number of sets of each exercise must be multiplied by the time it takes to perform each exercise. The question states that a set of squats lasts *for 6 minutes*, and a set of deadlifts lasts *for 4 minutes*. The question also states that *the first client performs 4 sets of squats and 3 sets of deadlifts*. In matrix multiplication, the numbers in the first row of the first matrix are multiplied by the numbers in the first column of the second matrix; then the resulting products are added together. For example, the first part of the matrix product below represents the calculation $AC + BD$.

$$[A \ B]\begin{bmatrix} C & E \\ D & F \end{bmatrix}$$

The total time it takes Sean to lead the first client's session can be calculated as $6(4) + 4(3)$. Look for a matrix product that represents the calculation $6(4) + 4(3)$. It will be the choice with a 3 in the lower left position of the second matrix. The correct answer is (E).

Reading

21. B This reasoning question asks which idea is emphasized by the first paragraph of Passage A. Read the first paragraph. The paragraph begins by stating that Jones collected material from *survival workshops* for his production, "*Still/Here*," and then it describes how he collected the words and gestures of the workshop participants and used their stories as raw material. Eliminate answers that don't match this prediction. Although the beginning of the paragraph suggests that Jones interviewed a large number of people, the function of the paragraph is to emphasize the content, not the quantity, of the material he collected. Since (A) doesn't answer the right question, eliminate (A). Keep (B) because it matches the prediction. Eliminate (C) because the paragraph does not state that Jones formed *personal relationships* with the workshop participants. Eliminate (D) because while it is reasonable to think that *organizational skills* would be required to coordinate Jones's travel, the paragraph does not discuss these skills. The correct answer is (B).

22. G This reasoning question asks for the performance piece that would be *most conceptually similar to Jones's performance piece discussed in the fourth paragraph of Passage A*. Read the fourth paragraph. The fourth paragraph says that "*Still*" *opens with the company reciting and demonstrating the movement vignettes created by the workshop participants* and that it includes video imagery. Therefore, the performance involves movement, spoken words, and video, and is based on the material created by the workshop participants. The first paragraph says that the workshop participants created material based on their experiences of living with *life-threatening illnesses*. Eliminate answers that don't match this prediction. Eliminate (F) because although the paragraph describes stories told through *dance*, it is based on many personal narratives, not one story that is known to many people, such as a *traditional folk tale*. Keep (G) because *a multimedia performance inspired by accounts of life-changing accidents* matches the idea of dance, spoken words, and video based on people's personal stories about living with challenging circumstances. Eliminate (H), which uses some words from the passage, but doesn't match the meaning in the text: though the performance described uses *words, gestures, and images*, the passage indicates that Bill T. Jones selected and arranged these pieces deliberately to reflect a particular theme; they were not *chosen by chance*. Eliminate (J) because a *performance based on the actors' own experiences* doesn't match the idea that the performers recreated words and gestures of other people (the *workshop participants*). The correct answer is (G).

23. A This vocabulary-in-context question asks what the word *raw* most nearly means in line 7. Go back to the text, find the word *raw*, and cross it out. Carefully read the surrounding text to determine another word that would fit in the blank based on the context. Lines 1–8 say that Jones collected the *words and gestures* of *workshop participants* and that *these became the raw material* for "*Still/Here*." Therefore, *raw* must mean something like "unedited." *Unfinished* matches "unedited," so keep (A). *Sore* means "painful," which does not match "unedited," so eliminate (B). Note that (B) is based on another meaning of *raw* that is not supported by the text. *Organic* means "natural," which does not match "unedited," so eliminate (C). *Unpleasant* means "disagreeable," which does not match "unedited," so eliminate (D). The correct answer is (A).

24. **J** This reasoning question asks for the *main reason Jones interviewed real people to create "Still/Here,"* according to Passage A. There is not a good lead word in this question, so work the question later. Use lead words from the answers to find the window. The words *therapy, living,* and *death* all appear in the first paragraph, so read the first paragraph. Lines 1–4 state that Jones conducted workshops in which he collected material from people who were living with *life-threatening illnesses.* The paragraph then quotes Jones: *"This isn't therapy,"* he says. *"It's about creativity."* Lines 16–17 say that "Still/Here" is a piece *about living—about how to live in the same house as death, when the house is your body.* Therefore, Jones interviewed real people because he wanted to use their stories as the basis for a performance piece about living with life-threatening illnesses. Eliminate answers that don't match this prediction. Choice (F) uses words from the passage but doesn't match what the passage says. The passage says *this isn't about therapy,* so eliminate (F). Eliminate (G) because the first paragraph does not mention the *similarities between postmodern and traditional dance.* Eliminate (H) because the first paragraph does not mention the *interplay between theater and dance.* Keep (J) because it matches the prediction. The correct answer is (J).

25. **D** This referral question asks for the *aspect* of *"Story/Time"* with which *the author of Passage B was least engaged.* There is not a good lead word in this question ("Story/Time" appears in several places throughout the passage), so work the question later. In the last paragraph, the author says, *As the clock approached 70 minutes, I realized that I had registered very little of what Jones had said* and that *I had forgotten to process what [Jones's] words meant.* Eliminate answers that do not match this prediction. Eliminate (A) because it uses words from the passage but doesn't match what the passage says: the author says that he was *distracted by the aesthetic of it all,* which contradicts (A). Eliminate (B) because the author describes the *dancers' movements* in detail in the fourth paragraph and does not indicate that he was *least engaged* with this aspect of the performance. Eliminate (C) because this passage does not mention *video imagery.* Keep (D) because it matches the prediction. The correct answer is (D).

26. **F** This reasoning question asks why the author of Passage B *references John Cage's "Indeterminacy" and contact improvisation* when describing *Jones's dance company.* Look for the lead words *John Cage's "Indeterminacy"* and *contact improvisation* to find the window for the question. The second paragraph says that *Bill T. Jones and Arnie Zane* drew upon *John Cage's "Indeterminacy"* and *contact improvisation* to challenge *notions about what kind of bodies belong on stage and how dancing should look.* It also states that *they gained international*

renown for their experimental theater-dance hybrid. Therefore, the author mentions *John Cage's "Indeterminacy" and contact improvisation* as examples of unique inspirational material for Jones and his dance company. Eliminate answers that don't match this prediction. Keep (F) because *innovative* matches *experimental*. Eliminate (G) because there is no discussion about the dance company being *balanced*. Eliminate (H) because, although the passage suggests that the author found Jones's dance piece *engaging*, the discussion about Jones's dance *company* in the second paragraph doesn't mention this idea. Therefore, (H) answers the wrong question. Eliminate (J) because the company is described as *experimental*, which contradicts *traditional*. The correct answer is (F).

27. **B** This vocabulary-in-context question asks what the word *struck* most nearly means in line 86. Go back to the text, find the word *struck*, and cross it out. Carefully read the surrounding text to determine another word that would fit in the blank based on the context. Line 86 says, *Finally, the clock struck 70 minutes*. Therefore, *struck* must mean something like "showed." *Attacked* does not match "showed," so eliminate (A). *Signaled* matches "showed," so keep (B). *Found* does not match "showed," so eliminate (C). *Impressed* does not match "showed," so eliminate (D). Note that (A), (C), and (D) are based on other meanings of *struck* that are not supported by the text. The correct answer is (B).

28. **H** This reasoning question asks for the statement that *best captures a difference in the purposes of the passages*. Because this question asks about both passages, it should be done after the questions that ask about each passage individually. Passage A describes Jones's creative process while making "Still/Here" and discusses his personal motivation for creating such a piece. Passage B discusses the author's thoughts on Jones's piece "Story/Time." Eliminate answers that don't match this prediction. Eliminate (F) because the main purpose of Passage A is not to provide *a history of Jones's evolution as a dancer*. Eliminate (G) because Passage A does not contrast *Jones's earlier and later works*, and Passage B does not discuss in detail *Jones's exploration of Cage's work*. Keep (H) because it matches the prediction. Eliminate (J) because Passage A discusses only one dance piece, and Passage B does not contrast *Jones and other experimental choreographers*. The correct answer is (H).

29. **D** This referral question asks for the idea that *Passage A provides more information* about than *Passage B* does. Because this question asks about both passages, it should be done after the questions that ask about each passage individually. Eliminate any answer choices that misrepresent either passage. Eliminate (A) because Passage A does not mention *contact improvisation*. Eliminate (B) because neither passage discusses how Jones *responds to creative analyses of his choreography*. Eliminate (C) because Passage A does not mention *John Cage*. Keep (D) because it is true that Passage A, more so than Passage B, discusses how Jones *uses people's stories to create dance pieces*. The correct answer is (D).

30. **H** This referral question asks what the *authors of Passage A and Passage B both remark on* about *Jones*. Because this question asks about both passages, it should be done after the questions that ask about each passage individually. Eliminate any answer choices that misrepresent either passage. Eliminate (F) because only Passage A mentions *survival workshops*. Eliminate (G) because only Passage B mentions that Jones used *silence during his narration*. Keep (H) because both passages discuss Jones's use of *multiple vignettes* in *one performance*: Lines 32–34 in Passage A say that *"Still" opens with the company reciting and demonstrating the movement vignettes created by the workshop participants*, and lines 48–50 in Passage B say that *"Story/Time" is the telling of 70, one-minute vignettes written and narrated by Jones*. Eliminate (J) because neither passage says that Jones uses *traditional dance methods and techniques*; in fact, both imply that his methods are innovative. The correct answer is (H).

31. **A** This reasoning question asks for one *main purpose of the passage*. Because this is a general question, it should be done after the specific questions. The passage is about the platypus genome and how it is helping scientists understand *how mammals evolved their particular traits* (line 26). Eliminate answers that don't match this prediction. Keep (A) because it matches the prediction. Eliminate (B) because the passage indicates that the platypus *split from mammals* 166 million years ago, and the passage does not indicate that platypuses have *not undergone significant evolutionary changes* since then. Eliminate (C) because there are not *two prominent hypotheses* in the passage. Eliminate (D) because the discussion of *egg-laying and lactation* is included in only two paragraphs and is therefore not a main purpose of the passage. This answer includes a correct detail from the passage, but it doesn't answer the question that was asked. The correct answer is (A).

32. **J** This reasoning question asks for the best summary of *the author's claim about the relationship between the platypus genome and mammal evolution*. Because this is a general question, it should be done after the specific questions. The passage discusses the platypus genome and how it relates to both reptiles and mammals. Lines 24–26 say, *"The platypus is critical to helping us understand what genes were present in the ancestral reptilian lineage and how mammals evolved their particular traits,"* Warren said. Eliminate answers that don't match this prediction. Eliminate (F) because according to the passage, the platypus did retain some of *its reptilian features*, such as egg-laying. Choice (G) uses words from the passage but doesn't match the passage's meaning. Although the passage indicates that the platypus is related to the *echidna*, it doesn't suggest that this relationship is the reason that the platypus genome *helps scientists to understand mammal evolution*. Eliminate (G). Eliminate (H) because it contradicts the prediction. Keep (J) because it matches the prediction. The correct answer is (J).

33. **C** This reasoning question asks what the phrase *early divergence* refers to. Read a window around the given line reference. The text says, *The group of animals called monotremes... is thought to have split from other mammals at least 166 million years ago. That early divergence means...* Therefore, the *divergence* refers to the point at which monotremes *split from other mammals*. Eliminate answers that don't match this prediction. Eliminate (A) because the lines don't specify whether the change was *rapid*, nor do they discuss a time of change for *all mammals*; the lines reference the split of only one group from other mammals. Eliminate (B) because the lines discuss *monotremes* and *mammals*, not a shift from *egg-laying* to *live birthing* in *aquatic animals*. Keep (C) because it matches the prediction. Eliminate (D) because there is no mention of *habitat* in the window. The correct answer is (C).

34. **H** This referral question asks what was *true of the platypus's genes for lactation and its genes for live-bearing a little less than 166 million years ago*. Look for the lead words *lactation* and *live-bearing* to find the window for the question. *Lactation* and *live-bearing* are both mentioned in the fifth paragraph. Lines 54–56 state, *"The presence of the full repertoire of milk genes confirms that lactation evolved at least 166 million years ago, way before live-bearing."* Therefore, a little less than 166 million years ago, the platypus had genes for *lactation* but not for *live-bearing*. Eliminate answers that don't match this prediction. Eliminate (F), (G), and (J) because they don't match the prediction. The correct answer is (H).

35. **B** This referral question asks what *the author concludes* about the importance of *sequencing the platypus genome*. Look for the lead word *sequencing* (or *sequence*) to find the window for the question. The last paragraph indicates that *in the human genome*, it is hard *to find sequences that are functional*. The text then says, *Comparing the human and platypus genomes...will enable researchers to locate functional DNA sequences more easily*. Therefore, the platypus genome helps researchers *locate functional DNA sequences* in the human genome. Eliminate answers that don't match this prediction. Eliminate (A) because the passage does not say that the functional DNA sequences are the *most important*. Keep (B) because it matches the prediction. Eliminate (C) because *echidnas* are not mentioned in the window. Eliminate (D) because *reptiles* and *birds* are not mentioned in the window. The correct answer is (B).

36. **F** This referral question asks which genetic process *is thought to have given snakes the ability to produce venom*. Look for the lead words *snake* and *venom* to find the window for the question. *Snake* and *venom* are discussed in the seventh paragraph. Lines 69–72 say, *Previous studies of venomous snakes had found that poison production is the result of evolutionary modifications to genes that once served other functions*. Therefore, the genetic process involved changes to genes that were not originally associated with venom production. Eliminate answers that don't match this prediction. Keep (F) because it matches the prediction. Choice (G) uses words from the passage but doesn't match the passage's meaning: *spurs* are found on platypus *males' hind legs* and are not related to venom production in *snakes*. Eliminate (G). Eliminate (H)

because the last sentence in the seventh paragraph says that the evolutionary process for the platypus is *separate from the evolution of venom in snakes*. Choice (J) uses words from the passage but doesn't match the passage's meaning: the reference to *19 substances* pertains to platypus venom, not snake venom. Eliminate (J). The correct answer is (F).

37. **D** This referral question asks what the *evolved traits* of *lactation and live-bearing* are *characteristic of*. Look for the lead words *lactation* and *live-bearing* to find the window for the question. *Lactation* and *live-bearing* are mentioned in the fifth paragraph. Lines 48–56 indicate that *lactation* means *milk production,* and they refer to *milk production* and *giving birth to live young* as *two common mammalian traits*. Therefore, *lactation* and *live-bearing* are characteristic of mammals. Eliminate answers that don't match this prediction. Eliminate (A), (B), and (C) because they do not match the prediction. The correct answer is (D).

38. **G** This referral question asks which genetic trait indicated that *the platypus inherited some of its genome from reptilian ancestors*. Look for the lead words *reptilian ancestors* to find the window for the question. Lines 43–47 say, *"The new genomic data makes a water-tight case for [platypus] egg-laying truly being a primitive retention from reptilian ancestors."* Therefore, the genetic trait that connects the platypus to reptilian ancestors is *egg-laying*. Eliminate answers that don't match this prediction. Eliminate (F), (H), and (J). The correct answer is (G).

39. **B** This vocabulary-in-context question asks what the word *served* most nearly means in line 71. Go back to the text, find the word *served*, and cross it out. Carefully read the surrounding text to determine another word that would fit in the blank based on the context. Lines 69–71 say that *poison production is the result of evolutionary modifications to genes that once served other functions*. Therefore, *served* must mean something like "satisfied" or "provided." *Attended* means "tended to the needs of," which doesn't match "provided," so eliminate (A). *Fulfilled* matches "provided," so keep (B). *Produced* does not match "provided," so eliminate (C). *Initiated* means "started," which doesn't match "provided," so eliminate (D). The correct answer is (B).

40. **H** This reasoning question asks what *platypuses developed to locate prey underwater* that surprised *scientists*. Look for the lead words *locate prey underwater* to find the window for the question. The sixth paragraph mentions *locating prey underwater*. Lines 59–64 say, *One big surprise was the discovery of a number of specialized genes associated with odor detection* and the fact that *platypuses also rely on chemical cues when navigating and locating prey underwater*. Therefore, the scientists were surprised that platypuses developed *odor detection* to locate prey underwater. Eliminate answers that don't match this prediction. Eliminate (F) because there is no mention in the passage of *echolocation*. Eliminate (G) because there is no mention of *eyesight*. Keep (H) because it matches the prediction. Eliminate (J) because there is no mention of *long dives* or *oxygen*. The correct answer is (H).

Science

1. **C** The question asks for the approximate *difference between the resistance at a cross-sectional area of 0.25 mm² and the resistance at a cross-sectional area of 0.50 mm²* for a *16 m* wire of *Alloy B*, based on Table 2. Look at Table 2, and determine the resistance of each wire using the column for Alloy B. At a 0.25 mm² cross-sectional area, an Alloy B wire has a resistance of 1.0944 ohms. At a 0.50 mm² cross-sectional area, an Alloy B wire has a resistance of 0.5472 ohms. Round 1.0944 ohms to 1.10 ohms and 0.5472 ohms to 0.55 ohms to make the calculation easier: the difference is approximately 1.10 ohms − 0.55 ohms = 0.55 ohms. The correct answer is (C).

2. **J** The question asks for the order of Alloys B, D, E, and F from the *largest resistance* to the *smallest resistance* at *32 m*, based on Table 1. Look at Table 1, and find the row for 32 m. Alloy E has the largest resistance at 32 m, so eliminate (F) and (G). Alloy F has the second-highest resistance at 32 m, so eliminate (H). Only (J) correctly lists the alloys in descending resistance. The correct answer is (J).

3. **C** The question asks for the alloy with a resistance *most similar* to the *resistance of Alloy A*, based on Tables 1 and 2. Look at Tables 1 and 2, and compare the resistance of Alloy A to the resistance of Alloys B, C, D, and E. At every length in Table 1, the resistance of Alloy D is closest to the resistance of Alloy A. At every cross-sectional area in Table 2, the resistance of Alloy D is closest to the resistance of Alloy A. The correct answer is (C).

4. **G** The question asks *how many alloys listed in Table 2* have a resistance *smaller* than 0.3650 ohms *at 0.75 mm² and 16 m*. All of the alloys in Table 2 have a length of 16 m, so look at Table 2 and find the row for 0.75 mm² cross-sectional area. At 0.75 mm², Alloy B has a resistance of 0.3648 ohms and all other alloys have a resistance above 0.3650 ohms. So, only 1 alloy listed in Table 2 has a resistance smaller than 0.3650 ohms at 0.75 mm² and 16 m. The correct answer is (G).

5. **A** The question asks, based on Table 1, for the alloy and length of wire that will have the greatest current, given that *current passing through a wire decreases as the resistance of the wire increases*. Since the answers refer to Alloys B and E, compare the resistance of Alloy B with the resistance of Alloy E in Table 1. At a cross-sectional area of 1.00 mm², Alloy B has a lower resistance than Alloy E at every length. Since the current decreases as the resistance increases, Alloy B will have a greater current than Alloy E. Eliminate (B) and (D), which both refer to Alloy E. At 2 m, Alloy B has a resistance of 0.0342 ohms and at 256 m, Alloy B has a resistance of 4.3776 ohms. Since the wire with the smallest resistance will have the greatest current, the 2 m wire will have the greatest current. The correct answer is (A).

6. **G** The question asks, given that both wires are made of Alloy D and each has a cross-sectional area of 1.00 mm², whether a wire with a *resistance of approximately 0.03 ohms* or a wire with a *resistance of approximately 4.40 ohms* would have shorter *transmission time for a signal to pass through the wire,* based on Table 1. Look at Table 1 and determine the length of an Alloy D wire with a resistance of approximately 0.03 ohms and the length of an Alloy D wire with a resistance of approximately 4.40 ohms. At 2 m, an Alloy D wire has a resistance of 0.0344 ohms. At 256 m, an Alloy D wire has a resistance of 4.4032 ohms. Eliminate (F) because it indicates that the longer wire has a resistance of 0.03 ohms, and eliminate (J) because it indicates that the shorter wire has a resistance of 4.40 ohms. Since the wire with a resistance of 0.03 ohms is shorter, the signal will not have to travel as far and therefore will have a shorter transmission time. The correct answer is (G).

27. **D** The question asks which statement about *modern spiders* both students *would likely agree* upon. Look at each student's viewpoint for references to modern spiders and use Process of Elimination. Both students state that spiders have a high gas exchange rate, so eliminate (A). Neither student states that modern spiders have few blood vessels, so eliminate (B). Neither student claims that spiders evolved from horseshoe crabs, so eliminate (C). Student 1 states that *the ancestors of spiders were closely related to eurypterids.* Student 2 also states that *the ancestors of spiders* were *closely related* to *eurypterids.* The correct answer is (D).

28. **F** The question asks whether Student 2 would expect to see *respiratory structures with few blood vessels in a horseshoe crab or a modern spider.* Look for the sentences in Student 2's viewpoint that discuss blood vessels. Student 2 states that *few blood vessels* indicate *a low gas exchange rate and can be found in horseshoe crabs.* Eliminate (H) and (J), which both refer to the modern spider. Eliminate (G), which states that respiratory structures with few blood vessels indicate a *high* gas exchange rate. The correct answer is (F).

29. **C** The question asks in which group of chelicerates would *Student 1 most likely expect to find convoluted respiratory structures.* Look for the sentences in Student 1's discussion that discuss *convoluted respiratory structures.* Student 1 states that *the respiratory structures of eurypterids* were *highly convoluted.* Eliminate (B) and (D), which do not contain eurypterids. Student 1 also states that *convoluted respiratory structures* are *also seen in modern spiders.* Eliminate (A) since it does not contain modern spiders. The correct answer is (C).

30. **G** The question asks whether a horseshoe crab or a modern spider *would likely produce less energy through cellular respiration,* based on Student 1's discussion. The answers refer to gas exchange rates, so look for the sentences in Student 1's discussion that refer to gas exchange rates. Student 1 states that *horseshoe crabs retained* a *low gas exchange rate.* Eliminate (F) and (H), which state that horseshoe crabs have a high gas exchange rate. To choose between the remaining answers, outside knowledge is necessary. Cellular respiration is a process by

which organisms combine oxygen with nutrients to create energy. Since the horseshoe crab has a low gas exchange rate, it would have less available oxygen and be less able to produce energy through cellular respiration. The correct answer is (G).

31. **C** The question asks whether the discovery that *the common ancestor of eurypterids and horseshoe crabs had a low gas exchange rate* would be *consistent* with Student 1's viewpoint or Student 2's viewpoint. Look for the sentences that discuss a low gas exchange rate in each student's viewpoint. Student 1 states that eurypterids are descended from an ancestor that had *a low gas exchange rate*. Eliminate (B) and (D). Student 2 also states that eurypterids are descended from an ancestor that had *a low gas exchange rate*. Eliminate (A). The correct answer is (C).

32. **H** The question asks which group of chelicerates has *gills*, according to *Student 2*. Look for the sentences that discuss gills in Student 2's viewpoint. Student 2 states that *horseshoe crabs are descended from a common ancestor that had gills*, and *horseshoe crabs retained* this *trait*. Eliminate (G) and (J). Additionally, Student 2 states that *eurypterids also had gills*. The correct answer is (H).

33. **A** The question asks whether the discovery of a rock formation *formed from fossilized mud that was above sea level at the time* that *contains fossil trackways made by eurypterids* would support Student 1's viewpoint or Student 2's viewpoint. Look for the sentences in each student's viewpoint that discuss whether the eurypterids could live on land. Student 1 states that *eurypterids had book lungs and could survive on land for extended periods*. Therefore, the finding that eurypterids left fossil trackways above sea level would support Student 1. Eliminate (B) and (D). Student 2 states that *eurypterids had gills and could not survive on land,* so this finding would weaken Student 2's viewpoint. Eliminate (C). The correct answer is (A).

34. **G** The question asks for the trend of the *oxygen partial pressure needed to saturate all of the hemoglobin,* as the *acetic acid increased from 10 mg to 30 mg,* based on Experiment 2. The results of Experiment 2 are shown in Figure 2, so look at Figure 2. The amount of acetic acid was 10 mg in Trial 5, 20 mg in Trial 6, and 30 mg in Trial 7. The percentage of hemoglobin saturated is shown on the vertical axis. For all hemoglobin to be saturated, the percentage of hemoglobin saturated must be 100, so find 100 on the *y*-axis. In Trial 5, the oxygen partial pressure was approximately 70 torr, in Trial 6, the oxygen partial pressure was approximately 49 torr, and in Trial 7, the oxygen partial pressure was approximately 38 torr. So, as the *acetic acid increased* from 10 mg in Trial 5 to 20 mg in Trial 6 to 30 mg in Trial 7, the oxygen partial pressure decreased only. The correct answer is (G).

35. **D** The question asks for the most likely *percentage of hemoglobin saturated* if *a sample from Trial 4 had been analyzed at an oxygen partial pressure of 100 torr*, based on Figure 1. Using Trial 4 in Figure 1, determine the relationship between oxygen partial pressure and the percentage of hemoglobin saturated. As oxygen partial pressure increased, the percentage of hemoglobin saturated also increased. At an oxygen partial pressure of 90 torr, the percentage of hemoglobin saturated was approximately 80%. So, an oxygen partial pressure of 100 torr would have greater than 80% percent of hemoglobin saturated. The correct answer is (D).

36. **G** The question asks for the trend of *oxygen partial pressure at which 20% of the hemoglobin remained unsaturated*, as *the concentration of carbon dioxide increased*, based on Experiment 1. The results of Experiment 1 are shown in Figure 1, so look at Figure 1. When *20% of the hemoglobin remained unsaturated*, the percentage of hemoglobin saturated would be 80%. The percentage of hemoglobin saturated is shown on the vertical axis, so find 80 on the y-axis and draw a horizontal line to each of the saturation curves. In Trial 1, the carbon dioxide concentration was 0.02 mol/L, and the oxygen partial pressure was approximately 35 torr. In Trial 2, the carbon dioxide concentration was 0.03 mol/L, and the oxygen partial pressure was approximately 45 torr. In Trial 3, the carbon dioxide concentration was 0.04 mol/L, and the oxygen partial pressure was approximately 69 torr. In Trial 4, the carbon dioxide concentration was 0.05 mol/L, and the oxygen partial pressure was approximately 90 torr. So, as the *concentration of carbon dioxide increased*, the oxygen partial pressure increased only. The correct answer is (G).

37. **A** The question asks for the number of trials in which *the percentage of hemoglobin saturated reaches 100%* at an oxygen partial pressure *less than 60 torr*, based on Experiments 1–3. The results of Experiments 1–3 are shown in figures 1–3, so look at Figures 1, 2, and 3. In each figure, the oxygen partial pressure is shown on the horizontal axis and the percentage of hemoglobin saturated is shown on the vertical axis. In each figure, find 60 on the x-axis and draw a vertical line up to 100 on the y-axis. In Figure 1, none of the trials reach 100% hemoglobin saturation at an oxygen partial pressure of less than 60 torr. In Figure 2, Trial 6 reached 100% hemoglobin saturation at approximately 50 torr, and Trial 7 reached 100% hemoglobin saturation at approximately 37 torr. Trial 5 did not reach 100% hemoglobin saturation until 70 torr. In Figure 3, none of the trials reach 100% hemoglobin at an oxygen partial pressure of less than 60 torr. So, only 2 trials reached 100% hemoglobin saturation at an oxygen partial pressure of less than 60 torr. The correct answer is (A).

38. **H** The question asks for *the resulting charge of each hemoglobin iron ion after it loses an electron*. The experiments do not show the charge on iron ions, so read the passage introduction to learn more about the charge on the iron ions in hemoglobin. The passage states that hemoglobin contains the *ferrous ion, Fe^{2+}*. A loss of a negative charge would increase positive charge, so eliminate (F). A loss of a positive charge would result in a decrease in positive charge, so eliminate (J). To choose between the remaining answers, outside knowledge is necessary. An electron has

a negative charge, so the resulting charge of each hemoglobin iron ion after it loses an electron would increase from 2+ to 3+. The correct answer is (H).

39. **A** The question asks *how many of the trials were performed at a pH of higher than 7.0* in Experiment 2, given that *the hemoglobin solution used in Step 1 of each experiment was measured to have a pH of 7.0.* The results of Experiment 2 are shown in Figure 2, so look at Figure 2 and the description of Experiment 2. The experiment's description states that acetic acid was added in each trial. An increase in pH would cause all three trials to be performed at a pH greater than 7.0, so eliminate (B). A decrease in pH would cause none of the trials to be performed at a pH greater than 7.0, so eliminate (C). To choose between the remaining choices, outside knowledge is necessary. Acidic solutions have a pH of less than 7.0, while basic solutions have a pH greater than 7.0. So, the addition of acid decreased the pH of the solution. Eliminate (D), which incorrectly states that the addition of acid would increase the pH of a solution. Since the pH was decreased, none of the trials would have a pH greater than 7.0. The correct answer is (A).

40. **F** The question asks which expression *best approximates the mass of the unsaturated hemoglobin remaining in the 40°C solution at 80 torr,* based on Figure 3. Look at Figure 3. In Figure 3, the oxygen partial pressure is shown on the horizontal axis and the percentage of hemoglobin saturated is shown on the vertical axis. In Trial 10, the temperature was 40°C. Find 80 torr on the x-axis and draw a vertical line to the saturation curve for Trial 10. In Trial 10, the percentage of hemoglobin saturated is approximately 95%, so approximately 5% of the hemoglobin in Trial 10 remained unsaturated at 80 torr. Eliminate (H) and (J) since these expressions do not contain 5%. Compare the expressions in (F) and (G). Notice that in (F), the units for mL and L cancel out when the expression is simplified. This results in units of mg, which is used to measure mass. When simplified, the expression in (G) would contain the units $mL^2 \times mg/L^2$, which is not a unit of mass. Eliminate (G). The correct answer is (F).

STEP 3: Determine Your Goals

Now that you are a little more familiar with the structure and content of the ACT, let's discuss the specifics. The ACT always follows the same structure:

Test	Time	Number of Questions	Score Range
English	45 minutes	75 questions	1–36
Math	60 minutes	60 questions	1–36
Reading	35 minutes	40 questions	1–36
Science	35 minutes	40 questions	1–36
Writing (optional)	40 minutes	1 question	2–12

> The ACT calls each section a "test" instead of a "section," but we'll use the terms interchangeably.

What's with the Writing Test?

The Writing Test is considered optional in that you can register to take the ACT with or without it. However, some schools require you to submit a Writing Test score. If you apply to one of those schools, you must take the ACT with the Writing Test. If you are not sure whether you will apply to a school that requires you to take the Writing Test, it's a good idea to take it just in case you do.

Can I take just one or two sections?

Eventually, yes. ACT has committed to allowing students to do Single Section Retesting in the near future. The key word here is *retesting:* you have to have taken a full ACT in order to then take a single section over again. Here's how it works. Once you have taken a full ACT (more on when and how to do that in Step 8), you will be able to register to retake up to three sections in a single day instead of taking a full ACT again. There's one catch, though: you'll have to take the tests on a computer. As you can imagine, this has its own pros and cons. For instance, you might find the Math Test to be more challenging because you aren't able to write directly on top of the problem. On the other hand, if you are very fast at typing, you might love the option to take the Writing Test on the computer. You don't need to worry about this too much yet; for now, keep in mind that if you take the test and are happy with one or more scores, you may have the option to retake just the sections you hope to improve. Check ACT's website for updates on when this option will be offered.

The Big One: The Composite

When people talk about a single "ACT score," they're talking about the composite score. The composite is the average of the scores from the four multiple-choice tests: English, Math, Reading, and Science (the Writing score is separate and doesn't factor into the composite). When you researched colleges, you were probably looking at the average composite score for each school. Based on this, you came up with your target composite score, which is some number out of 36. However, in addition to a composite score goal, you should also determine a score goal for each section of the ACT. Students could have the same composite score and do very differently on the sections of the test. Here are some examples:

Student A	Student B	Student C
English: 32	English: 25	English: 21
Math: 20	Math: 26	Math: 22
Reading: 30	Reading: 24	Reading: 35
Science: 18	Science: 25	Science: 22
Composite: 25	Composite: 25	Composite: 25

Student A is stronger in English and Reading, so those scores balance out weaker scores in Math and Science. Student B does about the same in all four sections. Student C has one extremely high area—Reading—which balances out the other three sections. But all three students score the same!

Use your practice test to see how you did on each section of the ACT. Then, consider your target score. Remember, the composite is the average of the four sections. To determine the average of a set of numbers, first add the numbers together. Then divide the result by the number of items you've added. So, if you start with the average (composite), you can multiply it by 4 (because there are four numbers) to get the total score you need for all four sections. Then determine your target scores for the individual sections. In the previous example, if the target composite score is 25, the total score is 4 × 25 or 100. Any combination of scores that add to 100 will get you a composite score of 25! Here is a worksheet to help you determine your personal target scores.

When calculating the composite, ACT will round any decimals. For example, if the average of your multiple-choice sections is 24.5, your composite will be rounded up to 25. On the other hand, an average of 25.25 will be rounded down to 25. Therefore, technically you only need a total of 98 to earn a composite score of 25.

Target composite score: _____

Multiply that number by 4 and circle the

answer: _____

Your four section scores need to add to the circled number.

English goal:_____

Math goal: _____

Reading goal:_____

Science goal: _____

As you can see from the examples above, there are many ways to get to your target composite score. You should have taken a full practice test at this point. If you scored about the same in each area, then you may decide your goal is about the same on each section—unless there are some areas you think will be easier to improve than others. If you really hate science, for example, you could decide not to work on science at all and improve on the other three areas instead. On the other hand, if you have some stronger areas, lean into them! You don't have to plan to improve your weaker areas to match the scores in your stronger areas. In fact, you may find that your stronger areas are easier to improve than your weaker areas are—if you already do well on a section, you may have only a few small things to work on, and (bonus!) you may enjoy working on that subject more since it's one you excel at. The bottom line: make goals that will work for you.

In the next chapter, we'll discuss how many more questions you need to get correct to achieve your target scores.

STEP 4: Make Your Goals Specific

In Step 3, you determined your goal score for each section of the ACT. Now that you know what *scores* you're aiming for, let's talk about how many more *questions* you need to get correct to achieve those scores.

On the next page, you'll find a scoring chart for the ACT that shows how the number of correct answers corresponds to the "scale score" in each section of the test. (The number of questions that corresponds to a certain score on the ACT varies a little from test to test, but this chart will give you a good basis for setting your goals.)

Look up your goal score for a section in either the first or last column; then read across the row to find the number of questions you need to get correct.

For illustration, let's imagine a student—we'll call him Joe. Joe's composite score goal is 25. He's set the following goals for his individual section scores:

English: 28

Math: 24

Reading: 26

Science: 22

To achieve a scale score of 28 on the English Test, Joe must answer 65–66 questions correctly.

To achieve a scale score of 24 on the Math Test, Joe must answer 39–40 questions correctly.

To achieve a scale score of 26 on the Reading Test, Joe must answer 28 questions correctly.

To achieve a scale score of 22 on the Science Test, Joe must answer 23–24 questions correctly.

How many questions do you need to answer correctly on each section to reach your goal scores?

English: _____

Math: _____

Reading: _____

Science: _____

Scale Score	English	Math	Reading	Science	Scale Score
36	75	60	40	40	36
35	73–74	59	39	39	35
34	72	58	38	38	34
33	71	57	37	37	33
32	70	56	36	—	32
31	69	54–55	34–35	36	31
30	68	53	33	35	30
29	67	51–52	32	34	29
28	65–66	49–50	30–31	33	28
27	64	46–48	29	32	27
26	62–63	44–45	28	30–31	26
25	60–61	41–43	27	28–29	25
24	58–59	39–40	26	27	24
23	55–57	37–38	24–25	25–26	23
22	53–54	35–36	23	23–24	22
21	50–52	33–34	22	21–22	21
20	47–49	31–32	21	19–20	20
19	44–46	28–30	19–20	17–18	19
18	42–43	25–27	18	15–16	18
17	40–41	22–24	17	14	17
16	37–39	18–21	16	13	16
15	34–36	15–17	15	12	15
14	31–33	11–14	13–14	11	14
13	29–30	9–10	12	10	13
12	27–28	7–8	10–11	9	12
11	25–26	6	8-9	8	11
10	23–24	5	7	7	10
9	21–22	4	6	6	9
8	18–20	3	5	5	8
7	15–17	—	—	4	7
6	12–14	2	4	3	6
5	9–11	—	3	2	5
4	7–8	1	2	—	4
3	5–6	—	—	1	3
2	3–4	—	1	—	2
1	0–2	0	0	0	1

Next, determine how many *more* correct answers you need in each section to achieve your goal scores. Compare the number of correct answers you need to the number of correct answers you got on your practice test. If you still have not taken one, do so now to make the most of the discussion that follows.

Let's see what this looks like for Joe. On his first practice test, Joe had

56 questions correct in English

33 questions correct in Math

23 questions correct in Reading

20 questions correct in Science

In order to achieve his goal scores, Joe needs

9–10 more questions correct in English

6–7 more questions correct in Math

5 more questions correct in Reading

3–4 more questions correct in Science

How many more questions do you need to answer correctly on each section?

English: _____

Math: _____

Reading: _____

Science: _____

As you can see, an increase of just a handful of correct questions can raise your ACT score significantly! In the next chapter, you'll make a plan for how to get those extra questions correct.

If you took the Free ACT Practice Test on The Princeton Review website, log into your account and open the score report from your test. As you click on the tab for each section, you will see the number of questions you answered correctly, the number you answered incorrectly, and the number you left blank.

STEP 5: Make a Plan

Now that you know how many more questions you need to get correct in each section, let's make a plan to focus your preparation.

There are two key ways to improve your accuracy on a test like the ACT. The first is to adjust your test-taking strategies. The second is to work on content and skills for specific sections or types of questions.

If you were going to devote your whole life to studying for the ACT, you could learn all of the content and skills for all of the questions in all four sections of the test. But we sincerely hope that is not your plan. After all, you have plenty of other things on your plate and better things to do! So, your mission is to design an efficient plan that focuses on a few areas that will have a significant impact on your score. How will you do that?

Begin with Test-taking Strategies

First, hone your skills for the ACT as a whole. Get to know the structure of the test and how it is scored. Learn strategies that maximize your score on the ACT—a standardized, timed, multiple-choice test. No matter your areas of strength or weakness, you will benefit from becoming a savvy test-taker.

> Use Step 6 to learn the strategies you need for the ACT as a whole.

Maximize Your Strengths

Whether you look at your score online or wait to get it in the mail, the biggest number on the page is always the composite. While admissions offices will certainly see the individual scores of all four tests (or five, if you are taking the ACT with Writing), schools will use the composite to evaluate your application, and that's why in the end it's the only one that matters.

The composite is an average. Add the scores for the English, Math, Reading, and Science Tests, and divide the total by four. The four tests are weighted equally to calculate the composite. But do you need to bring up all four equally to raise your composite? Do you need to be a superstar in all four tests? Should you focus more on your weakest tests than your strongest tests? No, no, and absolutely not. The best way to improve your composite is to shore up your weaknesses but exploit your strengths as much as possible.

> To lift the composite score as high as possible, maximize the scores of your strongest tests.

You don't need to be a rock star on all four tests. Identify two or three tests, and focus on raising those scores as much as you can to raise your composite score. Are you strongest in English and Math, or maybe in English, Reading, and Science? Then work to raise those scores as high as you can. You shouldn't ignore your weaknesses, but recognize that the work you put in on your strengths will yield greater dividends. Think of it this way: if you had only one hour to devote to practice the week before the ACT, you would put that hour toward your best subjects.

It's also a good idea to focus first on the topics and types of questions that appear often on the test, since those have the biggest impact on your score.

> Use Step 7 to learn the skills and strategies for the English, Math, Reading, and Science Tests.

Determine Your Strengths and Weaknesses

In order to maximize your strengths, you must know your strengths! If you took The Princeton Review's free ACT practice test, you can easily use the score report from your practice test to identify your strengths and weaknesses.

Remember Joe? Let's take a look at two sections of the score report from his first practice test.

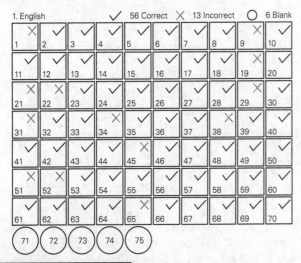

1. English — ✓ 56 Correct ✗ 13 Incorrect ○ 6 Blank

The takeaway: Joe should adjust his approach to use his time more effectively. He should pay attention to the "Pacing," "Personal Order of Difficulty," and "Guessing" strategies in Step 6. He should also focus on the pacing and order of difficulty information in the English section of Step 7.

> In this chapter, we mention the names of some strategies—such as Personal Order of Difficulty—that are covered in Steps 6 and 7. Don't worry that you don't know what the strategies are yet. You'll be familiar with them soon.

Next, let's view Joe's English score report by "Category."

English Responses by Category — ✓ 56 Correct ✗ 13 Incorrect ○ 6 Blank

- **STOP Punctuation 2/4:** 5 ✓, 49 ✓, 9 ✗, 51 ✗
- **GO Punctuation 2/6:** 10 ✓, 66 ✓, 21 ✗, 29 ✗, 31 ✗, 65 ✗
- **Commas: Unnecessary Info 1/1:** 41 ✓
- **Apostrophes 4/4:** 18 ✓, 33 ✓, 37 ✓, 47 ✓
- **Subject-Verb Agreement 2/3:** 59 ✓, 61 ✓, 34 ✗
- **Verb Tense 3/4:** 16 ✓, 64 ✓, 67 ✓, 19 ✗
- **Verb Forms 2/2:** 4 ✓, 43 ✓
- **Pronoun Agreement 3/3:** 7 ✓, 27 ✓, 57 ✓
- **Pronoun Case 0/1:** 71 ○
- **Diction 1/2:** 8 ✓, 74 ○
- **Idioms 2/3:** 14 ✓, 54 ✓, 1 ✗
- **Clauses: Conjunctions 1/1:** 13 ✓
- **Modifiers 1/1:** 30 ✓
- **Transitions 5/7:** 12 ✓, 24 ✓, 39 ✓, 53 ✓, 69 ✓, 70 ○, 73 ○
- **Focus: Sentence 3/4:** 32 ✓, 42 ✓, 68 ✓, 45 ✗
- **Focus: Passage 1/1:** 60 ✓
- **Add and Delete: Words 12/16:** 2 ✓, 6 ✓, 17 ✓, 26 ✓, 35 ✓, 36 ✓, 44 ✓, 46 ✓, 48 ✓, 50 ✓, 56 ✓, 58 ✓, 22 ✗, 38 ✗, 52 ✗, 72 ○
- **Add and Delete: Paragraphs 1/1:** 15 ✓
- **EXCEPT/LEAST/NOT 4/4:** 23 ✓, 25 ✓, 55 ✓, 62 ✓
- **Concision 3/4:** 3 ✓, 28 ✓, 40 ✓, 75 ○
- **Sentence Sequence 3/3:** 11 ✓, 20 ✓, 63 ✓

What can you learn from this view?

> If you don't have a Princeton Review score report, you can make a chart for yourself and mark which questions you answered correctly answered incorrectly, or skipped entirely in each section. Then you can try to identify these patterns on your own. You should do this for each of the four sections of the test.

This is the "Section" view of Joe's English Test. Questions with a check mark are correct, questions with an "x" are incorrect, and circled questions were left blank. What can you learn from this view?

You can see that Joe ran out of time at the end of the test—he left questions 70 through 75 blank.

Joe has several areas of strength on the English Test. For example, he got all of the questions correct in the categories Apostrophes, Verb Forms, Pronoun Agreement, and EXCEPT/LEAST/NOT. Notice that all of the questions that he answered in Transitions and Concision were correct, but he left three of the questions in those categories blank.

The takeaway: Joe should seek out the questions he is best at and be sure to answer all of them.

Joe also did well with questions in the categories Subject/Verb Agreement, Verb Tense, Idioms, Focus: Sentence, and both types of Add and Delete, although he missed a few questions in those categories.

The takeaway: Joe should focus his preparation on the types of questions we just mentioned—he's already good at them, and there are lots of them. So, if he can identify what went wrong with the few questions he missed and correct those errors, he'll boost his score significantly.

If Joe had answered all of the questions in his areas of strength correctly, he would have a total of 11 more correct questions. If you look back at Step 4, you'll see that Joe's goal was to get 10 more questions correct in the English Test. So, by focusing on basic strategy and on his areas of strength, Joe can reach his goal.

> If you don't have a Princeton Review score report with this category view, use these English categories to classify the questions on the test you took. Figuring out what each question tests is good practice to help you identify question types, and it will allow you to see your strengths and weaknesses more clearly. Repeat the process for the other sections of the test.

Finally, you can see that Joe had some trouble with the STOP Punctuation and GO Punctuation questions. Once Joe has maximized his score in his areas of strength, he could study the punctuation topics tested on the ACT. If he gains a better understanding of the punctuation rules and finds an efficient approach for those questions, he could potentially boost his score again. Since there are quite a few of these questions, this could also be a productive place to focus.

Next, let's take a look at Joe's Math Test.

2. Math ✓ 33 Correct ✗ 27 Incorrect ◯ 0 Blank

1 ✓	2 ✓	3 ✗	4 ✓	5 ✓	6 ✗	7 ✓	8 ✓	9 ✗	10 ✗
11 ✓	12 ✗	13 ✓	14 ✓	15 ✓	16 ✓	17 ✗	18 ✓	19 ✓	20 ✗
21 ✓	22 ✓	23 ✓	24 ✓	25 ✓	26 ✓	27 ✗	28 ✗	29 ✓	30 ✗
31 ✓	32 ✗	33 ✗	34 ✓	35 ✓	36 ✓	37 ✗	38 ✓	39 ✓	40 ✓
41 ✗	42 ✓	43 ✗	44 ✗	45 ✗	46 ✓	47 ✗	48 ✗	49 ✓	50 ✓
51 ✓	52 ✗	53 ✗	54 ✓	55 ✗	56 ✗	57 ✗	58 ✗	59 ✓	60 ✗

This is the view of Joe's Math Test by section. You can see that Joe answered all 60 Math questions and got just over half of them correct. The questions on the Math Test are arranged in a rough order of difficulty, with easier questions at the beginning of the section and harder questions nearer the end. Joe's accuracy was higher at the beginning of the test than at the end, but he missed several questions early in the section. There is a good chance that he made some careless errors on the easier questions because he was rushing to work all 60 questions in 60 minutes.

The takeaway: Joe should adjust his approach to use his time more effectively. He should pay attention to the "Pacing," "Personal Order of Difficulty," and "Guessing" strategies in Step 6. He should also focus on the pacing and order of difficulty information in the Math section of Step 7.

Next let's look at Joe's Math score by category.

Math Responses by Category · ✓ 33 Correct · ✗ 27 Incorrect · ○ 0 Blank

Category	Score	Responses
Solving for a Variable	0/4	✗3 ✗10 ✗38 ✗49
One-solution Inequalities	1/1	✓47
Two-solution Inequalities	0/3	✗44 ✗45 ✗57
Exponents	1/3	✓14 ✗30 ✗56
Quadratics	2/4	✗18 ✓22 ✓12 ✗17
Number Properties	1/6	✓11 ✗20 ✗32 ✗33 ✗43 ✗60
Functions	1/3	✓19 ✗27 ✗52
Order of Operations	1/1	✓13
Percents	1/2	✓7 ✗9
Statistics	2/2	✓4 ✓5
Patterns, Sequences, Series	1/2	✓15 ✗36
Right Triangles	4/4	✓2 ✓23 ✓34 ✓51
Similar Triangles	1/1	✓8
Circle Properties	1/1	✓50
Sectors and Circles	1/1	✓59
Quadrilateral Properties	3/3	✓16 ✓24 ✓40
Quadrilaterals & Polygons	1/1	✓21
Parallel Lines	0/1	✗6
Overlapping Figures	1/2	✓35 ✗58
Volume	0/2	✗48 ✗53
Basic Trigonometry	2/2	✓42 ✓54
Trigonometric Identities	1/1	✓46
Unit Circle	1/1	✓39
Slope	3/3	✓25 ✓29 ✓31
Linear Equations	0/1	✗41
Distance	0/1	✗55
Midpoint	1/2	✓1 ✗28
Parallel & Perpendicular Lines	1/1	✓37
Conics	1/1	✓26

Joe did particularly well on geometry topics. For example, he got all of the questions on Triangles, Circles, and Quadrilaterals correct. However, he did miss both Volume questions. Joe also did very well on trigonometry questions.

The takeaway: since geometry is a strength for Joe, he should seek out geometry problems in the Math Test and make sure he answers them. The volume formulas would be a good content review topic for Joe.

Joe correctly answered more than half of the coordinate geometry questions. He correctly answered all of the Slope questions and the Parallel and Perpendicular Lines question. but he missed the Linear Equations and Distance questions. He correctly answered one Midpoint question and missed the other.

The takeaway: coordinate geometry would be another good area for Joe to focus on. He has a good foundation, and probably just needs to review some facts and formulas.

If Joe could answer 2–3 more of the geometry and coordinate geometry questions correctly and eliminate 4–5 careless mistakes, he could achieve his goal of getting 6–7 more questions correct in the Math Test. So, by focusing on basic strategy and on his areas of strength, Joe can reach his goal.

Joe had more trouble with algebra questions, including Solving for a Variable, Two-Solution Inequalities, and Functions. Since there are a lot of these questions on the test, algebra would be another good area of focus. Once Joe has maximized his score in his areas of strength, he could study the strategies for algebra problems in Step 7. It's also possible that Joe missed some of these questions due to careless mistakes. As mentioned already, Joe can eliminate those errors by focusing on the pacing and Personal Order of Difficulty strategies in Steps 6 and 7.

Next let's look at Joe's Reading score report by section.

3. Reading   ✓ 23 Correct   ✗ 12 Incorrect   ◯ 5 Blank

1 ✗	2 ✓	3 ✗	4 ✗	5 ✓	6 ✗	7 ✓	8 ✓	9 ✗	10 ✗
11 ✓	12 ✓	13 ✓	14 ✓	15 ✓	16 ✗	17 ✗	18 ✓	19 ✓	20 ✓
21 ✓	22 ✓	23 ✓	24 ✓	25 ✗	26 ✓	27 ✓	28 ✓	29 ✗	30 ✓
31 ✓	32 ✓	33 ✓	34 ✗	35 ✓	36 ◯	37 ◯	38 ◯	39 ◯	40 ◯

What can you learn from this report?

Joe got 4 questions correct on the first passage (questions 1–10), 8 questions correct on the second passage (questions 11–20), 7 questions correct on the third passage (questions 21–30), and 4 questions correct on the last passage. Joe also ran out of time—he left 5 questions blank at the end of the test. Even though he ran out of time, Joe got as many questions correct on the last passage as he did on the first passage.

The takeaway: To maximize his efficiency, Joe should adjust the order in which he does the passages. He should pay attention to the "Pacing," "Personal Order of Difficulty," and "Guessing" strategies in Step 6. Chances are, if Joe had left the first passage for last and completed the fourth passage instead, he would have more questions correct overall.

Now let's look at Joe's Reading Test by category.

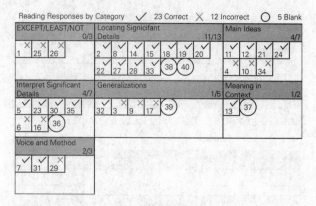

Reading Responses by Category   ✓ 23 Correct   ✗ 12 Incorrect   ◯ 5 Blank

EXCEPT/LEAST/NOT   0/3
| 1 ✗ | 25 ✗ | 26 ✗ |

Locating Significant Details   11/13
| 2 ✓ | 8 ✓ | 14 ✓ | 15 ✓ | 18 ✓ | 19 ✓ | 20 ✓ |
| 22 ✓ | 27 ✓ | 28 ✓ | 33 ✓ | 38 ◯ | 40 ◯ | |

Main Ideas   4/7
| 11 ✓ | 12 ✓ | 21 ✓ | 24 ✓ |
| 4 ✗ | 10 ✗ | 34 ✗ | |

Interpret Significant Details   4/7
| 5 ✓ | 23 ✓ | 30 ✓ | 35 ✓ |
| 6 ✗ | 16 ✗ | 36 ◯ | |

Generalizations   1/5
| 32 ✓ | 3 ✗ | 9 ✗ | 17 ✗ | 39 ◯ |

Meaning in Context   1/2
| 13 ✓ | 37 ◯ |

Voice and Method   2/3
| 7 ✓ | 31 ✓ | 29 ✗ |

What can you learn from this report?

Joe did very well on questions in the "Locating Significant Details" category and had more trouble with questions in the "Main Ideas," "Generalizations," and "EXCEPT/LEAST/NOT" categories. The category "Locating Significant Details" refers to questions that ask what was stated in the passage. (These are the "easy-to-answer" questions that you will read about in the Reading section of Step 7).

The takeaway: Joe should focus on the questions he is best at, making sure that he answers the easy-to-answer questions before spending too much time on questions that are less straightforward. Joe should learn the Basic Approach for Reading in Step 7, which will help him work the questions more efficiently and increase his accuracy on the harder-to-answer questions.

If Joe had focused on the passages and question types he is best at, he could have correctly answered 4 more questions from the final passage. If he correctly answered just 1 more question in one of the other passages, that would give him a total of 5 more correct questions. If you look back at Step 4, you'll see that Joe's goal for Reading was to get 5 more questions correct. By focusing on his strengths and his strategy, Joe can achieve his goal score.

Next, let's look at Joe's Science score report by section.

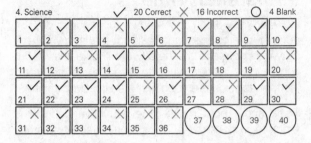

What can you learn from this report?

Overall, Joe had higher accuracy at the beginning of the section and missed more questions later in the section. He also ran out of time, leaving the last 4 questions blank. Joe may have started to rush later in the section and made careless mistakes as a result. His accuracy was also higher on some passages than others, indicating that Joe found certain passages easier and other passages more challenging.

The takeaway: Joe should adjust his strategy to maximize his accuracy and efficiency on the Science Test. He should pay attention to the "Pacing," "Personal Order of Difficulty," and "Guessing" strategies in Step 6. By focusing on the more straightforward passages, Joe can improve his accuracy.

Now let's look at Joe's Science score report by category.

What can you learn from this report?

Joe's accuracy was highest on questions in the "Data and Procedures" category and the two "Dual" categories. The "Data and Procedures" category includes the questions that ask about trends and relationships in charts and graphs. The "Standalone Scientist—Dual" and "Both/All—Dual" categories include the questions from the Science "reading" passage. (You'll learn more about the types of Science passages in Step 7.)

The takeaway: Joe should focus on the questions he is best at. He should learn the Basic Approach in the Science section of Step 7 to maximize his accuracy on the questions that ask about trends and relationships in the charts and graphs. This strategy will solidify his performance on the "Data and Procedures" questions and improve his accuracy on the "Predictions from Trends" questions. He should also learn the approach for the Science "reading" passage to maximize his accuracy on that passage. Joe had trouble with the "Outside Knowledge" questions, but there are only a few outside knowledge questions on the test, so they won't have a big impact on Joe's score. Therefore, focusing on the "Outside Knowledge" questions would not be the wisest use of Joe's preparation time.

If Joe had focused on the passages and question types he is best at, he could have correctly answered 2 more questions in the "Dual" categories and 2 more in the "Data and Procedures" or "Predictions from Trends"—a total of 4 more correct answers. If you look back at Step 4, you'll see that Joe's goal was to correctly answer 3–4 more questions in Science. So, by focusing on his strengths and his strategy, Joe can achieve his goal score.

Your Turn

Now, look at your own score report from your practice test. Look at both the "Section" and "Category" views for each section. Did you run out of time or rush through any section? Did you spend a long time on a very difficult problem, when you could have spent the time on easier questions? Which types of questions were you best at? Which topics did you struggle with?

Look back at your goals in Step 4. How many more questions do you need to get correct in each section? Which questions should you focus on to accomplish your goals? Make notes about which topics will be best for you to focus on during your preparation. Focus on maximizing your performance in your strong areas, and seek strategies to minimize missed questions in your weaker areas.

Grab a notebook or some scratch paper to make your notes about your strengths and weaknesses and what you will focus on during your preparation.

Planning Your Preparation Time

How will you fit in the study you need to do? Sit down with a calendar and map out the time you have between now and the date you will take the ACT. If you haven't decided when to take the test yet, making that decision is a good first step in your planning.

Think about how much time you have during the week to work on the ACT. It's more effective to study for a short time on several days during the week than to do a mega-session every once in a while. If you have several weeks or months before the ACT, you can set aside some days to take additional practice tests (you'll find sources for additional practice tests in Step 8). It's also important not to burn yourself out, so give yourself breaks, and leave time to eat, sleep, exercise, and relax!

What follows is a sample plan for a student who has five weeks before the ACT. This plan includes three or four study sessions per week. You can use this as a template, adjusting as you need for your schedule. You can also adjust this according to the areas of focus you choose or to include a bit of Writing prep if you are taking the essay portion of the test. If you have more time, you can supplement your practice with other resources—see Step 8 for ideas.

WEEK 1 (You may have already completed these sessions!)

Session One: Take the first practice test and score it.

Session Two: Review your score report and set your goals, using Step 4 as a guide.

Session Three: Review your score report and decide what areas to focus on, using Step 5 as a guide.

WEEK 2

Session Four: Read through Step 6, noting the shifts in strategy that will help you improve your accuracy and efficiency on all sections of the ACT.

Session Five: Read through the strategies for English in Step 7. Practice these strategies using a timed English section from one of the additional sources described in Step 8.

Session Six: Review your work on the timed English section. Which strategies did you apply well? How could you improve your accuracy and efficiency?

WEEK 3

Session Seven: Read through the strategies for Math in Step 7. Practice these strategies using a timed Math section from one of the additional sources described in Step 8.

Session Eight: Review your work on the timed Math section. Which strategies did you apply well? How could you improve your accuracy and efficiency?

Session Nine: Read through the strategies for Reading in Step 7. Practice these strategies using a timed Reading section from one of the additional sources described in Step 8.

WEEK 4

Session Ten: Review your work on the timed Reading section. Which strategies did you apply well? How could you improve your accuracy and efficiency?

Session Eleven: Read through the strategies for Science in Step 7. Practice these strategies using a timed Science section from one of the additional sources described in Step 8.

Session Twelve: Review your work on the timed Science section. Which strategies did you apply well? How could you improve your accuracy and efficiency?

WEEK 5

Session Thirteen: Take a full practice test. Use the techniques you've been learning and practicing for each section.

Session Fourteen: Score your test and go through the explanations for English and Math. Focus on where you may have missed the opportunity to use a technique and on your decisions about whether you should have attempted a question or not, given your pacing goals and Personal Order of Difficulty.

> Look for the Personal Order of Difficulty strategy in Step 6.

Session Fifteen: Go through the explanations for Reading and Science. Focus on where you may have missed the opportunity to use a technique and on your decisions about whether you should have attempted a question or not, given your pacing goals and Personal Order of Difficulty.

Session Sixteen: Review your pacing goals and major strategies for each section of the test. Do something fun and relaxing to de-stress before the test!

Grab a notebook, a calendar, or another way to plan your preparation and put it down in writing!

Now you have your plan in place. In the next chapter, you'll learn the strategies that apply to all sections of test.

STEP 6: Learn Big Picture Strategies

Now that you have a plan about how to focus your time, let's look at the strategies that will improve your accuracy and efficiency on all four multiple-choice sections of the ACT.

THE BASIC APPROACH

The ACT test is different from the tests you take in school, so you need to approach it differently. To be effective, ACT strategies have to be based on the ACT and not on any other test. You need to know how the ACT is scored and how it's constructed.

Scoring

You've already seen that each section of the ACT is scored on a scale of 1–36, and that the scale score is based on the "raw score"—the number of questions you get correct. There are a few other important details to consider about the way the ACT is scored.

How many raw points is an easy question worth? How many raw points is a difficult question worth? An easy question is worth 1 raw point, and a difficult question is also worth 1 raw point. So, you don't receive any more credit for working a hard question than you do for working an easy question.

How many points is a blank answer worth? If you guessed 0, you're right. But what about a wrong answer—do you lose points when you answer incorrectly? Nope! A wrong answer is also worth 0 points.

Structure

Let's review the structure of the ACT. The four tests (or five, if you're taking the ACT with Writing) are always given in the same order.

	Amount of Time	# of Questions
English	45 minutes	75 questions
Math	60 minutes	60 questions
Reading	35 minutes	40 questions
Science	35 minutes	40 questions
Writing	40 minutes	1 essay

ENEMY #1: TIME

How much time do you have per question on the Math Test? You have just one minute, and that's generous compared with the time given per question on the English, Reading, and Science Tests. But how often do you take a test in school with a minute or less per question? If you do at all, it's maybe on a quiz but probably not on a major exam or final. Time is your enemy on the ACT, and you have to use it wisely and be aware of how that time pressure can bring out your worst instincts as a test-taker.

ENEMY #2: YOURSELF

Many people struggle with test anxiety in school and on standardized tests. But there is something particularly evil about tests like the ACT and SAT. The skills you've been rewarded for throughout your academic career can easily work against you on the ACT. You've been taught since birth to follow directions, go in order, and finish everything. But that approach won't necessarily earn you your highest ACT score.

On the other hand, treating the ACT as a scary, alien beast can leave your brain blank and useless and can incite irrational, self-defeating behavior. When you pick up a No. 2 pencil, you may tend to leave your common sense at the door. Test nerves and anxieties can make you misread a question, commit a careless error, see something that isn't there, blind you to what is there, talk you into a bad answer, and worst of all, convince you to spend good time on "bad" questions.

There is good news. You can—and will—crack the ACT. You will learn how to approach it differently from how you would a test in school, and you won't let the test crack you. The structure and the scoring of the test shape the best strategies for the ACT.

Be warned that some of the approaches we're going to show you may seem counterintuitive or unnatural. Some of these strategies may be very different from the way you learned to approach similar questions in school, but trust us! Try tackling the problems using our techniques, and keep practicing until they become easier. When you do this, you'll see a real improvement in your score.

ACT STRATEGIES

Personal Order of Difficulty (POOD)

If time is going to run out, would you rather it run out on the hardest questions or the easiest? You know that hard questions are not worth any more than easy questions, so of course, you want time to run out on the questions you are less likely to get right.

You can easily fall into the trap of spending too much time on the hardest questions and either never getting to or rushing through the easiest (Remember Joe's English, Math, Reading, and Science Tests from Step 5?). You shouldn't work in the order ACT provides just because it's in that order. Instead, find your own Personal Order of Difficulty (POOD). Make smart decisions about which questions you'll do Now, Later, and Never as you move through each test. Make your decisions quickly and for good reasons. Here's a good approach to take to maximize your POOD.

NOW

Do you know how to do the question? Can you do it fairly quickly and accurately? Do it *Now*.

LATER

Will this question take more time to work, but you still think you know how to do it? Leave it and come back to it *Later*. Circle the question number so you can find it easily when you come back.

> If you are taking the ACT Online Test, flag Later questions.

NEVER

Test-taker, know thyself. Know the topics that are your worst, and learn the signs that flash danger. Don't waste time on questions you should *Never* do. Instead, use the time you save by skipping them to answer the Now and Later questions accurately. Later in this chapter, we'll show you what to do with Never questions.

Pacing

The ACT may be designed so that you run out of time, but you can't rush through it as fast as possible. All you'll do is make careless errors on easy questions you should get right and spend way too much time on difficult ones you're unlikely to get right (like Joe did!). Let your POOD help determine your pacing. Go slowly enough to answer correctly all the Now questions but quickly enough to get to the number of Later questions you need to reach your goal score.

In Step 4, you identified the number of questions you need to reach your goal score in each section. Practice your pacing on practice tests (see Step 8 for additional practice resources), going slowly enough to avoid careless errors and quickly enough to reach your goal scores.

> Slow down, score more. You're not scored on *the number of questions you do*. You're scored on *the number of questions you answer correctly*. Doing fewer questions can mean more correct answers overall!

Process of Elimination (POE)

Multiple-choice tests offer one great advantage: they provide the correct answer right there on the page. Of course, they hide the correct answer among 3–4 incorrect answers. It's often easier to spot the wrong answers than it is to identify the right ones, particularly when you apply a smart Process of Elimination (POE). As you work each question, actively look for answers that are wrong and physically cross them off on the page. This will help you avoid traps and make a better guess if you need to.

POE works differently on each test on the ACT, but it's a powerful strategy on all of them. For some question types, you'll always use POE rather than wasting time trying to figure out the answer on your own. For other questions, you'll use POE when you're stuck. ACT hides the correct answer among wrong ones, but when you cross off just one or two wrong answers, the correct answer can become more obvious, sometimes jumping right off the page. Try this example.

What's the capital of Azerbaijan?

Give up?

Unless you spend your spare time studying an atlas, you may not even know that Azerbaijan is a real country, much less what its capital is. If this question came up on a test, you'd have to skip it, wouldn't you? Well, maybe not. To find out if you can figure out the answer anyway, let's turn this question into a multiple-choice question—just like all the questions on the ACT.

1. What is the capital of Azerbaijan?
   A. Washington, D.C.
   B. Paris
   C. London
   D. Baku

The question doesn't seem that hard anymore, does it? Of course, we made our example extremely easy. (By the way, the ACT does not ask any questions on geography unless they are answered in the text that accompanies the question.)

But you'd be surprised by the number of people who give up on ACT questions that aren't much more difficult than this one just because they don't know the correct answer right off the top of their heads. "Capital of Azerbaijan? Oh, no! I've never heard of Azerbaijan!"

These students don't stop to think that they might be able to find the correct answer simply by eliminating all of the answer choices they know are wrong. As we just mentioned, wrong answers are usually easier to find than the right ones are. After all, there are more of them! Remember the question about Azerbaijan? Even though you didn't know the answer off the top of your head, you easily figured it out by eliminating the three obviously incorrect choices. You looked for wrong answers first.

It's Not About Circling the Right Answer

Physically marking in your test booklet (or on your whiteboard if you are taking the test on a computer) what you think of certain answers can help you narrow down choices, take the best possible guess, and save time!

Try using the following notations:

✔ Put a check mark next to an answer you like.

~ Put a squiggle next to an answer you kind of like.

? Put a question mark next to an answer you don't understand.

A̶ Cross out the letter of any answer choice you KNOW is wrong.

You can always come up with your own system and you may not need all these categories for every section of the test.

There won't be many questions on the ACT in which incorrect choices will be as easy to eliminate as they were on the Azerbaijan question. But if you read this book carefully, you'll learn how to eliminate at least one choice on almost any ACT question, if not two or even three choices.

What good is it to eliminate just one or two choices on a four-choice ACT question?

Plenty. In fact, for most students, it's an important key to earning higher scores.

Here's another example:

2. What is the capital of Qatar?
   F. Paris
   G. Dukhan
   H. Tokyo
   J. Doha

On this question you'll almost certainly be able to eliminate two of the four choices by using POE. That means you're still not sure of the answer. You know that the capital of Qatar has to be either Doha or Dukhan, but you don't know which.

Should you skip the question and go on? Or should you guess?

If you are taking the ACT Online Test, you can use the Answer Eliminator tool for POE.

CLOSE YOUR EYES AND POINT

There is no guessing penalty on the ACT, so you should bubble something for every question. If you get down to two answers, just pick one of them. There is no harm in doing so.

You're going to hear a lot of mixed opinions about what you should bubble or whether you should bubble at all. Let's clear up a few misconceptions about guessing.

FALSE: Don't answer a question unless you're absolutely sure of the answer.

You will almost certainly have teachers and school counselors who tell you this. Don't listen to them! The ACT does not penalize you for wrong answers. Put something down for every question: you might get a freebie.

FALSE: If you have to guess, guess (C).

This is a weird misconception, and obviously there is nothing magical about the letter (C). Since the ACT is a standardized test, there will be no way to game the system by just selecting a certain answer. The test-makers take great pains to have a fairly even answer distribution on each test, and we'll tell you how you *can* benefit from that in a minute.

FALSE: Always pick the [fill in the blank].

Be careful with directives that tell you that this or that answer or type of answer is always right. It's much safer to learn the rules and to have a solid guessing strategy in place.

As far as guessing is concerned, we do have a small piece of advice. First and foremost, make sure of one thing:

Answer every question on the ACT. There's no penalty.

Letter of the Day (LOTD)

Just because you don't work a question doesn't mean you don't answer it. Since there is no penalty for wrong answers on the ACT, you should never leave any blanks on your answer document. When you guess on Never questions, pick your favorite two-letter combo of answers and stick with it. For example, always choose A/F or C/H. Any letter will do, given the fairly even answer distribution on the test. If you're consistent in using the same letter combo throughout the test, you're more likely to pick up more points.

> The paper-and-pencil ACT alternates between A/B/C/D and F/G/H/J answers (or A/B/C/D/E and F/G/H/J/K answers on the Math Test). On the ACT Online Test, you will see only answers A/B/C/D (or A/B/C/D/E on the Math Test).

POOD, Pacing, POE, and LOTD all work together to help you spend your time where it does the most good: on the questions you can and should get right.

The Best Way to Bubble In

If you are taking the paper-and-pencil ACT, work a page at a time, circling your answers right on the test booklet. Transfer a page's worth of answers to the answer document at one time. It's better to stay focused on working questions rather than disrupt your concentration to find where you left off on the answer document. You'll be more accurate at both tasks. Do not wait until the end, however, to transfer all the answers of that test to your answer document. Go one page at a time on English and Math, and go a passage at a time on Reading and Science. In the last few minutes of each section, though, bubble the answer after working each question.

BE RUTHLESS

The worst mistake a test-taker can make is to throw good time at "bad" questions. You read a question but don't understand it, so you read it again. And again. If you stare at it really hard, you know you're going to just see the answer. And you can't move on, because really, after spending all that time it would be a waste not to keep at it, right?

Wrong. You can't let one tough question drag you down, and you can't let your worst instincts tempt you into self-defeating behavior. Instead, the best way to improve your ACT score is to follow our advice.

- Use the techniques and strategies in Step 7 to work efficiently and accurately through all your Now and Later questions.

- Know your Never questions, and use your LOTD. Know when to move on. Use POE, and guess from what's left.

In Step 7, you'll learn how strategies such as POOD, Pacing, and POE work on each section.

USE YOUR PENCIL

You own the test booklet, and you should write where and when it helps you. Use your pencil to physically cross off wrong answers on the page. On the Reading Test, use your pencil to underline predictions in the passage. On the Math Test, set up problems with pencil and paper and write down your work. On the Science Test, use your pencil to mark up the figures. You'll learn more details about how to use your pencil in Step 7.

If you're taking the ACT Online Test, write on your whiteboard, and use the Answer Eliminator tool to cross off wrong answers.

STEP 7: Learn Section-Level Strategies

ACT English

Structure

The ACT English Test consists of 75 multiple-choice questions spread out over 5 passages. It is always the first section on the ACT. The questions cover a variety of topics related to punctuation, grammar, and style, but they are not organized by topic or difficulty level.

Pacing

Of the four multiple-choice sections on the ACT, the English Test has the greatest number of questions. It also gives you the least amount of time per question. This means that the English Test is very fast-paced. Some people don't have much trouble getting through all 75 questions, but others find themselves rushing through the last passage. Of course, this means those students who rush will likely miss questions toward the end of the test that they could have gotten right, simply because they ran out of time. If you find that you fall into this group, it will be in your best interest to have a plan that involves skipping some questions as you go, especially if you don't have time to learn the rules that are tested on the English portion. How should you decide which questions to skip?

POOD

Earlier, we discussed POOD (Personal Order of Difficulty)—throughout the ACT, you should start with the questions and passages that are easiest for you in order to maximize your score. How does this work on the English Test? Well, the English Test does not follow an order of difficulty: there won't be harder or easier passages, and the easy and hard questions are all mixed together. Furthermore, it's a very fast-paced section, so you may waste time if you try to skip around. Lastly, you will need to answer questions that involve the structure and flow of ideas within a passage; this means that you should be reading the paragraphs in a passage in order.

With all of this in mind, it's in your best interest to complete the English section more or less in order. However, that does not mean that you have to *attempt* every question. You may find that skipping a few of the hardest English questions gives you more time to finish the test and get to those questions at the very end that you may not otherwise have had time to do—some of which are likely easy. The good news is that it is easy to identify many of the hardest and most time-consuming questions on the English test: they are much longer.

Take a look at these two questions:

55. The writer is considering deleting the preceding sentence. Should this sentence be kept or deleted?
   A. Kept, because it describes important information about Jackie Robinson's endorsement deals.
   B. Kept, because it helps the reader understand how Jackie Robinson sacrificed personal advancement in favor of civil rights work.
   C. Deleted, because it doesn't provide exact details about the civil rights laws that Jackie Robinson enacted.
   D. Deleted, because it draws focus toward other athletes and away from Jackie Robinson.

58. F. NO CHANGE
    G. very widely
    H. more widely
    J. widelier

Which question looks easier? #58! This question has only one or two words in each answer, and you can probably eliminate (D) without even reading the sentence. To answer it, all you'll need to do is read the sentence in the passage and see which option makes the most grammatical sense. On the other hand, question 55 requires you to read the preceding sentence *and the entire rest of the paragraph*, consider whether the sentence is consistent with the paragraph, and then read four long answer choices and use POE. Whew! Is one point worth all of that work? For many people, the answer will be no.

Here is the key pacing strategy for the English Test:

Make the obvious POOD choice and finish the English Test.

Skip the obviously more time-consuming questions as you go so that you will be able to make it to the end of the section in 45 minutes and not have to rush on easier questions at the end. Remember, bubble in the Letter of the Day for any questions you skip. Note that you can star or circle any questions you skip so that you can attempt them if you have extra time left at the end.

> Use the chart on page 105 to determine how many questions you can skip on the English Test.

The Basic Approach

The English Test is organized into five passages. You don't want to start by reading an entire passage—remember, you don't have a lot of time in this section. Instead, while you are reading each passage, you'll answer the questions as you come to them. Therefore, the first step for English is to...

STEP 1 » Read to the end of the sentence with an underlined portion.

Most English questions won't actually ask a question—they'll look like question 58 on the previous page. Rather than looking for errors and considering every possible rule related to punctuation, grammar, and style, take a peek at the answers: the similarities and differences among them will tell you what is being tested. For instance, if the words all stay the same but commas change, you know the question is testing you on commas, so you only need to remember comma rules and don't have to worry about any of the other topics to answer that question.

STEP 2 » Look to the answers to see what's changing.

Once you know what topic or topics are being tested, use the rules to determine which answer is correct. Here's the catch: don't try to fix the sentence in your head. You might decide, for example, that a period should be used instead of a comma. However, when you look at the answers, you don't see an answer that

has a period. Or worse yet, you may see an answer that does use a period but makes an error with grammar. To avoid picking a trap answer and to save time, therefore...

Use Process of Elimination.

Physically cross off any answer choices that you know are wrong, until you find the one answer that is correct.

Let's take a look at how to apply these steps.

Over two decades ago, in 1999, people around the world prepared for a momentous occasion: a new millennium. In the fifteen years leading up to this milestone, however, technologists noticed a potential problem and warned about it's effects.
                                                    1

1. A. NO CHANGE
    B. warn about its
    C. then warn about it's
    D. warned about its

Once you have read the entire sentence, look at the answer choices and determine what's changing: verb tense (*warn* versus *warned*) and apostrophes (*it's* versus *its*). You can start with whichever of those topics is more comfortable for you. Let's begin with tense. The other verb in the sentence is *noticed*, which is in past tense, so this verb needs to be in past tense to be consistent. Eliminate (B) and (C) because both use present tense. Now, determine whether an apostrophe is needed. The word *it's* means "it is." Do you want to say "it is effects?" No, so eliminate (A). The correct answer is (D).

Notice that in the question above, you could easily have made a mistake if you just spotted one of the errors. For instance, if you saw right away that *it's* should be changed to *its*, you could have accidentally picked (B) without realizing that (B) creates a new error by changing to present tense. This is why it's so important to look for what's changing in the answers and to do POE with the answers that are actually there. Remember, if you try to correct the sentence in your head, you may find that your correction doesn't actually appear in the answers. You're better off using POE!

In the previous question, you needed to know some rules about verb tense and apostrophes. What rules do you need to know for the ACT English? Let's take a look.

The Four C's

You don't need to learn every rule of English writing to do well on the ACT English Test: you need to know only the handful of rules that are actually tested on the ACT. Moreover, if you decided to study grammar, you would learn terms such as *independent clause*, *parallelism*, *past participle*, *subjunctive mood*, and *possessive determiners*. Just reading those words might start to make your head spin, but remember—no matter what the rules are called, the fancy-sounding names for those rules are NOT tested on the ACT. You should know what the rules are, but you don't need to have a special name for each one. Instead, you should focus on what we call the four C's: Complete, Consistent, Clear, and Concise. Let's take a closer look at each one and how it is tested on the ACT.

Complete

One of the main topics tested on the ACT English is punctuation. All of the types of punctuation, except for apostrophes, relate to the way sentences are constructed. As you have learned in school, all sentences must be complete. What does a complete sentence need?

Subject + Verb

A complete sentence needs a subject and a verb. Here are two examples:

> The reporter writes.

> My cat is sleeping.

Both of these could stand alone as complete sentences, so they are called complete ideas. Some sentences need more than just a subject and a verb. Consider the following:

> The reporter has

> My cat likes

Even though these phrases contain both a subject and a verb, some verbs, like *has* and *likes*, require an object. The sentence feels as if it's missing something—and it is. To make a complete sentence, you need to finish the idea by telling what the reporter has or what the cat likes.

Longer phrases can also be incomplete:

> Because I like being outside in warm weather

This idea is incomplete because it starts with *because*. Phrases beginning with *because*, *though*, *when*, *that*, and *since*, among other transition words, are incomplete and must be linked to a complete idea.

Let's take a look at how complete sentences could be tested on the ACT.

This problem—most commonly known as the Millennium bug or Y2K, short for Year 2000 Problem—involved how computers process <u>dates:</u>[2] programmers theorized that when the year changed from 1999 ("99") to 2000 ("00"), some computers would instead think the year was 1900.

2. **F.** NO CHANGE
   G. dates,
   H. dates. And
   J. dates; while

First, check what's changing in the answers—in this case punctuation. Next, determine whether the parts of the sentence are complete or incomplete ideas. The phrase *This problem—most commonly known as the Millennium bug or Y2K, short for Year 2000 Problem—involved how computers process dates* is a complete idea—it could be its own sentence. The phrase *programmers theorized that when the year changed from 1999 ("99") to 2000 ("00"), some computers would instead think the year was 1900* could also be its own sentence, so it is also a complete idea.

Let's start with a simple rule that is one of the most commonly tested punctuation rules on the ACT: you can never put just a comma between two complete ideas. You may remember from school that this creates a run-on sentence. What does that tell you here? Choice (G) is wrong, so cross it off. Next, you probably remember from school that starting a sentence with *And* is not allowed—choice (H) does exactly that, so eliminate it. Let's take a look at (J) next—it uses a semicolon. A semicolon works exactly the same as a

period. That might seem like a good idea here, since you have two complete ideas, but notice what else (J) does: it adds the word *while*. If you read the second part of the sentence with *while*, you'll see that it is no longer complete (remember—phrases beginning with a transition word like *while* are incomplete). If a semicolon works just like a period, then (J) does not work, since the second part of the sentence isn't complete anymore. Thus, you have to cross off (J), and (F) is the answer.

> Don't be afraid to pick NO CHANGE! It's correct about a fourth of the time that it appears.

While experts disagreed about exactly what could happen if computers thought the year was <u>1900, and technology</u>[3] companies and governments around the world evaluated their systems in an attempt to avoid a catastrophe.

3. **A.** NO CHANGE
   B. 1900, technology
   C. 1900; technology
   D. 1900. Technology

What's changing in the answers? Punctuation. You might notice an error right away from reading the sentence: it isn't correct to use the word *and* after the first part of the sentence beginning with *while*. This creates an incomplete sentence, so eliminate (A). Now, consider the parts of the sentence. *While experts disagreed about exactly what could happen if computers thought the year was 1900* is an incomplete idea, and *technology companies and governments around the world evaluated their systems in an attempt to avoid a catastrophe* is a complete idea. You might have noticed another answer choice that is easy to eliminate: (D). You already know that a period can come only at the end of a complete sentence, and the first part isn't a complete sentence. You may also remember from question 2 that a semicolon works just like a period, so if the period is wrong, so is the semicolon. Eliminate (C). That leaves you with the correct answer, (B).

> If you haven't mastered the different types of punctuation, check out *ACT Prep* for more on how each punctuation mark can be used.

Consistent

The next "C" word is Consistent. The underlined portion must always be consistent with the non-underlined portion. This is why you must read the whole sentence, and sometimes more than that. Many different grammar topics fall under consistency. You saw one already in question 1: tense. Let's take a look at a few more.

The number of devices and computer systems that could experience issues <u>were making</u> the task of reconfiguration daunting. [4]

4. **F.** NO CHANGE
   G. were to make
   H. made
   J. have made

First, look to see what's changing in the answer choices: verbs. We've discussed tense already, so let's take a look at number, another aspect of verbs that involves consistency. A verb must be consistent with its subject. Here, ACT is trying to trick you. The writers of the test want you to think the subject is *issues*, making the subject and verb combination "issues were making," which probably sounds okay. However, were the *issues* making the task daunting? No, it was the *number* of devices that made the task daunting. The subject of the sentence is *number*, and the phrase *of devices and computer systems that could experience issues* is just a describing phrase that separates the subject and the verb. Now that you know the subject is *number*, what do you think about the phrase "The number...were making?" You probably think it isn't correct, and you're right! Cross off (F), (G), and (J) because they are all plural—they might work with a word like *issues*, but they don't work with a singular subject such as *number*. Therefore, the answer is (H), *made*, which does work with the subject *number*.

Programmers identified a second potential source of error: many devices mistakenly did not recognize the year 2000 as a leap year in <u>its</u> calendars. [5]

5. **A.** NO CHANGE
   B. one's
   C. those
   D. their

What's changing in the answers? Pronouns. You may remember from school that pronouns stand in for nouns. This means they must be consistent with the noun they are supposed to be replacing. Start by identifying whose *calendars* are being discussed: it's the calendars of the *devices*. Because *devices* is plural, the correct pronoun must also be plural. Eliminate (A) and (B) because both are singular. The word *those* doesn't work here because *those* can refer only to something that was previously mentioned, and the calendars weren't mentioned before. Eliminate (C). Therefore, (D) is the answer: it correctly uses *their* to refer to the devices' calendars.

Worldwide, it is estimated that over $300 billion was spent on fixing these programming glitches to prevent the forecasted problems, which ranged from incorrect clocks to a collapse of the banking system.

6. Which choice provides the clearest and most specific information about how much money was spent on the Y2K problem?

   F. NO CHANGE
   G. a great deal of money
   H. a certain amount of money
   J. some money

First off, do you notice what's different about this one? It actually asks a question! Although the majority of the questions will look like the ones you've already seen, in which there was no question, some English questions will actually ask you something. **The most important thing you can do is notice when you're being asked a question**—otherwise, if you go straight to the answer choices, you can easily pick an answer that you personally like but that does not do what the question is asking you to do. Let's see what you are being asked to do here: choose an answer that *provides the clearest and most specific information about how much money was spent*. Choice (F) provides a specific number, so keep that one. Choice (G) indicates that it was a large amount, but this is not as specific as (F). Choices (H) and (J) are vague and don't provide any specific details. Therefore, (F) does the best job at answering the question. Notice that the wrong answers here aren't grammatically wrong, but they just don't do what the question is asking. It's a good habit to underline what these questions are asking, and then cross off any answers that are not consistent with that purpose.

> Note that while (J) is the shortest option, it's wrong because it doesn't fulfill the purpose stated in the question. Never automatically pick the shortest option—it's not always right!

You will also see questions that involve the order of ideas, main points of paragraphs and passages, and adding or deleting text. These, too, all come down to consistency. Be sure to pay attention to what you are reading about, as you will need to understand the main idea of the paragraph for many of the ones that ask a question.

Clear

The next topic focuses on clarity: does the sentence provide a clear meaning? This type of question is testing word choice—in other words, of the choices provided, which one provides the best choice, or the clearest meaning. Let's see how this topic can be tested.

One of the first mainstream predictions of Y2K was a 1993 article titled "Doomsday 2000," and this melodramatic take <u>covered</u> the tone for much of the media coverage that followed in the years leading up to the millennium.

7. **A.** NO CHANGE
   B. revealed
   C. completed
   D. set

Here, vocabulary is changing in the answer choices. Don't worry—in most cases, you will know the words that appear in the answers on the English Test. However, you will need to determine which one provides the clearest meaning within the sentence. The sentence describes *one of the first* sources of Y2K information and explains how its *tone* related to that of *the media coverage that followed* it. The underlined word should mean something like "was the foundation for." Choice (A), *covered*, doesn't match with "was the foundation for," so eliminate it. Neither do choices (B) and (C). However, to "set" the tone is consistent with the idea of being a foundation for something else, so (D) is the correct answer. As you can see, for these questions it's a good strategy to determine what the underlined portion should be like

before you use POE in the answers. This way you know what you are looking for. The correct answer needs to make the meaning of the sentence clear.

As news media speculated about the worst possible outcomes of the computer malfunctions, many Americans stockpiled food and emergency supplies, and some religious groups <u>prophesied at the turn about the apocalypse of the millennium they expected.</u>

8. **F.** NO CHANGE
   G. prophesied about the turn of the millennium the apocalypse they expected.
   H. at the apocalypse prophesied about the turn of the millennium they expected.
   J. prophesied about the apocalypse they expected at the turn of the millennium.

Here, notice that the answer choices use all of the same words, but they put those words together in different ways. This question is testing clarity. You must choose the answer that provides the clearest meaning. Choice (F) uses the phrase *at the turn*, which doesn't provide a clear meaning—*turn* of what? Choice (G) says *prophesied about the turn of the millennium*, which also doesn't provide a clear meaning—the turn of the millennium was definitely going to happen, so it doesn't make sense that people would *prophesy* or make predictions that it would happen. Choice (H) says that the groups *at the apocalypse* prophesied, which makes it sound like an apocalypse happened, which isn't the correct meaning of the sentence. Choice (J) makes the meaning clear, and it's the correct answer.

Concise

Some of the ACT English questions on the English section of the ACT will ask you to choose the option that is concise and doesn't repeat the same words twice or use more words than it needs to. Whew, that was a mouthful! We probably could have said that in a more concise way. You saw in some of the previous questions that the shortest option isn't always correct, but once you have dealt with Complete, Consistent, and Clear, you can then consider which option is the most Concise. Let's take a look.

As it turned out, after the clock struck midnight on December 31, 1999, very few serious Y2K-related problems were brought to the attention of authorities and reported.
                                                         9

9. **A.** NO CHANGE
   B. reported.
   C. reported to authorities and announced.
   D. reported by making them known publicly.

> If you spot one short answer and three longer answers, it's a good clue that the question could be testing concise wording.

As you read this sentence, you might have noticed an error right off the bat: the underlined portion is a bit wordy. Doesn't *brought to the attention of authorities* mean the same thing as *reported*? Yes, so eliminate (A). Choice (B) is concise, so keep that one. Choices (C) and (D) make the same mistake as (A): they use too many words or phrases that have the same meaning. Therefore, (B) is the answer.

Remember, do not automatically choose the shortest option. Ask yourself whether the extra words clarify the meaning. If they do, then you want the additional words. In this case, the extra words do not make the meaning clearer.

Some argue that the Y2K fears were overblown, while others contend that the threats were real and that the massive time and money put into avoiding the predicted glitches had the intended effect and prevented major problems. In addition, Y2K has
                                              10
now become a historical event largely remembered only by those who actually experienced it.

10. **F.** NO CHANGE
    G. For example,
    H. By contrast,
    J. DELETE the underlined portion.

First, determine what's changing in the answers: transition words. You probably noticed something different here as well. Choice (J) gives the option to delete the transition entirely. Transitions connect two sentences, so read the two sentences without the underlined portion, as they would be for (J). This seems to work, but check the other options just in case. *In addition* is used for another point, but the second sentence isn't another point that follows the previous sentence. Eliminate (F). This sentence also isn't an example, and it doesn't draw a contrast compared to the previous sentence. This eliminates (G) and (H). Therefore, the answer is (J). None of the provided transitions works in this context, and a transition is not really needed anyway. Choice (J) is concise and correct.

When you have the option to DELETE, look for a reason not to choose it. If the underlined portion is necessary to make the sentence complete, consistent, or clear, then don't choose DELETE. However, if the underlined portion isn't necessary within the sentence, then go with that option.

ACT Online English

The Basic Approach to English requires no changes on the ACT Online Test. When you decide to skip a question to come back to it Later (for example, a question asking for the introduction to the topic of the passage before you've read any part of the passage), flag the question so you can easily jump back to the question before moving on to the next passage.

Another useful feature is the Highlighter tool. When a question asks you to fulfill a specific purpose, you can highlight the purpose stated in that question (for instance, in question 6 on page 134 you would highlight *clearest and most specific* as well as *how much money was spent*). This way, you can focus your eyes on what the question is asking you to do, much like you might underline those words on the paper version of the test. You may also find it helpful to highlight the subject in a question in which the verb is underlined (such as number 4 on page 133), and so on.

Lastly, as with every section on the ACT Online Test, you should use the Answer Eliminator tool for Step 3 of the Basic Approach to aid with Process of Elimination, rather than looking for the correct answer.

That's All, Folks!

As you can see, you don't need to be a grammar expert to do well on the ACT English. By focusing on the four C's and some basic rules, you can boost your English score.

Summary

- Aim to finish the English section, even if that means skipping a few obviously time-consuming questions as you go.

- Follow the Basic Approach for English:

  1. Read to the end of the sentence with an underlined portion.

  2. Look to the answers to see what's changing.

  3. Use Process of Elimination.

- Use the four C's:

  ❏ **Complete**—follow punctuation rules to avoid run-on sentences and fragments.

  ❏ **Consistent**—make the underlined portion match up with the non-underlined portion.

  ❏ **Clear**—choose an answer that makes the meaning 100% clear.

  ❏ **Concise**—after applying the other C's, then choose the option that provides the correct meaning with the fewest words.

ACT Math

Structure

The ACT Math Test consists of 60 questions in a rough order of difficulty. Some questions will be grouped together based on the same information, but most are stand-alone questions. All questions on the Math Test have 5 answer choices, unlike questions on the other sections of the ACT which only have 4 options.

Pacing

The Math Test is only 60 minutes long, allowing for a mere 60 seconds to answer each question. Of course, some questions will take less time than that, but others will take more. Unless you are an ACT Math superstar, you are unlikely to be able to work through and answer all 60 questions within the time limit. In fact, most students should be skipping some questions. Say you rush through the Math Test, trying every question and making a lot of careless mistakes. You may end up getting only 30 of the 60 questions right, which would give you a Math score of about 19. What if, instead of trying to tackle everything, you slowed down and worked only the 40 questions that you felt most comfortable with? You'd likely get most or all of them right, and you would never even have to think about those harder questions. If you were able to get 35 of those correct, your score would jump to a 22 or so, and you'd get there with a lot less stress! Sounds great, but how do you know which ones to do and which to skip?

POOD

Although the questions in the Math Test are in an approximate order of difficulty, knowing that is not very helpful to you as a test-taker. It is much more useful for you to determine your Personal Order of Difficulty (POOD). While the first 20 Math questions on the ACT are generally easier than those that come later, you can count on seeing some easy questions among the final 10 questions as well. There are also usually a few pretty tough questions early in the test. Don't let yourself get stuck on those hard questions, no matter where they show up. The worst thing you can do is spend a long time on a hard question when there are still easy questions you have yet to answer. The way to avoid this is to use a two-pass system.

The Two-Pass System

Do the Math Test in two passes. On your first pass through the section, decide if each question is one you want to do Now, Later, or Never. Answer the easy questions in the first pass because they're easy, and you don't want to miss any of the easy points. All questions have the same value, so you don't get bonus points for struggling successfully to answer a really tough question. Therefore, make sure you get to all the Now questions that you know how to do. Because they don't put all the questions that you know how to do in one place, the only way to find them is to use this two-pass system.

On the first pass, you also "do" the Never ones because they're impossible. Let's say you can't do trig graphing, and on your first pass you come to a trig graphing question. Spending any time on this question would be a waste, so you don't want to come back to it later. You also don't want to leave it blank on your answer sheet, because you might get lucky and

> Your Letter of the Day (LOTD) is a single letter/letter pair (A/F, B/G, etc.) that you choose whenever you're purely guessing on a question.

guess correctly (remember that there's no penalty for wrong answers). So, put in your Letter of the Day (LOTD) and move on, looking for more questions you know how to do.

That leaves the Later questions. On the first pass, as you identify questions you think you can do but that will take some work, circle them in your test booklet but don't work them. You don't want to get hung up on them before you are sure you've answered all the easy questions, but you want to be able to easily find them again. Once you've worked your way through the entire test in this way (finishing your first pass), you're going to come back and work on the questions you circled and skipped.

On the second pass, go back and work on the questions you circled in the first pass, starting with the ones in which you are most confident. Spending time on questions you think you may be able to figure out is much wiser than taking a 10-minute nap at the end of the section. When you have 5 minutes left, stop and make sure to enter your answers for questions you've worked but not marked on your bubble sheet yet. Also put in your LOTD for any questions you're not going to have time to finish.

Using your LOTD along with proper pacing is a very powerful strategy. In our previous pacing example, getting 35 of the 60 questions correct would give you a Math Test score of 22. If you got there by doing only 40 questions, you would use your LOTD on the remaining 20 questions. The odds are that you'd get about one-fifth of them right, gaining you about 4 more points. This could boost your score up to a 24 with no additional work!

Content

Knowing which topics will come up on the test and focusing first and foremost on the ones you know you can nail will help you to improve your score. Here is the topic breakdown according to ACT.

Preparing for Higher Math (34–36 questions)

- Number and Quantity (4–6 questions)
- Algebra (7–9 questions)
- Functions (7–9 questions)
- Geometry (7–9 questions)
- Statistics and Probability (5–7 questions)

Integrating Essential Skills (24–26 questions)

This is what the ACT calls the math you learned before high school, including percentages, rates, proportions, and much of geometry.

Modeling (15+ questions)

This is what the ACT calls word problem questions that require you to make equations to represent situations. These questions are also counted in the above two categories, as they may also test Higher Math or Essential Skills. That's why the total number of questions in the three categories is greater than 60.

So now you know the topics you'll see on the ACT on test day. What you *don't* know is which questions will be the hard ones and which will be the easy ones, but this breakdown does tell you what you need to be studying. Because there's no calculus, don't bother with studying calc. Because there are only a handful of trig questions, you probably don't want to spend too much time on trig either.

Most of the questions are in geometry and algebra—stuff you probably finished studying in 10th grade. The fact of the matter is, there is a lot of math on the ACT that you last studied before high school. You're going to need to review those topics in order to do well on the test.

Remember Your Calculator

You are allowed to use a calculator on the ACT's Math questions. Sometimes it will be useful, and sometimes it won't. Although every question on the test can be done without a calculator, doing the test this way is no fun at all, so remember to take your calculator.

> If you don't have your calculator handy right now, you should. You'll need it to do the Math questions in this book. Remember: Always have your calculator when doing ACT Math problems.

Keep in mind that not all calculators are permitted on the ACT. You can check the ACT website (www.act.org) for the specifics. Basically, if your calculator has a Computer Algebra System (like the TI-89, HP-40G, and Casio CFX-9970G do), you can't use it on the ACT. Don't think that you'll be able to sneak a banned calculator by the proctors, either. ACT has been pushing its proctors to crack down, and they are checking more carefully than they used to.

Even though you *can* use your calculator on all the Math questions, that doesn't mean that you *should* always use it. Let's look at an example of a question on which you may be tempted to use your calculator, but doing so may be more trouble than it is worth.

13. What is the value of $3(a)^2 + \dfrac{2b}{c} - \dfrac{a}{c}$ if $a = -2$, $b = 3$, and $c = 4$?

  A. -11
  B. -10
  C. 12
  D. 13
  E. 14

In this kind of question, all of the pieces are given to you. All you need to do is the math—carefully. ACT likes to use negatives, so keep your eyes open for those. Remember to set up the problem on paper before you begin stabbing at your calculator: ACT knows exactly the types of mistakes that can occur when you rush to punch numbers into your calculator too quickly and will have those incorrect solutions waiting for you in the answer choices. You should recopy the equation with the numbers in place of every variable, like so:

$$3(-2)^2 + \frac{2(3)}{4} - \frac{(-2)}{4}$$

When solving an equation, follow the order of operations (PEMDAS), which says to take care of calculations inside Parentheses first and then apply Exponents. There are no calculations inside parentheses here, so do the exponent first. A negative number to an even power becomes positive, so you get this:

$$3(4) + \frac{2(3)}{4} - \frac{(-2)}{4}$$

Next, handle Multiplication and Division, from left to right. Remember that a negative multiplied by a negative gives a positive. Finally, do any Addition and Subtraction, from left to right.

$$12 + \frac{6}{4} + \frac{2}{4} = 12 + \frac{8}{4} = 12 + 2 = 14$$

The correct answer is (E), and writing the steps out on paper was a much more foolproof way to solve it than using a bunch of parentheses on your calculator. Now let's look at another way to avoid a lot of calculations.

The Big Technique: Ballparking

As you already know, every Math question on the ACT has one right answer and four wrong answers. Your job is to eliminate those wrong answers and pick the right one, rather than just hoping the right one jumps out at you. When the people who write the ACT are constructing a Math question, the first answer they come up with is the right answer. Then, they build the wrong answers by working the problem and making the sorts of mistakes that a careless (or rushing) student might make. The wrong answers they get are what they use as the wrong answers on the test. That's why when you make an error on a question, you frequently find your wrong answer listed. Sneaky, eh?

In order to reduce the chance of this happening, and in order to help you get rid of some wrong answers on questions you're not exactly sure how to do (which will help you guess better), you're going to use a technique called Ballparking.

Ballparking is the name for the process of reading a question, figuring out roughly what the right answer will be (without actually working the problem), and then crossing out any answers that are too big, too small, or too obviously trying to trick you.

For example, if a question says that the price of something increases 20 percent from $300, you can immediately cross out anything less than $300, because the price is going up, not down. You could also get rid of anything bigger than $600, because it goes up

only 20 percent, which is much less than doubling. It's likely that $320 would be an answer choice on this question because that's what you get when you add $20 instead of 20%. They're trying to trick you, so turn the tables and cross off that answer.

Ballparking will rarely eliminate all four wrong answers, but it will frequently eliminate two or three wrong answers, and that's a real help. Try it out on these problems. (Don't work them out—right now just practice eliminating answers that are too large or too small.)

---

3. A rectangle has a length of 7 inches and an area of 56 square inches. What is its width, in inches?

   A. 392
   B. 49
   C. 21
   D. 8
   E. 7

23. A pair of running shoes, regularly priced at $75.00, is marked down 20% for summer clearance. If a sales tax of 8% is added to the final purchase price, how much will a customer pay for these shoes during the sale?

   A. $55.20
   B. $60.00
   C. $64.80
   D. $74.88
   E. $81.00

A Note on Question Numbering

You may notice that the practice questions in this book, particularly in the Math chapters, are not always numbered sequentially. In other words, you may see Math questions numbered 6, 7, 13, 32, and 37, for example. We've done this to indicate where a given question may show up on the actual exam and thus help you anticipate where a certain topic may be tested and how.

In question 3 you can quickly eliminate (A) and (B) because they are too large. Area is found by multiplying length and width, and 7 times either of those answers will be way bigger than 56. Once you get rid of those answers, you have a better chance of guessing the correct one (it happens to be (D)) or avoiding traps if you make a mistake calculating the answer.

In question 23 you know that the shoes will cost less than $75, so eliminate (E) right away. Because they're being marked down by 20%, and the 8% sales tax won't make up that much of the difference, (D) is also too high. Choice (A) is close to $20 less but the question is about 20%, so (A) is a trap and can be crossed out. That leaves you with (B) and (C), and if you don't know how to do percentages, you now have a fifty-fifty chance of getting this question right anyway.

Since such word problems can often be wordy and difficult, let's examine a consistent approach to use when you are faced with them.

The Big Technique: Word Problem Approach

Use the following steps every time you are faced with a word problem.

 Know the question.

Read the whole question before calculating anything, and underline the actual question at the end.

Let the answers help.

Look for clues on how to solve and ways to use Process of Elimination.

Break the problem Into bite-sized pieces.

When you read the question a second time, pause to calculate at each step and watch out for tricky phrasing.

For question 23, you've already done the first two steps. Let's work through Step 3 to determine whether the correct answer is (B) or (C). Start by calculating the exact value of 20% of $75.00 by multiplying $\frac{20}{100}$ by $75 to get $15. This is the amount of the markdown, so subtract this from $75 to get $75 − $15 = $60. A sales tax of 8% will be added to this, but WAIT! Don't rush into calculating this exact value. The correct answer must be slightly more than $60, so it must be (C). Using those answers (Step 2) can really help you avoid unnecessary work and save precious seconds on the test.

Now let's look at two more related techniques that can help you break down tricky questions, even difficult ones, and make them much more manageable.

The Big Technique: Plugging In

Here is the sort of algebra question that ACT loves to test.

---

17. Which of the following correctly gives the

    average of x, $x + 3$, $2x - 5$, and $6x - 1$?

    A. $2x - 5$

    B. $x - \dfrac{3}{4}$

    C. $\dfrac{5}{2}x + \dfrac{9}{4}$

    D. $10x - 3$

    E. $\dfrac{5}{2}x - \dfrac{3}{4}$

If you came across this question while taking the ACT, you might think to yourself, "Gaah! I don't want to do this—there are way too many x's here." Well, we agree with you, so we're going to teach you a way to eliminate all of the variables from this question and turn it into a simple arithmetic problem. We'll do it by using one of our most powerful techniques—Plugging In.

The thing about question 17 that makes it troublesome is the variable, right? If the question were asking you to find the average of four integers, it would be a snap, wouldn't it? So, what you're going to do is make up a value for x and change all the terms you're averaging into real numbers. Let's use 5 for x and work the problem out.

If $x = 5$, then the question is asking you to find the average of 5, 8, 5, and 29. That's easy enough. Add them up to get 47; then divide by the number of things, 4, to get that the average is 11.75. So, when $x = 5$, the correct answer is 11.75. This is your target answer. Circle it.

Now go to the answer choices, plug in 5 for every x to see which answer works out to 11.75. (Because you chose 5 for x at the beginning, you must use it all the way through. Don't change your value for x in the middle of a problem).

Choice (A) is $2(5) - 5 = 5$. That's not 11.75, so cross it out. Choice (B) works out to $5 - 0.75 = 4.25$—too small; eliminate it. Choice (C) is $\dfrac{5}{2}(5) + \dfrac{9}{4} = 12.5 + 2.25 = 14.75$. That's too big, so cross out (C). Choice (D) $10(5) - 3 = 47$—way too big. That leaves only (E), which works out like this:

$\dfrac{5}{2}(5) - \dfrac{3}{4} = 12.5 - 0.75 = 11.75$—exactly what you are looking for! Choice (E) is the correct answer.

So maybe you're thinking that you got lucky here. Nope, not at all. Plugging In will work on almost any question with variables in the answer choices. As long as you follow the simple steps, you'll get the right answer on Plugging In questions on the test. See next page for steps on how to do it.

The Big Technique: Plugging In Approach

STEP 1 » Assign numbers to the variables.

Pick a number for one of the variables, following any requirements in the question. Then see what else you can figure out. If you can determine no other values, assign a number to the remaining variable(s). Write your numbers above the variables to keep track of what's what.

STEP 2 » Solve the question using your numbers.

Circle whatever value you get. This is the target value, and you're going to check the answer choices to see which one matches your target value.

STEP 3 » Put your numbers into the answer choices and solve them.

Find the one that matches your target value from Step 2.

STEP 4 Check all five answer choices.

Always check every answer choice. If you get more than one that works, just use a different set of numbers and try again (this doesn't happen very often, but we'll demonstrate how to handle it later in this chapter anyway).

That's all there is to it.

Pick Easy Numbers

Remember that you still have to do some math when you're plugging in, so pick numbers that are going to make your life easier. We picked 5 in that average question, not 137.92. It would have worked if we had picked 137.92 (go ahead and try it out if you don't believe us), but why make life so hard? By picking 5, we kept the math simple and barely worked up a sweat finding the right answer.

Keeping that in mind, then, take a look at this:

---

20. If $q = \dfrac{3(s-5)}{t}$, then what is s in terms of q

and t ?

F. $qt + 8$

G. $\dfrac{8q}{t}$

H. $\dfrac{qt + 5}{3}$

J. $\dfrac{qt}{3} + 5$

K. $\dfrac{3qt}{5}$

This problem has three different variables. No problem—plugging in will handle this easily. Whenever you have multiple variables, plug in for the variable that's buried in the middle of stuff first and work your way out to the other ones. That means starting with s here. If you make $s = 10$, the top of that fraction will be 15. Make $t = 5$, and that will make $q = 3$.

The question asks what s is, so circle 10 because that is the value of s. Now it's on to the answer choices. Plug in carefully to avoid making a mistake.

F. $(3)(5) + 8 = 15 + 8 = 23$
Nope, not 10.

G. $\dfrac{8(3)}{5} = \dfrac{24}{5}$
Nope, still not 10.

H. $\dfrac{(3)(5) + 5}{3} = \dfrac{15 + 5}{3} = \dfrac{20}{3}$
Again, nope.

J. $\dfrac{(3)(5)}{3} + 5 = \dfrac{15}{3} + 5 = 5 + 5 = 10$
Yes! But always check all five answers.

K. $\dfrac{3(3)(5)}{5} = \dfrac{45}{5} = 9$
Still nope.

Choice (J) is your answer. So when do you want to plug in? Every single time you can. Just look for variables in the answer choices as your clue to plug in. It's a foolproof way of getting the questions right, and that's what it's all about on the ACT, right? Right.

Try to plug in on this question before reading the explanation that follows:

32. Which of the following is equal to $\dfrac{2}{x} - \dfrac{2}{1-x}$ for all $x \neq 0$ and $x \neq 1$?

F. 0

G. 2

H. $\dfrac{4}{x}$

J. $\dfrac{2}{x(x-1)}$

K. $\dfrac{2(1-2x)}{x(1-x)}$

Did you do the question? Don't start reading this explanation unless you actually picked a number for x and plugged in until you got the answer. Plugging In, like all of our techniques, will work only if you practice it.

Okay, let's plug in 4 for x. The expression then works out like this:

$$\frac{2}{4} - \frac{2}{1-4} = \frac{1}{2} - \left(-\frac{2}{3}\right) = \frac{3}{6} + \frac{4}{6} = \frac{7}{6}$$

So, now it's on to the answer choices. Right away, (F) and (G) are out. If you look more closely, you'll notice that you need a 7 in your numerator. Choices (H) and (J) can also be eliminated. Plug in 4 for x in (K) to make sure it matches your target.

K. $\dfrac{2[1-2(4)]}{4(1-4)} = \dfrac{2(1-8)}{4(-3)} = \dfrac{2(-7)}{-12} = \dfrac{-14}{-12} = \dfrac{7}{6}$
YES!!!

If you didn't get (K) when you plugged in, go back and check your math. You made a miscalculation at some point. It's important to find out where so that you see what type of mistake you tend to make. That way, you'll be more sensitive to avoiding similar missteps in the future.

Geometry Plugging In

Plugging In is a hugely powerful technique (on one recent ACT we counted more than 10 questions that you could do with Plugging In), and you should use it at every available opportunity. In other words, don't use it on algebra questions only—use it on geometry questions, too.

Plugging In works on geometry questions the same way that it works on other questions. You plug in your numbers, solve for the answer, and then check the answer choices. Remember not to violate any of the rules of geometry, though—no triangles with 300 degrees or squares with five sides!

> Whenever you have variables in the answers, plug in!

14. A triangle with a base of 4 and a height of 6 has both of these dimensions increased by z. What is the area of the new triangle, in terms of z ?

    F. $12 + z$

    G. $12 + \dfrac{z}{2}$

    H. $6z^2$

    J. $\dfrac{z^2}{2} + 5$

    K. $\dfrac{z^2}{2} + 5z + 12$

You know how this works by now. Let's use 2 for z and then find the area of the new triangle. The new base is $4 + 2 = 6$ and the new height is $6 + 2 = 8$. The formula for the area of a triangle is $A = \dfrac{1}{2}bh$, so the new area is $\dfrac{1}{2}(6)(8) = 24$. This is the target value; circle it and move on to the answers.

F. $12 + 2 = 14$
Nope, not 24.

G. $12 + \dfrac{2}{2} = 12 + 1 = 13$
Still not 24.

H. $6(2)^2 = 6(4) = 24$
Yes, but don't stop there!

J. $\dfrac{2^2}{2} + 5 = \dfrac{4}{2} + 5 = 2 + 5 = 7$
Nope.

K. $\dfrac{2^2}{2} + 5(2) + 12 = \dfrac{4}{2} + 10 + 12 = 2 + 22 = 24$
Oh no, this is also 24!

So, two answers worked—what should you do? Cry? Give up? No! You can either guess and go from here, or you can finish this one out by picking a new value for z. If $z = 4$, the new dimensions are 8 and 10, and the new area is $\dfrac{1}{2}(8)(10) = 40$. There is no need to try this in all five answer choices. Just check the two that remain.

F. ~~12 + z~~

G. ~~12 + \dfrac{z}{2}~~

$$12 + \dfrac{z}{2}$$

H. $6(4)^2 = 6(16) = 96$
That no longer works.

J. ~~\dfrac{z^2}{2} + 5~~

$$\dfrac{z^2}{2} + 5$$

K. $\dfrac{4^2}{2} + 5(4) + 12 = \dfrac{16}{2} + 20 + 12 = 8 + 32 = 40$
YES!!!

Once you've plugged in the first time, you know the steps to take to check the answers, so plugging in again is easy if you need to do it.

Some good numbers to plug in are 2, 4, 5, or 10. Make sure to follow the restrictions in the question when picking your numbers. It is usually best to avoid plugging in 0 or 1, as they make weird things happen with the math.

The Big Technique: PITA

No, it's not snack time. PITA stands for Plugging In The Answers, another type of Plugging In strategy that you can use on the ACT.

PITA is a technique you can use when the ACT tells you a little story and then asks you how many or how much. All the answers are real numbers, and only one of them works in the story ACT told (of course—otherwise there'd be more than one right answer). So,

what you're going to do on this type of question is try the answers out in the little story. Plug the Answers Into The story. (Okay, so that way it spells PAIT, but you get the idea.)

These are the steps to follow when using PITA.

Underline what the question asks for and label the answers accordingly.

If the question asks how many movie tickets were sold to adults, write "*adult tickets*" above the answers. If it asks for the value of *x*, write "*x*" above the top answer. Any time the final question asks for a specific value or number, that quantity is what the answers represent, and you can use PITA to answer the question.

Start with the middle answer choice.

Unless the question asks for the *least* value or the *greatest* value, start in the middle and use that number to work through the story. If it is too big or too small, you can eliminate other answers as well.

When you find an answer that works, STOP!

Unlike with Plugging In, there is only one answer that can possibly work on PITA questions. Once you find it, even if it is just because you've eliminated the other 4 answers, stop and bubble that answer in.

Here's how it works on a real question:

---

40. David, Heidi, and Shawn are shopping for a gift for Cindy. If David pays $\frac{1}{3}$ as much as Heidi does, Shawn and Heidi pay the same amount, and the gift costs $210, how much does David pay? (Disregard taxes when figuring your answer.)

F. $30
G. $70
H. $90
J. $140
K. $180

When using PITA, start with the middle answer choice. Because the answer choices are almost always listed in ascending or descending order, if the middle choice is too big or too small, you can immediately cross off two more wrong answers above or below it. Always label the answer choices before you start solving the problem, and work horizontally so you can easily see what to do on later answer choices. Let's try it on this one. you're looking for what David paid, so label the answers "David" and then start working on (H), the middle answer. Because David

pays $\frac{1}{3}$ of what Heidi does, you should start solving by tripling 90 (David's amount in (H)) to get 270. Put that under a label for Heidi. Because Heidi and Shawn paid the same amount, add a label for Shawn and put 270 under it. The last thing you'll need is the total. Add the three together to see if it equals 210 (the amount given in the story).

You should write it like this:

	David	Heidi	Shawn	Total	210?
	F. $30				
	G. $70				
Start:	H. $90	270	270	630	NO WAY!
	J. $140				
	K. $180				

Okay. Choice (H) is way too big, so (J) and (K) are out, too. Cross them out. Now you can work on (G) or (F). Try (F) next, since you need a much smaller number.

	David	Heidi	Shawn	Total	210?
	F. $30	90	90	210	YES!
	G. $70				
Start:	H. ~~$90~~	270	270	630	
	~~J. $140~~				
	~~K. $180~~				

At this point, you're done. If you had tried (G) next and it was also too big, you would still be done—if (G) doesn't work, (F) must be right. If you have been careful with your work, you don't even need to check the last answer as you do with Plugging In. PITA questions always have numbers in the answers, and you only need to check all five answers when using Plugging In because the answers contain variables, and more than one expression with variables could happen to equal the same number.

PITA also works very well on questions that ask you to determine what point fits a given equation.

---

35. Which of the following points lies on the circumference of the circle given by the equation $(x - 2)^2 + (y + 5)^2 = 16$?

  A. (2,–5)
  B. (2,–1)
  C. (–2, 5)
  D. (–2, 1)
  E. (2, 5)

To use PITA on a question like this, try the points in the equation given. Unlike when you choose your own number with regular Plugging In, only one of them will work, so stop when you find one that does. These answers are not in ascending order in the same way they were on the last question, so just start with (A) and move on from there as needed.

A.   (2,–5) $(2 - 2)^2 + (-5 + 5)^2 = 0^2 + 0^2 \neq 16$
No good.

B.   (2,–1) $(2 - 2)^2 + (-1 + 5)^2 = 0^2 + 4^2 = 16$
This looks good. You're done.

C.   (–2, 5)

D.   (–2, 1)

E.   (2, 5)

Because (B) worked, there was no point in trying the three answer choices remaining.

Try PITA on your own on this next question (remember to start with (C) when the answers are in order so you can use Process of Elimination).

---

37. A cookie recipe calls for flour and sugar to be combined in a 9:1 ratio. If the recipe yields 3 dozen cookies for each pound of this flour and sugar mix, how many pounds of sugar will be needed to make 27 dozen cookies?

  A. $\dfrac{81}{100}$

  B. $\dfrac{9}{10}$

  C. 9

  D. 27

  E. 81

Work it out on your own before continuing.

Here's what you should have:

	Sugar	Flour	Total	Cookies	27 Dozen?
A.	$\dfrac{81}{100}$				
B.	$\dfrac{9}{10}$	$\dfrac{81}{10}$	$\dfrac{90}{10} = 9$	27 dozen	Yep!
~~C.~~	~~9~~	81	90	270 dozen	No
~~D.~~	~~27~~				
~~E.~~	~~81~~				

Choice (B) is the correct answer because it works out to make 27 dozen cookies. Because the flour to sugar ratio is 9:1, you find the amount of flour by multiplying the sugar by 9. Add them to get the total number of pounds. The question says that each pound of mix makes 3 dozen cookies, so multiply Total by 3 to get the number of cookies in dozens that you could make from that much mix.

ACT Online Math

The Math Test is the place where you will have to adjust your approach the most when taking the Online Test instead of the paper-and-pencil test. No matter how you take the test, you should be writing things down as you solve the Math questions to keep track of your information and avoid careless errors. When you take the Online Test, you will have a small whiteboard to write down your work instead of the paper test booklet.

As you read each Math question, use the Highlighter tool to highlight any information you may forget, like restrictions on the value of x or the final question asked in a Word Problem. When using a technique like Plugging In or Plugging In the Answers, write the answers on your whiteboard to set up your work. If the question contains an equation to solve or a geometry figure to work with, carefully copy that down onto your whiteboard before getting to work.

As you work through a Math question, make sure to use the Answer Eliminator tool on any answers that you know are not correct. This helps you to make a better guess if you need to or to avoid falling for trap answers, just as when you use Process of Elimination on the paper-and-pencil test. Another handy feature of the online test is the Flag tool. Use that to mark any Later questions that you know will take a bit more time or work. Once you've done all the easier questions, you can see all those that you flagged in the Nav window.

Getting comfortable with these tools and the whiteboard will take some practice, so make sure to start using them right away if you plan to take the ACT Online Test.

You're On Your Way!

These simple Math techniques will do a lot to improve your score. If you want more great techniques or a more thorough review of Math content, check out The Princeton Review's *ACT Prep* book.

Summary

- Use the two-pass system to work through the Math section efficiently.

- Use your Personal Order of Difficulty to find all the Now questions and work them first.

- Mark questions that you want to work Later, and use your LOTD for any Never questions.

- Use your calculator wisely. Make sure to set up the question first and use your calculator only if you need to do so to avoid making mental math mistakes.

- Use Ballparking to eliminate any answers that are too big or too small to help you avoid falling for trap answers or to improve your odds if you need to guess.

- For Word Problems, follow this approach:

  1. Know the question—read the entire question and underline the actual question at the end.

  2. Let the answers help—look for clues about how to solve it or for ways to use POE.

  3. Use Bite-Sized Pieces—read carefully and do one small step at a time.

- For questions with variables in the answer choices, Plug In following these steps:

  1. Pick numbers for all the variables, making sure to fit any requirements given, and write them down.

  2. Solve the question using the numbers you picked to get a target value that answers the question. Circle the target value.

  3. Plug your numbers into the answer choices to eliminate any choices that don't work.

  4. Check all 5 answer choices. If more than one works, plug in again.

- For questions that ask for a specific value, Plug In the Answers following these steps:

  1. Underline the final question and label the answers.

  2. Start with the middle number unless asked for the *least* or *greatest* value. Use that value to work through the steps of the question and eliminate answers.

  3. When you find an answer that works, STOP!

ACT Reading

Structure

The ACT Reading Test consists of four passages, each with 10 questions. The passages always come in this order: Literary Narrative (or Prose Fiction), Social Studies, Humanities, Natural Science. One of the passages will be a "dual" passage: it will contain two shorter passages that are related in some way. Each passage in the ACT Reading Test begins with a blurb that gives the author, title, and date of the passage. The passages are all roughly the same length—about 700–900 words.

Pacing

Once you have determined your goal score for the Reading Test, there are two possible approaches to pacing: choose passages or choose questions. Some people have very high accuracy when they take their time working a passage; these people get their highest scores by working the more straightforward passages, spending a bit more time per passage, and using their Letter of the Day on harder passages. Other people maximize their scores by working the question types they are best at from all four passages. For example, a person may choose to answer all of the questions whose answers are easy to find in each passage. (You'll learn more about easy-to-find questions in this chapter.)

For illustration, imagine that your goal is to work 30 questions and guess your Letter of the Day on 10 questions. If you choose passages, you will work all of the questions from three passages and guess your Letter of the Day on all of the questions from one passage. If you choose questions, you will work 30 questions selected from all four passages and guess your Letter of the Day on 10 questions. You can try both strategies on practice tests to see which works better for you.

POOD

Neither the passages nor the questions are written in order of difficulty, so you must determine your Personal Order of Difficulty.

POOD for Questions

When determining your POOD for questions, think about whether it will be easy or hard to find the question's reference in the passage. Then, think about whether it will be easy or hard to answer the question once you find it.

Questions are easy to find if they mention a specific set of lines or a specific paragraph. We call these "line references" or "paragraph references." Here's an example of a question with a line reference.

> The ACT Online Reading Test does not include line references. Instead, a portion of the text is highlighted for certain questions, making them easy to find.

The author most likely includes the quote in lines 7–13 in order to:

Questions are also easier to find when they have good "lead words." Lead words are words that appear in the passage and are easy to spot. Good lead words include dates, words that are capitalized or italicized, and words that appear only once in the passage. Here is an example of a question with good lead words.

According to the passage, *The Catcher in the Rye* was written when the author:

Notice what stands out in this question—the book title—which is written with capital letters and in italics. Likewise, the italicized, capitalized title will stand out in the passage, making it easier to find.

Questions that are harder to find won't have line references or lead words.

> The passage's focus is primarily on the:

Notice the difference? This question doesn't have any good words to grab onto as you read the passage.

Questions with lead words that are not easy to spot in the passage can also be harder to find.

> According to the passage, stars and galaxies are most greatly affected by:

This question has lead words—"stars and galaxies"—but they won't be as easy to spot as *The Catcher in the Rye*.

Now that we've considered how easy or hard it is to find a question, let's think about what makes a question easy or hard to answer once you find it.

Questions are usually **easy to answer** when they ask for something that is explicitly stated in the text. These questions often include phrases such as "according to the passage," "the passage states," or "the passage indicates," and they often have short answers. We call these "referral" questions because they ask you to refer to what is explicitly stated in the passage.

Questions that are harder to answer will typically include words such as "means," "suggests," or "in order to," and they often have longer answer choices. These are called "reasoning" questions because they require you to first read information from the passage and then to think (or reason) about why that

information is there. Note that the answers to reasoning questions *will still be supported by the text*, even though they will typically not be explicitly stated.

Usually, people do best at questions that are easy to find, easy to answer, or both. Of course, Personal Order of Difficulty is *personal*, so choose the questions that you do best at.

POOD for Passages

When determining your POOD for entire passages, consider the passage's genre and topic. For example, if you love science and never choose to read fiction, you may want to start with the Natural Science passage and leave the Literary Narrative passage for last.

You can also consider the number and length of the paragraphs in a passage. It's typically easier to work a passage with 8–10 medium-sized paragraphs, as opposed to a passage with just a few very long paragraphs or a lot of very short paragraphs.

Finally, consider the questions and answer choices. Questions with line references, good lead words, and short answers tend to be easier, so a passage with lots of those kinds of questions will likely be easier overall.

Choose your Personal Order of Difficulty for the four passages described on the next page.

LITERARY NARRATIVE: This passage is adapted from the novel *The Old Drift* by Namwali Serpell (©2019 by Namwali Serpell).

10 paragraphs, 2 line-reference questions and 4 lead-word questions, 4 questions with short answers.

SOCIAL SCIENCE: Passage A is adapted from the book *National Parks* by Alfred Runte (©2010 by Alfred Runte). Passage B is adapted from the article *U.S. National Parks Could Be Privatized* by Adina Solomon (©2020 by National Geographic Society).

12 paragraphs divided between two passages, 4 line-reference questions and 1 lead-word question, 3 questions with short answers.

HUMANITIES: This passage is adapted from the book *The Visual Arts: A History* by Hugh Honour and John Fleming (©2009 by Fleming-Honour Ltd).

5 paragraphs, 1 line-reference question and 5 lead-word questions, 2 questions with short answers.

NATURAL SCIENCE: This passage is adapted from the article *Do We Live in a Lopsided Universe?* by Lee Billings (©2020 by Scientific American).

6 paragraphs, 2 line-reference questions and 5 lead-word questions, 4 questions with short answers.

Your order:

1st _____

2nd _____

3rd _____

4th _____

There's no right answer—it's whatever makes sense for your POOD.

6-Step Basic Approach

No matter your pacing goals and Personal Order of Difficulty, you will need an efficient approach to the Reading Test.

Your task on the ACT Reading Test is quite different from what you're asked to do in your English class at school. In your English class, you might spend days or even weeks reading a book. You might learn about its author and the time in which it was written. You discuss the book in class, and your teacher might help you uncover its central themes. You might be graded on your thoughtful participation in class discussions. Perhaps you take a test during which you're expected to remember key points about the book. Maybe you write an essay about the book in which you're rewarded for your independent, critical thinking.

On the ACT Reading Test, not so much. On the ACT, you get points for bubbling in the right answer, period. Your task is different, so your approach needs to be different.

You get points for answering questions, not for reading the passage, so you shouldn't spend your time deeply contemplating the passage and committing each detail to memory. On the other hand, the correct answers to the questions are based on the passage, so you need to read the relevant parts of the passage carefully. To balance these goals, you need an approach that helps you efficiently find information in the passage in order to answer the questions. The following 6-step process is designed to do just that.

> The ACT Online Reading approach is a little different. See "ACT Online Reading" later in this chapter for more information.

STEP 1 » Preview: Read the blurb and map the questions.

Read the blurb that precedes the passage; then map the questions by 1) putting a star next to line reference questions and 2) circling lead words.

Previewing the blurb and questions gives you some context for what you are about to read. Without this step, it's as though you've walked into the library, grabbed a random book, opened to a random page, and then started to read. Not a very friendly way to begin!

When you map the questions, you also prepare yourself to work the passage more efficiently.

Try Step 1 with the following blurb and set of questions. We left out the passage text and the answer choices. Focus on the questions as you look for line references and lead words.

SOCIAL STUDIES: This passage is adapted from the book *The Great Depression* by T. H. Watkins (©1993 by Blackside, Inc. Reprinted by permission of Little, Brown and Company).

11. The passage as a whole can best be described as:

12. According to the passage, Norman Bel Geddes was:

13. As it is used in line 47, the word *distinguished* most nearly refers to:

14. Which of the following best describes how the author uses the reference to the Trylon and Perisphere (lines 58–59)?

15. The New York World's Fair was inspired by which of the following events?

   I. The success of Chicago's World's Fair
  II. The inauguration of George Washington
 III. A vision of world peace

16. The theme presented by Chicago's "Century of Progress" celebration (lines 6–7) was that:

17. As it is used in line 79, the word *busy* most nearly means:

18. All of the following statements concerning Chicago's fair are true EXCEPT:

19. According to the passage, which of the world's fairs took place in two cities?

20. The author suggests that the timing of the four world's fairs was:

Which line reference questions did you star, and which lead words did you circle?

The line reference questions are questions 13, 14, 16 and 17. The lead words are Norman Bel Geddes, *distinguished*, Trylon and Perisphere, New York World's Fair, Chicago's "Century of Progress" celebration, *busy*, Chicago's, world's fairs, two cities, and timing. Notice how the lead words are those in the question that will lead you to the part of the passage with the answer. Things like "main idea" and "passage as a whole" are not lead words.

STEP 2 ≫ Work the passage.

The goal in this step is to prepare yourself to answer the questions efficiently. Do this by getting a sense of where you will find the answers in the passage. Read the passage, but don't try to absorb every detail. Your main job is to look for the lead words that you mapped in the questions—when you see one, circle it in the passage so you can find it quickly later. It's especially important to look for the lead words from the questions that don't have line references. If you also get a sense of the main idea while working the passage, that's a nice bonus, but it isn't necessary. If you see the answer to a specific question while you're working the passage, it's okay to stop and answer the question!

You should spend no more than three minutes on this step. If you have trouble getting through the passage in three minutes, try reading just the first sentence of each paragraph. You may also find that it works best for you to skip this step and simply read the passage one chunk at a time as you go through the questions.

Try Step 2 with the following passage, timing yourself to see how long it takes.

One of the peculiarities of the years of the Great Depression was the fact that in the middle of the worst economic period Americans had ever seen, four cities somehow found the time, money, and energy to produce
5 four world's fairs—more than during any other ten-year period in the nation's history. The first, Chicago's "Century of Progress" celebration, opened for business on a 400-acre landfill on the edge of Lake Michigan on April 29, 1933. The fair, said its president, Rufus C. Dawes,
10 on opening day, was "the spontaneous expression of the pride of citizenship of Chicago" and, furthermore, demonstrated man's "power to prevail over the perils that beset him." Over the two years of the fair's life, 38 million people came to witness its attractions, giving

15 the city of Chicago a helpful shot of income for several months (although the fair itself lost money, as world's fairs tend to do).

Hoping to duplicate Chicago's economy-boosting success, on June 6, 1936, Texans celebrated the hundredth
20 anniversary of their independence from Mexico by producing the Texas Centennial Exposition in Dallas and a smaller, though related, Frontier Centennial Exposition in Fort Worth. Before closing down in December, the combined expositions drew some 7 million visitors,
25 and if that appeared insignificant when compared to the Chicago fair, the celebration accomplished its principal task, according to Stanley Marcus, cofounder of the mercantile empire of Neiman-Marcus. "I've frequently said that modern Texas history started with the celebration of
30 the Texas Centennial," he remembered, "because it was in 1936 . . . that the rest of America discovered Texas."

Then there were the two great fairs that marked the end of the decade—San Francisco's Golden Gate Exposition, which opened on February 18, 1939, and
35 the New York World's Fair, which opened on April 30, 1939; both ran until the fall of 1940. Neither brought in anywhere near the number of people Chicago's fair had in 1933, but each stood at the cusp between two historical epochs and consequently would shine forth
40 more brilliantly in the national memory, both burdened and enhanced by their roles as symbols.

San Francisco's exposition was designed to celebrate the completion of the Oakland–San Francisco Bay Bridge and the Golden Gate Bridge across the entrance to
45 the San Francisco Bay, two of the certifiably triumphant engineering accomplishments of the age. The fair itself was distinguished particularly by the fact that it was erected on a 400-acre landfill.

The inspiration for the New York World's Fair, built
50 5 miles from downtown Manhattan on a 1,200-acre Long Island refuse site called the Corona Dump, was the inauguration of President George Washington 150

years before, which the fair's leaders chose to identify as the true moment when the United States of America
55 opened for business. The theme of the fair was "The World of Tomorrow," and it featured the definitive futuristic symbols of the age: a 750-foot-high spike called the Trylon and, by its side, an enormous globe called the Perisphere, 200 feet in diameter. The fair was crawling
60 with its own forward-looking exhibits—a robot named Elektro, a simulated trip to the moon, and the first public demonstration of television, among others—but the most ambitious was "Futurama," a $7.5 million exhibit funded by General Motors and designed by Norman Bel Geddes.
65 With 500,000 miniature buildings, a million little trees, and 50,000 tiny automobiles that ran like beetles over complex highway networks, the huge exhibit pictured what Bel Geddes thought America would be like in the year 1960.

70   If the great industrial designer's vision of the future was not entirely reliable (he predicted that his teardrop-shaped automobiles would cost only $200, for one thing), it was no more flawed than the vision of the current world that both the Golden Gate Exhibition
75 and the New York World's Fair presented. The ornate mix of Mayan, Cambodian, Burmese, Malayan, and Polynesian architectural styles that characterized most of the buildings on San Francisco's Treasure Island, for example, was called "Pacific Basin," and the fair's busy
80 publicity machine repeatedly emphasized the wonderful unity of prosperity and cooperation that the peoples of the Pacific Rim nations enjoyed and presumably would continue to enjoy. For its part, the New York fair's own publicity people touted the beauty and hope represented
85 by its Lagoon of Nations, its Hall of Nations, and its Court of Peace bordered by the flags of the 58 foreign countries that had chosen to participate in the fair, 21 of which had erected their own buildings or pavilions, including Italy, the USSR, France, Great Britain, Japan,
90 and Belgium. So had the League of Nations, that engine of universal peace that had been established (without the participation of the United States) after the first World War.

Which lead words did you circle? How long did working the passage take you?

Mark this page so you can flip back to the passage easily as you work through the rest of the chapter.

Select and understand «STEP 3
a question.

Work the questions according to your POOD, starting with the questions that seem easy to find and easy to answer. Do questions that are harder to find later. Do general questions (such as *main idea* and *primary purpose*) last.

You'll notice that ACT likes to phrase questions as odd, half-finished sentences.

16. The theme presented by Chicago's "Century of Progress" celebration (line 6–7) was that:

Rephrase these half-sentences as actual questions that begin with words such as "What" or "Why." Be sure you understand the question you should answer.

How would you rephrase question 16?

_____

_____

_____

_____

One possible way to phrase the question is "What was the theme of Chicago's "Century of Progress" celebration?"

STEP 4 » Read what you need.

The answers to most ACT Reading questions are based on 5–10 lines from the passage—we call this the "window" for the question. You usually don't need to read more than this, but you also should not read less. Even if the question mentions line 4, you can't get the answer by reading *only* line 4.

Go back to the passage, locate the window for question 16, and draw a bracket around it to remind yourself of how much you need to read. You're looking for about 5–10 lines around lines 6–7.

Which lines did you bracket as the window for question 16?

Lines 1–13 work well.

We'll reprint the window for question 16 for convenience.

> One of the peculiarities of the years of the Great Depression was the fact that in the middle of the worst economic period Americans had ever seen, four cities somehow found the time, money, and energy to produce
> 5 four world's fairs—more than during any other ten-year period in the nation's history. The first, Chicago's "Century of Progress" celebration, opened for business on a 400-acre landfill on the edge of Lake Michigan on April 29, 1933. The fair, said its president, Rufus C. Dawes,
> 10 on opening day, was "the spontaneous expression of the pride of citizenship of Chicago" and, furthermore, demonstrated man's "power to prevail over the perils that beset him."

Predict the correct answer. « STEP 5

If possible, underline the answer to the question in the passage. Even if the question is not explicitly answered in the text, predict the correct answer based on what you read. Do not rely on your memory or your interpretation of the passage.

Underline the lines in the paragraph that describe the theme of the "Century of Progress" celebration; then check your prediction below.

The following sentence provides an answer to the question and would be a good one to underline:

> The fair, said its president, Rufus C. Dawes,
> 10 on opening day, was "the spontaneous expression of the pride of citizenship of Chicago" and, furthermore, demonstrated man's "power to prevail over the perils that beset him."

Notice that this sentence is *not* included in the line reference mentioned in the question! The evidence for the answer is often found just before or just after the line reference in the question, so you must read a window around the line reference.

Use POE. « STEP 6

Eliminate answer choices that don't match the prediction from the passage. Be sure to read all four answers, even if you see one that looks good right away. The best answer is the one that is best supported by the passage.

Try eliminating the answers that don't match the prediction you made.

F. humankind can triumph over adversity.
G. the Depression was almost over.
H. the future held world peace.
J. prosperous times were ahead for all Americans.

Did you eliminate (G), (H), and (J)? None of those answers matches the prediction. Notice that (F)—the correct answer—doesn't use the exact words from the passage. It's a paraphrase of the text, but it's a close match. The word *humankind* matches *man's*, the phrase *can triumph over* matches *power to prevail over*, and the word *adversity* matches *the perils that beset him*. This type of paraphrase is typical of the correct answer to a referral question on the ACT.

Repeat Steps 3 through 6

Continue to work through the questions according to your Personal Order of Difficulty, repeating steps 3 through 6 for each question.

Try the next question on your own. It's a referral question with a lead word. When you've worked the question, check the explanation that follows.

12. According to the passage, Norman Bel Geddes was:

F. a prolific inventor.
G. an industrial designer.
H. a renowned clairvoyant.
J. an economic theorist.

Rephrase the question: "*What was Norman Bel Geddes?*" Use the lead words *Norman Bel Geddes* to find the window for the question. His name appears in line 64. Read a window of 5–10 lines around his name.

The text says, *The fair was crawling with its own forward-looking exhibits...but the most ambitious was "Futurama," a $7.5 million exhibit...designed by Norman Bel Geddes. With 500,000 miniature buildings, a million little trees, and 50,000 tiny automobiles that ran like beetles over complex highway networks, the huge exhibit pictured what Bel Geddes thought America would be like in the year 1960.*

Underline information in the text that helps to answer the question: it says that the *"Futurama"* exhibit was *designed* by *Norman Bel Geddes*. Make a prediction for the correct answer based on the text: Norman Bel Geddes was a designer. Next, eliminate answers that don't match the prediction.

Eliminate (F) because there is no evidence in the text that Geddes invented anything. He designed an exhibit that illustrated what might be created in the future, but he did not actually invent the things shown in the exhibit.

Keep (G) because it matches the prediction. It includes the word *industrial*, which was probably not part of your prediction, but the fact that Geddes's design included buildings, cars, and highways supports the idea that Geddes was *an industrial designer*.

The word *clairvoyant* means "psychic." Although Geddes imagined the future, the text doesn't say that he actually saw the future. Eliminate (H).

Eliminate (J) because there is no evidence in the passage that Geddes studied the economy.

The correct answer is (G).

Another type of easy-to-find question you will see on ACT Reading is a "vocabulary-in-context" question. These questions usually involve a common word that has multiple definitions. The key to answering a vocab-in-context question correctly is to pay attention to the way the word is used in the passage. Let's take a look at one.

17. As it is used in line 79, the word *busy* most nearly means:

Rephrase the question: "What does the word *busy* mean in line 79?" Read a window around the line reference. For vocabulary-in-context questions, you can usually read just a sentence or two. The text says that *the fair's busy publicity machine repeatedly emphasized the wonderful unity of prosperity and cooperation* of the *Pacific Rim nations*. Next, cross out the word *busy* and jot down another word or phrase that has a similar meaning. Be sure to base your prediction on the text. The fair's *publicity machine* was *repeatedly* emphasizing something, so it was very active. The word *busy* could be replaced by "active." Now eliminate answers that don't match the prediction.

    A. crowded.
    B. meddling.
    C. bustling.
    D. unavailable.

The word *crowded* doesn't match "active," so eliminate (A). Notice that this answer is based on a different meaning of *busy* that might be used in another context. Although it could be a valid definition, "crowded" doesn't answer the question about how *busy* is used in line 79. Alternative definitions are very common wrong answers on vocabulary-in-context questions, so be sure to make a prediction based on the way the word is used in the passage.

The word *meddling* doesn't match "active," so eliminate (B). The word *meddling* means "interfering," which is a different definition of *busy* that doesn't fit the context.

The word *bustling* matches "active," so keep (C).

The word *unavailable* does not match "active." At this point, you're probably not surprised to see yet another definition of *busy* that doesn't fit the context! Eliminate (D).

The correct answer is (C).

Next, let's take a look at a reasoning question that is easy to find but may be a bit harder to answer.

13. As it is used in line 47, the word *distinguished* most nearly refers to:

First, rephrase the question: "What does the word *distinguished* refer to?" Although this question looks a lot like a vocabulary-in-context question, notice that it doesn't ask what the word *means*, but what it *refers to*. Use the line reference to find the window, and read 5–10 lines.

> San Francisco's exposition was designed to celebrate the completion of the Oakland–San Francisco Bay Bridge and the Golden Gate Bridge across the entrance to
> 45 the San Francisco Bay, two of the certifiably triumphant engineering accomplishments of the age. The fair itself was distinguished particularly by the fact that it was erected on a 400-acre landfill.

Underline information in the text that helps answer the question: it says that the *fair itself was distinguished particularly by the fact that it was erected on a 400-acre landfill*. Then eliminate answers that don't match the text.

A. an elegant person.
B. a notable feature.
C. a vision of the future.
D. a pair of bridges.

Eliminate (A) because there is no mention of a *person* in this paragraph. Eliminate (C) because there is no mention of the *future*. That leaves you with (B) and (D).

Getting down to two answers is a common occurrence on ACT Reading. On harder-to-answer questions, the match between the correct answer and the passage might not be as easy to spot, so you'll need a good strategy for working with tougher answer choices. Let's pause for a minute and talk about ACT's answers before we finish this question.

Getting Underneath the Answers

The answers can be one of the trickiest elements of the ACT Reading Test. Think about it: if the wrong answers were easy to eliminate, or if the correct answer were obvious, then everyone would get just about every question correct. When the ACT Reading authors create a question, they use specific strategies to make the correct answer less obvious and to make the wrong answers more tempting.

On many questions, the correct answer will be a paraphrase of what was in the passage. You'll need to match the paraphrased words of the answer back to the words of the passage.

On the other hand, wrong answers often use exact words from the passage. That makes them sound like what you've read, and they can be tempting if you're working too quickly. However, if you pay attention to each word of a wrong answer, you'll see that it doesn't quite match what the passage said. Or, you may see that it matches something stated in the passage, but that it doesn't answer the right question.

POE: Use Two Passes and Compare

Now that you know what the ACT is up to, what can you do to improve your accuracy? Make sure your predictions are based on what is actually stated in the passage. Then, focus on Process of Elimination. Make two passes through the answers. On the first pass, eliminate answers that clearly don't match the prediction (just as we did with question 13). Leave an answer in if you're not sure about it or if it's confusing and you need more time to read it carefully.

On the second pass, take your time. At this point, you have probably narrowed it down to the right answer and a tricky wrong answer that sounds a lot like the right answer. Use a comparison process: compare the remaining answers to each other and focus on what is different. Compare the answers to the passage. Consider every word of the answer as you match it back, and eliminate answers that don't match the passage. Compare each answer to the question that was asked and eliminate answers that don't answer the right question.

Now, try a comparison strategy with the two remaining answers from question 13.

A.
B. a notable feature.
C.
D. a pair of bridges.

Compare (B) and (D), looking for differences between them.

Choice (B) is about a *feature* (the answer doesn't say which feature) and (D) is about *a pair of bridges*. A *pair of bridges* is more specific, so (D) will probably be easier to work with than (B).

Compare (D) to the passage. What does the text say about the *two bridges*? It says that *San Francisco's exposition* celebrated *the completion of* the two bridges.

Now compare (D) to the question. The question asks what the word *distinguished* refers to. Although the two bridges are mentioned near the word *distinguished* in the text, the word doesn't refer to the two bridges; it refers to the fair. Eliminate (D).

Compare (B) to the question and to the passage. The text says, *The fair itself was distinguished particularly by the fact that it was erected on a 400-acre landfill.* So, the word *distinguished* refers to the *fair* and to the fact that it was built on a *landfill.* The fact that the fair was built on a landfill is an unusual characteristic, or *notable feature* of the fair. The correct answer is (B). Again, notice how the correct answer didn't use words directly from the text. Instead, you had to first read the text and then think about the fact that the fair being built on a landfill is unusual, or notable.

The comparison process will help you choose between tricky answers. However, if you get stuck, take a guess and move on to a question that will give you an easier point.

Try another reasoning question; then check the explanation below.

---

14. Which of the following best describes how the author uses the reference to the Trylon and Perisphere (lines 58–59)?

   F. It is one example among several of the way the designers of the New York World's Fair envisioned the future.
   G. It provides descriptions of the kind of buildings that were built in America in the 1960s.
   H. It highlights a difference between the world's fairs held in San Francisco and New York.
   J. It specifies how the world's fairs symbolized two different periods in history.

The question asks *how the author uses the reference to the Trylon and Perisphere.* Read 5–10 lines around the given line reference. Lines 55–60 describe the *New York World's Fair,* saying that it *featured the definitive futuristic symbols of the age: a 750-foot-high spike called the Trylon and, by its side, an enormous globe called the Perisphere, 200 feet in diameter...* along with other *forward-looking exhibits.* In other words, the author uses the *Trylon* and *Perisphere* as examples of the *futuristic symbols* that characterized the *New York World's Fair.* Eliminate answers that don't match this prediction. Keep (F) because it matches the prediction. Eliminate (G) because the passage doesn't indicate that buildings like the Trylon and Perisphere were built outside of the World's Fair. Eliminate (H) because there is no comparison with the San Francisco World's Fair in the window that describes the *Trylon* and *Perisphere.* Eliminate (J) because the passage doesn't discuss *two different periods in history* that were symbolized at the world's fairs. The correct answer is (F).

Later

Now let's take a look at some questions that are harder to find. These questions are best done later because they can be more time-consuming than easy-to-find questions are. It's also easier to find what you need once you've become familiar with the passage by working the easy-to-find questions.

19. According to the passage, which of the world's fairs took place in two cities?

This question may be harder to find because it includes neither a line reference nor a good lead word. The whole passage is about *world's fairs*, so those words appear in several paragraphs, and the passage never actually uses the phrase *two cities*. Fortunately, there are some other tools you can use to find the window for a harder-to-find question. Let's look at the answers for this question.

    A. The New York World's Fair
    B. The "Century of Progress" celebration
    C. The Texas Centennial Exposition
    D. The Golden Gate Exposition

In this case, the answers include better lead words than the question! So, you can look for the lead words from the answers to narrow down the chunks of the passage you need to read.

Let's start with (A): scan the passage looking for the *New York World's Fair*. It is mentioned in line 49. Read a short window around this reference: *the New York World's Fair, built 5 miles from downtown Manhattan on a 1,200-acre Long Island refuse site called the Corona Dump*. The fair was built 5 miles from downtown Manhattan, and there is no mention of a second city, so eliminate (A).

Next, scan the passage for the *"Century of Progress" celebration*. It is mentioned in lines 6–7, which say that *Chicago's "Century of Progress" celebration… opened for business on a 400-acre landfill on the edge of Lake Michigan*. Again, there's no mention of a second city, so eliminate (B).

Now scan for the *Texas Centennial Exposition*. It appears in lines 18–23, which say, *Texans celebrated the hundredth anniversary of their independence from Mexico by producing the Texas Centennial Exposition in Dallas and a smaller, though related, Frontier Centennial Exposition in Fort Worth*. Two cities—*Dallas* and *Fort Worth*—are mentioned, so keep (C).

Finally, scan for the *Golden Gate Exposition*. It appears in lines 32–36, which say that *there were the two great fairs that marked the end of the decade— San Francisco's Golden Gate Exposition…and the New York World's Fair*. The next paragraph also discusses *San Francisco's exposition*, saying, *The fair itself was distinguished particularly by the fact that it was erected on a 400-acre landfill*. Though the passage mentions *two* fairs, it indicates that there was only one location for the Golden Gate Exposition, so eliminate (D).

The correct answer is (C). You can see why this question is more time-consuming—you have to look up four windows instead of just one.

Let's look at another Later question.

15. The New York World's Fair was inspired by which of the following events?

    I. The success of Chicago's World's Fair
    II. The inauguration of George Washington
    III. A vision of world peace

    A. I only
    B. II only
    C. I and II only
    D. I and III only

As you can see, this "Roman numeral" question involves making decisions about multiple events. Focus on one event at a time and use Process of Elimination. Sometimes, you don't have to think about all three possibilities in order to answer the question.

Start by finding the window for the question, using the lead words *New York World's Fair*. You found these lead words while working the previous question. Lines 49–55 state, *The inspiration for the New York World's Fair…was the inauguration of President George Washington*. Roman numeral (II) is true, so eliminate any answers that don't include (II). Eliminate (A) and (D).

Now there are only two answers left—(B) and (C). One of them includes Roman numeral (I) and the other doesn't, so consider (I). There is no reference to the success of the *Chicago's World's Fair* related to the New York World's Fair, so (I) is not true. Eliminate (C). The correct answer is (B).

Another type of question that can be time-consuming is an EXCEPT/LEAST/NOT question. These take more time because they require you to locate three true statements in the passage. They can also be confusing because they ask you to choose the answer that is **not** supported by the passage. Let's try one.

18. All of the following statements concerning Chicago's fair are true EXCEPT:

Note that the question asks which statement is **not** true. Use the lead word *Chicago's* to find the window for the question. *Chicago's "Century of Progress" celebration* is discussed in the first paragraph. Now, look each answer up in the first paragraph. Rather than crossing out wrong answers as you normally would, mark each answer as "T" for "True" or "F" for "False."

    F. It was the first world's fair of the decade in the United States.
    G. It promoted progress made during the twentieth century.
    H. It was a source of pride for Chicago's citizens.
    J. It generated a significant profit.

Lines 6–9 identify *Chicago's "Century of Progress" celebration* as the *first* of the world's fairs. Mark (F) as true.

The fair was held in 1933 and called the *"Century of Progress" celebration*, which suggests that it *promoted progress made during the twentieth century*. Mark (G) as true.

Lines 9–13 quote the fair's president saying that the fair *was "the spontaneous expression of the pride of citizenship of Chicago."* This supports (H), so mark (H) as true.

Lines 13–17 state that Chicago's fair *lost money*. Therefore, the fair did not generate *a significant profit*. Mark (J) as false.

Looking at your "T/F" notes, you'll see that (J) is the odd one out. The correct answer is (J).

Try one more Later question on your own; then check the explanation below.

---

20. The author suggests that the timing of the four world's fairs was:

    F. ironic.
    G. admirable.
    H. contemptible.
    J. unrealistic.

The question asks what the author suggests about the *timing* of the *four world's fairs*. Since this question doesn't have a good lead word, use what you've learned about the passage while working the other questions to find the window. Only the first part of the first paragraph discusses the *four world's fairs* as a group. All the other parts of the passage discuss the fairs individually. So, read the beginning of the first paragraph and look for information about the timing of the fairs. The first sentence states, *One of the peculiarities of the years of the Great Depression was the fact that in the middle of the worst economic period Americans had ever seen, four cities somehow found the time, money, and energy to produce four world's fairs—more than during any other ten-year period in the nation's history.* This statement suggests that the author finds the timing of the fairs surprising. Eliminate answers that don't match this prediction. Keep (F) because *ironic* means "contrary to what's expected," which matches the prediction. Eliminate (G) because the author doesn't express admiration for the timing of the fairs. Eliminate (H) because the author doesn't express contempt for the timing. You might leave (J) in on your first pass because it seems unlikely that a city could afford to produce a big event during the Depression. However, the author says that the *four cities somehow found the time, money, and*

energy to produce four world's fairs. Since the cities were able to produce the fairs, the timing was not *unrealistic.* Eliminate (J). The correct answer is (F).

Last

Leave general questions that ask about the passage as a whole for last. Once you've worked the specific questions, you'll have a better sense of the main idea of the passage.

---

11. The passage as a whole can best be described as:

The question asks for a description of the *passage as a whole.* Use what you've learned from working the specific questions to make a prediction for this general question. The passage describes four world's fairs that took place during the Great Depression and included exhibits that celebrated accomplishments and imagined the future. Eliminate answers that don't reflect the passage as a whole.

    A. a critique of inaccurate exhibits presented at the world's fairs.
    B. a celebration of the most successful world's fairs.
    C. an assessment of an economic strategy employed during the Great Depression.
    D. an overview of a series of historically interesting cultural events.

Choice (A) may remind you of what you read in the last paragraph of the passage: *If the great industrial designer's vision of the future was not entirely reliable...it was no more flawed than the vision of the current world that both the Golden Gate Exhibition and the New York World's Fair presented.* However, this answer does not reflect the passage as a whole, so eliminate (A).

Choice (B) mentions the *most successful world's fairs*, but the passage doesn't indicate which fairs were the *most successful*. Furthermore, the author is neutral, discussing both positive and negative aspects of the events, so it isn't accurate to say that the passage as a whole is a *celebration* of the fairs. Eliminate (B).

Choice (C) may remind you of the discussion in the first and second paragraphs, which stated that the Chicago World's Fair gave *the city of Chicago a helpful shot of income for several months* and that the Texas Centennial Exposition hoped *to duplicate Chicago's economy-boosting success*. However, the rest of the passage doesn't focus on the economic impact of the world's fairs. Eliminate (C).

Choice (D) doesn't use any words from the passage—for example, there is no mention of *world's fairs*. This might make (D) seem unlikely, but don't be too hasty. The passage discusses four world's fairs, which are *a series of cultural events*. Additionally, the author calls the world's fairs *peculiarities of the years of the Great Depression*, which supports the idea that they are *historically interesting*. The correct answer is (D).

Dual Passage

One passage in the Reading Test will be a dual passage, that is, two shorter passages on a common topic. The passages will be followed by some questions that are only about one passage or the other and some questions that ask you about both passages. Thinking about one passage at a time is easier than thinking about two at once, so the best strategy is as follows:

1. Work the questions about Passage A using the 6-Step Basic Approach.

2. Work the questions about Passage B using the 6-Step Basic Approach.

3. Jot down the main idea of each passage.

4. Work the questions that ask about both passages.

When you work the questions about both passages, it may help to do Process of Elimination based on one passage at a time. Remember, if you run out of time, or if you find the questions about both passages especially tough, you can use your Letter of the Day.

ACT Online Reading

There are a few differences between the paper-and-pencil ACT Reading Test and the ACT Online Reading Test. In the ACT Online Reading, there are no line references; instead, the relevant part of the text is highlighted. The passage will also "jump" to the highlighted text if it's off the screen when you go to that question. This may disorient you at first; be prepared for this to happen.

The biggest change is that you can see only one question on the screen at a time. Rather than looking over the questions at a glance, you must click from question to question. This feature means that the Reading Basic Approach needs to be modified in order to be as time efficient as possible.

ACT Online Reading Basic Approach

STEP 1 » Preview.

Read only the blurb—do not go through and map the questions. Instead, write the question numbers on your whiteboard to prepare to work the passage.

STEP 2 » Work the passage.

This step is even more optional on the ACT Online Test than on the paper-and-pencil ACT. You haven't mapped the questions, and your highlights show up on only one question. If you do decide to work the passage, ensure that you're getting through the passage in 2–3 minutes. More likely, you'll find it best to just skip this step and move on to the questions after reading the blurb and setting up your whiteboard.

Select and understand a question. « STEP 3

If the answer to a question is easy to find (a portion of the text is highlighted or you know where to find the content you need from working the passage), do it Now. Understand the question; then move on to Step 4.

If the answer to the question is not easy-to-find (in other words, you don't immediately know where in the passage to go), write down the question's lead words on your whiteboard next to the question number. Include EXCEPT/LEAST/NOT if the question includes those words. If there are no lead words, flag the question.

After you do all the easy-to-find questions, then work the passage, scanning actively for your lead words. Once you find a lead word, do the corresponding question. After answering the questions with lead words, finish with the flagged questions.

Read what you need. « STEP 4

Find the 5–10 lines you need to answer the question. If you find the Line Mask tool helpful, use it to frame your window. As you read, look for the evidence for the answer to the question in your window and highlight it using the Highlighter tool. (You can highlight text that ACT has already highlighted—the color will change to "your" highlighting color.)

STEP 5 ≫ Predict the correct answer.

As always, base your prediction on the words in the passage as much as possible.

STEP 6 ≫ Use POE.

For most questions, use the Answer Eliminator tool to eliminate choices you know are incorrect. For EXCEPT/LEAST/NOT questions, write ABCD on your whiteboard and mark each answer T or F (or Y or N) and choose the odd one out.

That's a Wrap

As you have seen, everything you need to answer the questions on the ACT Reading section is located in the passage. Focus on finding the evidence and eliminating the answers that don't match it, and you will improve your ACT Reading score!

If you want more practice right now, you can do the following questions based on the World's Fair passage. There are only 10 questions per passage on ACT Reading, but we're providing some bonus questions here for extra practice. Follow your Personal Order of Difficulty as you work these questions. Follow Steps 3–6 of the Basic Approach. When you use POE on tougher questions, use two passes and compare the remaining answers.

1. As used in the passage, the phrase *opened for business* (line 55) refers to:

   A. the repurposing of an old dump.
   B. purchases made by visitors to Futurama.
   C. an important moment in the history of the United States.
   D. the start of the New York World's Fair in 1939.

2. The exhibits shown at the U.S. world's fairs portrayed Americans as:

   F. unimaginative.
   G. realistic.
   H. ambitious.
   J. timid.

3. According to the passage, which of the fairs had the greatest attendance?

   A. Chicago's "Century of Progress"
   B. The New York World's Fair
   C. San Francisco's Golden Gate Exposition
   D. The Texas Centennial Exposition

4. Stanley Marcus would most likely agree with which of the following statements about Texas and its place in the United States?

   F. The world's fairs opened Marcus's department stores to business from across the country.
   G. Most Americans knew little about Texas until the Centennial Exposition in 1936.
   H. Texas was just as important as Illinois, California, and New York because it was chosen to host a world's fair.
   J. Texas became independent from Mexico and joined the United States in 1936.

5. Which one of the following would the author most likely see as an example of the flawed visions seen at the world's fairs?

   A. A joint French and German exhibition
   B. A building that is designed but never constructed
   C. Robots that are only able to crawl
   D. Cars that are too expensive

6. According to the passage, the Golden Gate Exposition and the New York World's Fair were both notable for:

   F. bringing in record numbers of visitors.
   G. having extraordinarily long runs.
   H. losing large amounts of money.
   J. bridging two eras of history.

Check the answers and explanations on the following page.

Bonus Questions Answers and Explanations

1. **C** The question asks what the phrase *opened for business* refers to. Read a window around the given line reference. Lines 49–55 refer to *the inauguration of President George Washington 150 years before, which the fair's leaders chose to identify as the true moment when the United States of America opened for business.* The phrase *opened for business* refers to the moment of George Washington's inauguration, which was an important milestone in the early history of the United States. Eliminate answers that don't match this prediction. Eliminate (A); although the World's Fair repurposed a dump, the phrase *opened for business* refers to the United States, not to the dump. Eliminate (B); although the "Futurama" exhibit is mentioned in this paragraph, purchases at the exhibit are not what the phrase *opened for business* refers to. Keep (C) because it matches the prediction. Eliminate (D); although the paragraph discusses the New York World's Fair, the phrase *opened for business* doesn't refer to the opening of the fair. The correct answer is (C).

2. **H** The question asks how the *exhibits shown at the U.S. world's fairs portrayed Americans.* Since there is not a good lead word in the question, work it later. Use what you've learned about the passage from working other questions to help you find descriptions of the exhibits at the world's fairs. Lines 59–64 describe the exhibits at the New York World's Fair: *The fair was crawling with its own forward-looking exhibits—a robot named Elektro, a simulated trip to the moon, and the first public demonstration of television, among others—but the most ambitious was "Futurama."* Therefore, the exhibits shown at the world's fairs portrayed Americans as *forward-looking* and *ambitious.* Eliminate answers that don't match this prediction. Eliminate (F) because *unimaginative* doesn't match *forward-looking* and *ambitious.* Eliminate (G); in the last paragraph, the author mentions that some of the exhibits' ideas about the future were not accurate. Therefore, the description *realistic* is not supported. Keep (H) because it matches the prediction. Eliminate (J) because *timid* doesn't match *forward-looking* and *ambitious.* The correct answer is (H).

3. **A** The question asks *which of the fairs had the greatest attendance.* Use lead words from the answers to find the windows for the question. Lines 13–17 state that *38 million people* attended Chicago's "Century of Progress" celebration. Lines 32–41 indicate that neither *San Francisco's Golden Gate Exposition* nor the *New York World's Fair…brought in anywhere near the number of people Chicago's fair had.* Eliminate (B) and (C). Lines 18–28 state that the *Texas Centennial Exposition in Dallas and a smaller, though related, Frontier Centennial Exposition in Fort Worth…drew some 7 million visitors.* Since the Chicago World's Fair had 38 million visitors, eliminate (D). The correct answer is (A).

4. **G** The question asks which statement *about Texas and its place in the United States Stanley Marcus would most likely agree with*. Use the lead words *Stanley Marcus* and *Texas* to find the window. Lines 28–31 quote Stanley Marcus as saying, *"I've frequently said that modern Texas history started with the celebration of the Texas Centennial…because it was then that the rest of America discovered Texas."* Eliminate answers that don't match this prediction. Eliminate (F) because this answer is about *department stores* instead of *Texas*, and because it is not supported by the passage. Keep (G) because it matches the prediction: if the *rest of America discovered Texas* during the Texas Centennial, then it is reasonable to infer that *most Americans knew little about Texas* before the event. Eliminate (H) because the passage doesn't indicate that Marcus thought particular states were *chosen to host* world's fairs or that hosting a fair made a state *important*. Eliminate (J) because the passage states that the Centennial Exposition in 1936 *celebrated the hundredth anniversary* of Texas's independence from Mexico. The correct answer is (G).

5. **A** The question asks what the author would *most likely see as an example of the flawed visions seen at the world's fairs*. Use the lead words *flawed visions* to find the window. The last paragraph says, *If the great industrial designer's vision of the future was not entirely reliable…it was no more flawed than the vision of the current world that both the Golden Gate Exhibition and the New York World's Fair presented*. It goes on to describe exhibits that emphasized the *unity of prosperity and cooperation* between nations. The author would most likely consider an exhibit that emphasized unity between nations as an example of flawed vision. Eliminate answers that don't match this prediction. Choice (A) matches the prediction because a *joint exhibit* between France and Germany would emphasize unity between them. Keep (A). Eliminate (B) because the author doesn't mention designs that were not carried out as an example of flawed vision. Eliminate (C) because the author doesn't critique inventions with limited abilities as examples of flawed vision. Eliminate (D); although the author suggests that an inexpensive car was an inaccurate prediction of the future, there is no mention of a car that is *too expensive* as an example of flawed vision. The correct answer is (A).

6. **J** The question asks what the *Golden Gate Exposition and the New York World's Fair were both notable for*. Use the lead words *Golden Gate Exposition* and *New York World's Fair* to find the window. Lines 32–41 discuss *San Francisco's Golden Gate Exposition…and the New York World's Fair*, and state that they *each stood at the cusp between two historical epochs and consequently would shine forth more brilliantly in the national memory, both burdened and enhanced by their roles as symbols*. Eliminate answers that don't match this prediction. Eliminate (F) because the text says that neither of these two fairs *brought in anywhere near the number of people Chicago's fair had*. Eliminate (G) because the text indicates that both fairs ran for more than a year, but the first paragraph states that *Chicago's "Century of Progress" celebration* ran for two years. Therefore, the length of the runs was not the most notable feature of the New York World's Fair and Golden Gate Exposition. Eliminate (H) because the passage says that *world's fairs tend to* lose money, but there is no mention of the New York and Golden Gate fairs losing unusually large amounts of money. Keep (J) because *bridging two eras of history* matches *stood at the cusp between two historical epochs*. The correct answer is (J).

Summary

- Decide which pacing approach works best for you: choose passages or choose questions.

- Use your Personal Order of Difficulty to choose the easier passages and work them first.

- Work easy-to-find questions Now. Work hard-to-find questions Later. Work general questions Last.

- Follow the 6-Step Basic Approach (for paper and pencil):

    1. Preview—read the blurb and map the questions.

    2. Work the passage—circle your lead words in the passage (optional step).

    3. Select and understand a question—restate the question stem as an actual question.

    4. Read what you need—5–10 lines.

    5. Predict the correct answer—try to underline a prediction in the text.

    6. Use POE—eliminate answers that don't match the prediction.

        ■ If there is more than one answer left, use comparison.

- Follow the approach for the Dual Passage:

    1. Work the questions about Passage A using the 6-Step Basic Approach.

    2. Work the questions about Passage B using the 6-Step Basic Approach.

    3. Jot down the main idea of each passage.

    4. Work the questions that ask about both passages.

- Follow the 6-Step Basic Approach (for ACT Online):

  1. Preview—read the blurb and write the question numbers on your whiteboard.

  2. Work the passage (optional step).

  3. Select and understand a question—restate the question stem as an actual question.

     - Do questions that come with highlighted portions of the text first.

     - Write the lead words for other questions down on your whiteboard.

     - Flag questions that do not have a lead word.

  4. Read what you need—read 5–10 lines.

  5. Predict the correct answer—try to highlight a prediction in the text.

  6. Use POE—eliminate answers that don't match the prediction.

     - If there is more than one answer left, use comparison.

ACT Science

Structure

The ACT Science Test consists of 40 multiple-choice questions spread out over 6 passages. Two or three of those are charts and graphs passages, two or three are experiments passages, and one is a "conflicting viewpoints" passage. These passages are never in any particular order, though, unlike the Reading section. The Science Test is always the last multiple-choice part of the ACT.

Pacing

The Science Test is only 35 minutes long, allowing less than 6 minutes to answer the questions on each passage. Of course, some passages will take less time than that, but others will take more. Within a given passage, some questions will be quick and easy, and others will be difficult or time-consuming. Unless you are an ACT Science superstar, you are unlikely to be able to work through and answer all 40 questions within the time limit. In fact, most students should be skipping some questions or even some entire passages. Say you rush through the Science Test, trying every question and making a lot of careless mistakes. If you ended up getting only 20 of the 40 questions right, that would give you a Science score of about 20. What if, instead of trying to tackle everything, you slowed down and worked only the 30 questions that you felt most comfortable with? You'd likely get most or all of them right, and you would never even have to think about those harder questions. If you were able to get 28 of those correct, your score would jump to a 25 or so, and you'd get there with a lot less stress! Sounds great, but how do you know which ones to do and which to skip?

POOD

There are many things to consider when determining your Science POOD. You need to start by knowing the number of raw points you need and how many passages you will tackle to get those points. Here are some guidelines.

Target Score	# of Passages to Attempt
< 20	4 passages
20–23	4–5 passages
24–27	5–6 passages
> 27	6 passages

Notice we aren't extremely specific here. That is because sometimes you will get the points you need by skipping a hard question here and there, and sometimes you can get them by skipping one entire passage. The first thing you need to do when confronted with the Science section is to flip through all 6 passages and see what ACT has given you. Try to identify the three passages that seem the most straight-forward—the Now passages. These will generally feature the following:

- Small tables and graphs

- Easy-to-spot, consistent trends

- Numbers, not words or symbols

- Short answers to the questions

When determining your Science POOD, you should also consider your own strengths, weaknesses, and preferences. If there is a topic you find interesting among the Science passages, that is a better place to start than with a topic that puts you to sleep or that you've never even seen before.

Notice that we aren't telling you to find the "Easy" passages. We use the term "Now" passages because you want to do them Now, but they may still feature a hard question or two. Make sure you do not get hung up on a difficult or time-consuming question while working your first few passages. If you are doing one of your first few passages and it seems too tricky once you get into it, move on to the next Now passage. You can always come back later to the one you skipped.

After you tackle the Now passages, move on to the Later ones. These are ones that may take a bit more time or understanding, but you still feel they are manageable. On these, make sure you are focusing on the easier questions and possibly skipping the harder ones.

You will also need to be flexible about when, or if, you do the Science Reading passage, known as "conflicting viewpoints" by ACT. If you are a strong reader and tend to do well on this passage, you may want to do it before you tackle any passage with complicated charts and graphs. If you are a slow reader or more of a visual person, you may push this passage into the Never category.

On your initial look through the Science section, you may find that there is a passage that seems very difficult. If this is the case, you may have to do more of the questions on the remaining passages and skip that one entirely to get the number of raw points you need. Knowing this going in is crucial to allowing you an aggressive yet flexible approach to the Science section.

So, whether you are skipping random difficult questions across all 6 passages or leaving one entire passage alone, make sure to put in your Letter of the Day (LOTD) on any questions you are not actually working.

> Your Letter of the Day (LOTD) is a single letter/letter pair (A/F, B/G, etc.) that you choose whenever you're purely guessing on a question.

Using your LOTD along with proper pacing is a very powerful strategy. In our previous pacing example, getting 28 of the 40 questions correct would give you a Science Test score of 25. If you got there by only doing 30 questions, you would use your LOTD on the remaining 10 questions. The odds are that you'd get about one-fourth of them right, gaining you another 2 or 3 points. This could boost your score up to a 26 with no additional work!

Content

Knowing what is and is not tested on the ACT Science Test can help you prepare and feel confident going into the test. Although it sounds strange, you actually need very little science knowledge to do well on the Science Test. ACT claims it is a measure of your *science reasoning* skills, focusing specifically on "interpretation, analysis, evaluation, reasoning, and problem-solving."

The best way to improve all those skills is to focus on finding trends and relationships in the passages. Questions on the ACT Science Test may ask you to look up a value, predict a value or trend, or synthesize information. Knowing the trends and relationships can help with all those question types. Almost every question on the Science Test can be answered by the text and figures provided by the passages, but two or three questions involve outside knowledge. Never fear, though! These topics are those from biology, chemistry, physics, and the Earth/space sciences that are things the average high school student has already learned.

Because the science passages don't require scientific knowledge, doing many of the questions becomes largely a matter of looking up information and drawing conclusions about the data presented. With questions like these, the test writers are forced to find some way to make the test difficult, and what they've chosen to do is fill the passages with junk in hopes of distracting you and wasting your time.

The Big Technique: Ignore the Intro

With the exception of the Science Reading passage, every science passage has a generous amount of useless and often confusing information in it. This extra information is usually presented in the introduction to the passage. In these introductions, the test writers will give lengthy and complex explanations of the science on which the passage is based. Rarely will any questions refer to these explanations, however. So why are they there? To intimidate you and slow you down.

Most test takers expect the information on a test to be useful or at least important, so when they are taking a test, they read what is presented and attempt to understand it before going to the questions. That's what the test writers expect you to do, and that's what you must not do. As with the Reading Test, all the points are given for doing questions, not reading stuff. And because most of the questions involve looking up information in the charts and tables—not referring back to the introduction—reading the introduction at all is a waste of your time. What's worse is that the introductions are frequently quite confusing, and reading them can frustrate you, which is never how you want to take a test.

For every science passage you do, with the exception of the Science Reading passages (which we'll discuss later), skip the introduction and go directly to the rest of the passage. For charts and graphs passages, that will mean looking at the charts, and for experiments passages, that will mean looking at the experiments (we'll deal with experiments passages in greater detail later as well).

Note: If you come to a question that seems unrelated to the charts and experiments, then you should look at the intro, but not before that.

The Basic Approach

Well, if you don't want to read the intros, what should you do to efficiently work a Science passage? There are three main steps to follow on all passages except the Science Reading passage.

STEP 1 » Work the figures.

The first thing you want to do is take a look at the charts or tables. Read only enough of them to determine what is being represented. This usually means reading the labels on the sides and any labels that are on the graphs themselves. Take a few seconds to mark any clear trends or relationships in the data. If the numbers increase, add a small "up" arrow at the bottom of the column. If the numbers decrease, add a small "down" arrow. If they stay constant, use a flat line to indicate the lack of trend. As soon as you complete that, go directly to the questions.

STEP 2 » Work the questions.

Start with the easier questions on the passage. Ones with short answers like numbers or "increase" and "decrease" are good ones to start with, as are those with variables from the figures in the questions or answers. Ones that ask about the reasoning behind the experiment or study are generally trickier.

STEP 3 » Work the answers.

Work in bite-sized pieces and use Process of Elimination.

Charts and Graphs

There are two or three charts and graphs passages on the Science Test, with a total of about 12–20 questions. These passages usually have a preponderance of *Look it up* questions, so they are usually great places to start. The charts and graphs passages have introductions, which you should ignore.

Once you read the labels on all the charts and graphs and mark any trends, you are well along the path to tackling the questions. The method for answering the questions is not as involved as that for the Reading Test. In the Science Test, the questions will typically tell you exactly where to go to find the information you need and what to do when you get there. The majority of the questions are testing your ability to look up information and draw conclusions about it, so if you're careful when doing that, you should be able to do well. The thing to keep in mind is that everything you need in order to answer the questions is given to you. You don't need to know how atomic decay works to do a passage about atomic decay; you just need to know how to read. Everything you need is provided, so relax! Let's do a passage now, keeping all of this in mind.

Passage I

Newton's law of universal gravitation says that any two bodies attract each other according to a force that varies inversely as the square of the distance between them. Thus, when scientists try to launch a rocket (or any such projectile) into space, they must make sure that the rocket has enough energy to overcome the gravitational force on it due to the planet below. The minimum velocity necessary to be able to escape the planet's gravity is called the escape velocity. Escape velocity depends only on the radius and mass of a given planet; the mass of the projectile is irrelevant. Table 1 lists some escape velocities, masses, and radii of different planets.

Table 1				
Planet	Mass ($\times 10^{24}$ kg)	Radius ($\times 10^6$ m)	Escape velocity (km/s)	Average surface temperature (°F)
Venus	4.9	6.1	10.3	860
Earth	6.0	6.4	11.2	59
Mars	0.6	3.4	5.0	−81
Jupiter	1,900.0	10.0	60.0	−101
Neptune	103.0	22.0	24.0	−350

Work the Figures

Remember: don't read the introductions for science passages unless you're doing a Science Reading passage. This is a charts and graphs passage, so you should skip the intro. The first thing you should do is look at the table. After seeing that it lists mass, radius, escape velocity, and average surface temperature for a bunch of planets, and not seeing any obvious trends

or relationships, you are done with that and ready to go on to the questions.

Work the Questions

There are three types of questions on the Science Test (except with the Science Reading passage, which is a separate issue altogether). We call these types of questions Look It Up, What If?, and Why?

Look It Up questions are the easiest types of questions to do. They ask you to look up a specific piece of information in one of the charts or tables. Sometimes you'll be looking up multiple pieces of information and comparing them.

What If? questions ask you to make predictions, draw conclusions, and analyze data. Don't get worried about this, though. The predictions are extensions of the data you're already given with no tricks thrown in. If something is getting hotter as time goes by and you're asked to predict its temperature after some more time passes, usually only one of the answer choices will give a higher temperature. What is being tested is your ability to look at the data and figure out how it is changing.

Why? questions tend to be the trickiest. They deal with the ideas behind how experiments are set up and how the scientific process works. You might be asked to identify a control, explain an assumption, or determine the best way to study a particular variable.

3. A space agency is designing a rocket that will need to launch from the surface of several different planets. The maximum velocity this rocket can reach while launching is 15.8 km/s. From which of the following planets would the rocket NOT be able to escape?

   A. Venus
   B. Earth
   C. Mars
   D. Neptune

This question is good to do first, as it is a *Look It Up* question and the answers are short. The question wants you to find the planet from which the rocket would not be able to escape. Be very careful on these NOT questions to keep track of exactly what they are looking for. To do this, then, look at the escape velocity for each of the planets in the answers. According to Table 1, Venus has an escape velocity of 10.3 km/s, Earth has an escape velocity of 11.2 km/s, Mars has an escape velocity of 5.0 km/s, and Neptune has an escape velocity of 24.0 km/s. When compared to the given velocity of 15.8 km/s, three of these values are less than that and only one is greater. On the planet with the greater escape velocity, the rocket would not be able to surpass it. Often, these NOT questions come down to finding the odd answer out, which is (D).

2. Based on the information in Table 1, the order of the average surface temperature from hottest to coolest is:

   F. Mars, Venus, Earth, Neptune, Jupiter.
   G. Jupiter, Neptune, Earth, Venus, Mars.
   H. Neptune, Jupiter, Mars, Earth, Venus.
   J. Venus, Earth, Mars, Jupiter, Neptune.

This is another *Look It Up* question with short answers. Here, the question asks for the order of the planets from hottest average surface temperature to coolest average surface temperature. In Table 1, the planet with the highest average surface temperature is Venus, so that should be the first planet listed in the correct answer choice. From this, you can eliminate answers (F), (G), and (H). The only remaining answer is (J), so that must be correct.

> On ACT Science questions, stop to eliminate answers as soon as you figure something out; then compare the remaining answers. Chances are you will not have to work through all four answers in order to get down to one correct choice, saving you a lot of time and effort.

1. Scientists discover a new planet beyond Neptune, which they call Rupert. Based on Table 1, if Rupert's mass measured 3.2×10^{24} kg and its radius measured 5.4×10^6 m, its escape velocity would most likely be closet to which of the following?

   A. 2.8 km/s
   B. 7.4 km/s
   C. 12.5 km/s
   D. 17.3 km/s

This is a *What If?* question. You need to prove that you understand something about the information presented by applying it to a new planet Rupert, given it has a mass of 3.2×10^{24} kg and a radius of 5.4×10^6 m. In Table 1, you haven't seen many trends, but this question forces you to find some. When you rearrange the planets based on mass and radius, you can see that as both mass and radius increase, the escape velocity also increases. Both the mass and radius of planet Rupert are between the masses and radii of Mars and Venus, so you can conclude that the escape velocity will also be between the velocities of Mars and Venus. The escape velocity of Mars is 5.0 km/s, and the escape velocity for Venus is 10.3 km/s. Only (B) is between 5.0 km/s and 10.3 km/s, so that must be correct.

---

4. The Sun has a mass of $1{,}991{,}000.0 \times 10^{24}$ kg and a radius of 700.0×10^6 m. Based on the information provided, the escape velocity from the sun would be:

   F. slower than the escape velocity from all the planets in Table 1 because both its radius and mass are larger than the radius and mass of all the planets in Table 1.

   G. slower than the escape velocity from all the planets in Table 1 because both its radius and mass are smaller than the radius and mass of all the planets in Table 1.

   H. faster than the escape velocity from all the planets in Table 1 because both its radius and mass are larger than the radius and mass of all the planets in Table 1.

   J. faster than the escape velocity from all the planets in Table 1 because both its radius and mass are smaller than the radius and mass of all the planets in Table 1.

Here's another *What if?* question. The question asks what the escape velocity of the Sun would be, given that the mass is $1{,}991{,}000.0 \times 10^{24}$ kg and the radius is 700.0×10^6 m. As you saw for question 4, there is a trend among mass, radius, and escape velocity in Table 1: as the mass and radius increase, the escape velocity also increases. The mass and velocity of the Sun are greater than those of any of the planets listed in Table 1. Thus, you can eliminate any answer choices

that say that the mass and radius of the Sun is smaller than those of the planets in Table 1. This gets rid of (G) and (J). Because the mass and velocity increase together or are "directly proportional," the escape velocity from the Sun would be larger than the escape velocities of the planets in Table 1. Now you can eliminate (F), and the correct answer is (H).

Try the next two questions on your own before looking at the explanations that follow. Use the table as much as possible, and focus on eliminating wrong answers.

---

5. A scientist predicts that surface temperature of a planet also affects escape velocity. The scientist's hypothesis is that as the surface temperature of a planet increases, escape velocity increases. Which of the following best refutes this hypothesis?

   A. Jupiter has a faster escape velocity than does Neptune.

   B. Earth has a faster escape velocity than does Mars.

   C. Mars has a slower escape velocity than does Venus.

   D. Venus has a slower escape velocity than does Earth.

---

6. A scientist hypothesizes that atmospheric density affects escape velocity from a planet. What would the scientist need in order to test this hypothesis?

   F. Evidence of a consistent relationship between surface temperature and gravity

   G. Evidence of a consistent relationship between surface temperature and radius

   H. Access to data from additional planets with a wider variety of masses and radii

   J. A method of measuring atmospheric density on each planet

Question 5 asks which statement best refutes the hypothesis that as surface temperature increases, so does escape velocity. You should have read each answer choice and used Process of Elimination. According to Table 1, Jupiter has a greater surface temperature than Neptune and has a higher escape velocity than Neptune. This supports the hypothesis rather than refuting it, so you should have eliminated (A). Earth has a greater surface temperature than Mars and has a greater escape velocity, which also supports the hypothesis: eliminate (B). Mars has a lower average temperature and escape velocity than Venus, which supports the hypothesis and eliminates (C). Venus has a greater average temperature than Earth but a lower escape velocity, so it refutes the hypothesis. The correct answer is (D).

Question 6 is a *Why?* question that asks what the scientist would need in order to test the hypothesis that atmospheric density affects escape velocity. In order to determine a potential relationship between escape velocity and atmospheric density, the scientists must have both of these values for multiple planets. The escape velocities are shown in Table 1, but the atmospheric density is not. Therefore, the scientists must be able to obtain the atmospheric density. Only (J) addresses the values for atmospheric density. The correct answer is (J).

Experiments

There are two or three experiments passages in every Science Test, with a total of 13–21 questions. They usually have graphs or tables for you to work with to answer the questions. The structure of an experiments passage is fairly consistent. An experiment is conducted, and results are given to you. Then, some aspect of the experiment is usually changed (maybe the temperature, maybe the weight of something),

the experiment is repeated, and the results are given to you again. Sometimes, something else is changed and the experiment is run again; then it's on to the questions. That's nothing to worry about; the pattern of experiment-change-experiment is always followed.

The key to the questions in the experiments passages is knowing which experiments they refer to. The types of questions are the same as those described in the Charts and Graphs section, so you'll use the same techniques. All you need to add to the mix is determining which experiment to refer to when doing each question. Because each experiment is essentially the same as the first one with only a slight change, focusing on those changes is going to be your mission in the experiments passages.

The Big Technique: Spot the Difference

To do the questions quickly, you need to know where to find the information they require. To do that, you need to know what is going on in each experiment. As with most science passages, you'll ignore the introduction on the experiments passages, but you will need to find the trends in the data that goes with each one. Use arrows to mark the trends in the data as increasing or decreasing, use flat lines for data that stays the same, and make no mark for data having no trend.

When you're marking the data trends of the experiments, you need to notice what makes each one different and maybe even note that next to the experiment. This will be evident in the different variables on each table or figure. Sometimes, you won't write anything at all next to the first one; the other experiments are the "different" experiments. Your notes should be just that—notes. Don't write a whole bunch of stuff, if you write down anything at all.

Look at the tables for these three experiments and determine how each one is different. Also mark the trends in the data as increasing, decreasing, staying the same, or having no trend.

Experiment 1

In the first experiment, a 0.5 m long bar was rotated at different angular velocities in a 10 tesla magnetic field.

Table 1	
Angular velocity (radians/second)	Electric potential difference (volts)
10	12.6
15	18.8
20	25.0
25	31.2
30	37.4

Experiment 2

In the second experiment, bars of various length were rotated at an angular velocity of 40 radians/second in a 30 tesla magnetic field.

Table 2	
Length of bar (m)	Electric potential difference (volts)
0.25	37.5
0.50	150.0
0.75	337.5
1.00	600.0

Experiment 3

In the third experiment, a 0.75 m long bar was rotated at an angular velocity of 20 radians/second in magnetic fields of varying strength.

Table 3	
Magnetic field strength (tesla)	Electric potential difference (volts)
10	56.25
20	112.50
30	168.75
40	225.00
50	281.25

In this example you probably wrote something by the first experiment. You could have written "diff. vel." by the first experiment, "diff. length" by the second, and "diff. mag. field" by the third. Anything similar to this would be fine. If you wrote more than three or four words, you're probably overthinking things. If you didn't write anything, that's okay, too, as long as you noticed the different variables on each table.

Did you notice that there are clear trends in the data? In each table as one value increases, the other *also* increases. Do not overlook such trends; write them down instead of keeping them in your head. Mark increases in data with an up arrow at the bottom of the column and decreases with a down arrow. After you've determined how the experiments differ and what the trends in the variables are, it's time to head for the questions.

Here's the rest of the passage for your reference. DON'T read it now (after all, you may never need it to answer the questions)! Just know it is there if you come across a question that cannot be answered from the information in the tables.

Passage II

When charged particles move through a magnetic field, they are acted on by a force, the strength of which is determined by the charge and velocity of the particles and the strength of the magnetic field. A charged conductor, an object capable of conducting electricity, moving through a magnetic field, will become polarized and an electric field will form inside of it. If a metal rod—a conductor—rotates at a constant speed (angular velocity) in a magnetic field, the two ends of the bar will have a difference in electric potential. Figure 1 shows a view of this setup as though looking down on it.

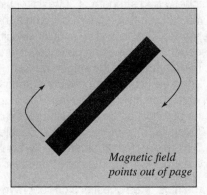

Magnetic field points out of page

Figure 1

Now let's move on to the questions!

7. Which of the following hypotheses was tested in Experiment 2 ?

   A. Magnetic field strength is directly related to potential difference.
   B. Length is directly related to angular velocity.
   C. Angular velocity is directly related to potential difference.
   D. Potential difference is directly related to length.

A question about the hypothesis is really asking, "What did the scientists mess around with and what did they measure?" Anything that was held constant cannot be what was being studied because, on the ACT, the only way to study something is to fool around with it. So what did they mess with in Experiment 2? They changed the length of the bar. Eliminate (A) and (C) because they don't mention length. What was being measured? Potential difference—the correct answer is (D).

8. According to the data taken, one way to increase the potential difference between the two ends of a given bar rotating in a magnetic field would be to:

   F. use steel bars instead of iron ones.
   G. decrease the strength of the magnetic field.
   H. decrease the length of the bar.
   J. increase the bar's angular velocity.

Right away, you should cross off (F). It's ridiculous and has nothing to do with what was mentioned in the experiments. The question asks you about a way to increase potential difference, so check out what made that happen in the experiments. In Experiment 1, increased angular velocity resulted in increased potential difference. This matches (J), so it is probably right, but check the other experiments. In Experiment 2, increased length resulted in increased potential difference. That's the opposite of (H), so cross (H) out. In Experiment 3, increased field strength resulted in increased potential difference. That's the opposite of (G), so (G) is out. Choice (J) is correct.

---

11. Based on the passage, which of the following magnetic fields would cause the largest electric potential difference in a 0.5 m long bar rotated at 40 radians/second?

    A. 25 tesla
    B. 35 tesla
    C. 45 tesla
    D. 55 tesla

The question asks which magnetic field strength would cause the largest electrical potential difference in a 0.5 m long bar rotated at 40 radians/second, based on the passage. Based on the trends you've already discovered, you know that as the magnetic field strength increases, so does the electrical potential difference. Thus, the largest magnetic field strength will give the largest electrical potential difference. The correct answer is (D).

---

13. Based on the results of Experiments 1 and 2, what would be the electric potential difference of a 1.0 m iron bar with an angular velocity of 20 radians/second in a 10 tesla magnetic field?

    A. 25 volts
    B. 100 volts
    C. 150 volts
    D. 600 volts

This *What If?* question involves synthesizing information from two different experiments. The question asks what the electric potential difference of a 1.0 m iron bar with an angular velocity of 20 radians/second and a magnetic field strength of 10 tesla would be. In Table 1, you can see that a 0.5 m bar with a magnetic field strength of 10 tesla and an angular velocity of 20 radians/second has an electric potential difference of 25 volts. This length is half the length you want, so look at Table 2 to see how length affects potential difference. When the length is doubled from 0.5 m to 1.0 m, the electric potential difference quadruples from 150 volts to 600 volts. Thus, if the length is doubled from 0.5 to 1.0 m, the potential difference will quadruple from 25 volts to 100 volts. The correct answer is (B).

Now try the next three questions on your own. Again, focus on trends and use Process of Elimination.

---

9. Based on the results of Experiment 1, if a 0.5 m long bar is rotated at 19 radians/second in a 10 tesla magnetic field, the electric potential difference between ends would be:

    A. less than 12.6 volts.
    B. between 12.6 volts and 18.8 volts.
    C. between 18.8 volts and 25.0 volts.
    D. greater than 31.2 volts.

10. Based on the results of Experiment 3, when the magnetic field strength doubles, the potential difference:

F. quadruples.

G. doubles.

H. remains the same.

J. halves.

12. A scientist hypothesized that the thickness of a bar rotating in a magnetic field affects the potential difference between the ends of the bar. Which of the following experiments would test this hypothesis?

F. Observing rotating bars made of different materials in a magnetic field

G. Observing rotating bars of varying thicknesses through a magnetic field

H. Observing stationary bars made of different materials in a magnetic field

J. Observing stationary bars of varying thicknesses in a magnetic field

---

Question 9 asks what the electric potential difference between the ends would be if a 0.5 m long bar is rotated at 19 radians/second in a 10 tesla magnetic field, based on the results of Experiment 1. That word *if* in the question tells you this is a *What If?* question based on the trends. In all of the trials of Experiment 1, the bar is 0.5 m long and is in a 10 tesla magnetic field, and as the angular velocity increases, so does the potential difference. Therefore, the potential difference at 19 radians/seconds will fall between the values at 15 radians/second and 20 radians/second. At 15 radians/second, the potential difference is 18.8 volts, and at 20 radians/second, the potential difference is 25.0 volts. The correct answer is (C).

Question 10 asks what happens to the potential difference when the magnetic field strength doubles, according to Experiment 3. In Table 3, when the

magnetic field strength doubles from 10 tesla to 20 tesla, the potential difference doubles from 56.25 volts to 112.5 volts. The correct answer is (G).

Question 12 asks about a way to test the hypothesis that the thickness of the bar affected the resulting potential difference. Any time the ACT asks you what the best way to study something is, the answer is always the same—mess with whatever it is you want to study. If you want to investigate the effect of temperature on something, run a bunch of trials at different temperatures. If you want to investigate the effect of thickness, then run a bunch of trials that vary the thickness. Both (G) and (J) mention the thickness of the bars, so compare them to see what is different. Choice (G) refers to rotating bars while (J) refers to stationary ones. The question asks about a rotating bar, so the answer is (G).

Whew, you did it! And you didn't even need to look at the intro or diagram to answer the questions. Good thing you skipped those, huh?

Science Reading Passage

Each Science Test will have one Science Reading passage (or "conflicting viewpoints" to use the ACT's term). This passage will have seven questions and can come at any point in the section. There are two major ways in which it is different from the other passages. First, it often doesn't have graphs or charts of any kind, though it may include them. Second, all the written material, including the scientists' arguments, is important and must be read.

Every Science Reading passage features a number of scientists or students debating some issue. There are usually two to four viewpoints represented, and the topic can be anything from any area of scientific study. What you must remember is that the topic is irrelevant. What matters is understanding how the argument is constructed, because that's what the questions will hinge on. You need to know how each argument is put together and what each scientist's point is.

The Big Technique: Read Carefully

Here are the steps to deal with Science Reading passages, and they are similar to the steps for the Dual Reading passage.

STEP 1» ## Read the introduction.

It is important to know the topic of the debate.

STEP 2» ## Group the questions.

Label them according to which hypothesis they refer to or "both/all" if they do not ask about just one hypothesis.

STEP 3» ## Read one hypothesis.

Start with the hypothesis that has the most questions associated with it, and answer all those questions that are just about that hypothesis.

Read another hypothesis.

Work the the remaining hypothesis or hypotheses one at a time, reading each and answering the stand-alone questions before moving on to another.

Save the questions about two or more hypotheses for last.

When you get to the Science Reading passage, you are in for some reading. It's the only way to do the questions. This alone may be enough to make you decide to put this passage last when you order the passages. That's fine, but when you get to it, you'll still have to read it.

There are two parts to a Science Reading passage: the introduction and the hypotheses. Step 1 is to read the introduction, because it will set the stage for you. Let's look at one.

Passage VI

For centuries, people have been interested in the nature of light. Seemingly one of the most fundamental entities in the universe, its exact nature has been a matter of debate in the scientific community for centuries. Below, three scientists discuss the behavior of light.

Okay, the "conflicting viewpoints" are about the nature of light. Once you've got that, skip over the hypotheses and go to the questions.

To make the most efficient use of your time, Step 2 is to group the questions according to the hypothesis they are based on. The questions come in two varieties: those that are concerned with only one hypothesis and those that are concerned with multiple hypotheses. There are three hypotheses in this passage—the theories of Scientists 1, 2, and 3. Write the number of the theory in each question next to the question number, or write "All" next to the question if it refers to all three theories.

2, 3   **28.** Upon which of the following points do Scientists 2 and 3 agree?

2   **29.** Which of the following predictions of Scientist 2's theory would be the most difficult to test experimentally?

ALL   **30.** Which of the following does Scientist 1's theory have that the other two theories lack?

3   **31.** Which of the following assumptions does Scientist 3 make?

1, 2   **32.** Which of the effects predicted by Scientist 2's theory would Scientist 1's theory not be able to explain?

3   **33.** X-rays are electromagnetic waves that behave the same way as light rays. According to Scientist 3's theory, which of the following would be true about x-rays?

ALL?   **34.** A scientist does experiments measuring the frequency of visible light and finds that as the frequency increases, the wavelength decreases. What color light would have the lowest frequency?

Question 34 is not clearly about any one theory, but you can look for the idea of the color of light as you work through the rest of the questions. For Step 3, read a hypothesis—carefully. Fortunately, they are pretty short—usually less than 20 lines long. Start with the one that has the most stand-alone questions. As you can see, Scientist 3's theory has two stand-alone questions, so that's a good place to begin. As you read the hypothesis, note the supporting points, either on the side or by underlining within the hypothesis. When you get to the end of a hypothesis, summarize the scientist's main idea.

Scientist 3

Light is merely one type of an electromagnetic wave, consisting of changing electric and magnetic fields. Thus, light can travel through a vacuum—a region of empty space. The speed of light in a vacuum is almost exactly 3×10^8 meters per second, but the speed of light in different media such as water or glass is always less than this number. Visible light (that is, light humans can see) is merely one type of electromagnetic wave. The color of light depends on its wavelength; the wavelength of visible light ranges from 400 nm (violet) to 700 nm (red), with all other colors in between. Visible light exhibits all familiar properties of wave behavior, such as diffraction, reflection, and refraction.

The important things you should have noted in this theory are that light is a type of electromagnetic wave, and light displays the properties of wave behavior. There is also some information about the speed and color of light, but don't worry about those specific numbers until you need them, if you ever do, to answer a question.

Now let's look at the questions related to this theory.

---

31. Which of the following assumptions does Scientist 3 make?

- **A.** The speed of light depends on its color.
- **B.** Electric and magnetic fields can exist in a vacuum.
- **C.** No one has been able to detect luminescent ether.
- **D.** Animals can see certain kinds of light that humans cannot.

Use Process of Elimination on a question that asks what assumption the author of a theory makes. For (A), the theory mentions *speed* and *color*, but the author says that the speed differed depending on media, not color. You can eliminate (A). Choice (B) refers to *a vacuum*, something that is mentioned in the passage. Scientist 3 states that *light is one type of electromagnetic wave consisting of changing electric and magnetic fields* and that *light can travel through a vacuum*. Therefore, electric and magnetic fields must exist in a vacuum. Keep (B) but check the remaining answers. Eliminate (C) because luminescent ether is not even mentioned in this theory. Eliminate (D) because there is no information about any animals other than humans. The correct answer is (B).

---

33. X-rays are electromagnetic waves that behave the same way as light rays. According to Scientist 3's theory, which of the following would be true about x-rays?

- **A.** X-rays propagate through luminescent ether.
- **B.** It is impossible for x-rays to bend around the edges of objects.
- **C.** A human being should not be exposed to x-rays for more than three hours at a time.
- **D.** X-rays can exhibit diffraction.

The question asks which of the following would be true about x-rays according to Scientist 3's theory given that x-rays behave the same as light rays. Again, use Process of Elimination. Eliminate (A) because luminescent ether is still not in this theory (it must be in one of the other two, but since you haven't read those yet, you avoid that confusion). Eliminate (B) because Scientist 3 states that visible light *exhibits all familiar wave behaviors such as diffraction*, which is defined earlier in the passage as the bending of light around the edges of objects. For this reason, (D) is looking good. Eliminate (C) because the dangers of x-rays are not discussed anywhere in the passage. The correct answer is (D).

Scientist 3 also mentions the color of light, so see if you have enough information to answer question 34.

---

34. A scientist does experiments measuring the frequency of visible light and finds that as the frequency increases, the wavelength decreases. What color light would have the lowest frequency?

   F. Violet
   G. Green
   H. Yellow
   J. Red

The question asks which color light would have the lowest frequency given that the frequency increases as the wavelength decreases. According to the passage, red light has the highest wavelength of visible light. Thus, due to the inverse relationship indicated by the question, red light would have the lowest frequency. The correct answer is (J).

Question 28 also mentions the theory of Scientist 3 in relation to that of Scientist 2, so read Scientist 2's theory next. As you do, look for the main point and ways it agrees or disagrees with Scientist 3's theory. Questions involving both scientists usually ask about the similarities and differences of the hypotheses. Sometimes you'll be asked how one scientist would react to another scientist's argument. That tests the same thing—your understanding of the underlying arguments.

Scientist 2

Light behaves in much the same way other waves (for example, water waves and sound waves) do. Like any wave, light requires a medium in which to propagate. Waves on the ocean propagate through the medium of water and sound waves propagate through the medium of air. Light propagates through space through the medium of luminescent ether, an invisible substance that is undetectable by any known means. There are many known experimental phenomena, which only the wave nature of light can explain. For example, it has been shown that light rays can bend around the edges of objects slightly; this is called diffraction. Diffraction has been observed for both water waves and sound waves; thus, light must be a wave as well.

This second theory says that light moves in waves through *luminescent ether*. Scientist 2 agrees with Scientist 3 in terms of wave behavior such as diffraction, but the medium of luminescent ether is unique to this theory. Always try to note the similarities and differences between the theories or hypotheses. Those will help you answer questions like the next one.

---

28. Upon which of the following points do Scientists 2 and 3 agree?

   F. Light rays consist of a great number of small particles.
   G. There are many instances in which light behaves like a wave.
   H. The color of light depends on its wavelength.
   J. The speed of light is 3×10^8 meters per second.

The question asks on which points the two theories agree. Use Process of Elimination to get rid of any answers you know are not true for one or the other theory. Neither one mentions small particles, so eliminate (F). Eliminate (H) and (J) because only Scientist 3 mentions the color or speed of light. Both theories mention that light exhibits wave characteristics such as diffraction. The correct answer is (G).

Now on to question 29, the stand-alone question about the theory of Scientist 2.

---

29. Which of the following predictions of Scientist 2's theory would be the most difficult to test experimentally?

   A. Light can bend around the edges of objects.
   B. Water waves and sound waves travel at exactly the same speed.
   C. Luminescent ether exists.
   D. There exist many other types of electromagnetic waves other than visible light.

The question asks which of Scientist 2's predictions would be most difficult to test experimentally. Eliminate (B) and (D) since that theory does not mention the speed of waves or electromagnetic waves. The passage states that *it has been shown that light rays can bend around the edges of objects*. Eliminate (A) because the text indicates that the prediction must have already been tested experimentally. According to the passage, *luminescent ether is undetectable by any known means*. Therefore, it would be most difficult to test the prediction that luminescent ether exists. The correct answer is (C).

Almost there! Question 32 contrasts the theory of Scientist 1 with that of Scientist 2, so read Scientist 1's theory now. As before, note where it lines up

with or diverges from the other theories in addition to determining the main point of the theory.

Scientist 1

A beam of light is composed of many small particles (called corpuscles) that travel in straight lines through space. When this stream of corpuscles enters the eye, it stimulates the sense of sight. This is how people see light sources. Corpuscles behave in the same way a small ball of matter would. For example, when one shines light on a mirror, the light gets reflected off the mirror with an angle exactly equal to the one with which the light hit the mirror. The same behavior can be seen in billiard balls—when one hits a ball off the side of a pool table, the reflected angle is the same as the incident angle. This provides experimental proof of the corpuscular theory.

The main idea of this theory is that light is composed of particles moving in straight lines. This contrasts with the other two theories, which say that light moves in waves. This is also the first theory to mention light in relation to sight.

---

32. Which of the effects predicted by Scientist 2's theory would Scientist 1's theory not be able to explain?

   F. The bending of light rays during diffraction
   G. The reflection of light off a mirror
   H. The existence of different colors of light
   J. The speed of light being exactly 3×10^8 meters per second

---

The question asks which of the effects predicted by Scientist 2 could not be explained by Scientist 1. Eliminate (H) and (J) because different colors of light and the speed of light are mentioned only in Scientist 3's theory. Eliminate (G) because Scientist 1 explains that the light is reflected from a mirror in the same way that billiard balls are reflected off the side of a pool table. Scientist 1 states that the *small particles (called corpuscles) travel in straight lines through space*. Therefore, this theory would not be able to explain the bending of light, called diffraction, described by the theory of Scientist 2. The correct answer is (F).

---

30. Which of the following does Scientist 1's theory have that the other two theories lack?

   F. An explanation of why there are different colors

   G. An example of something light does that supports the theory

   H. An explanation of why light requires a medium to propagate

   J. An explanation of how sight works

The question asks what the theory of Scientist 1 has that the other two theories lack. Remember that you already noted this was the only theory to mention sight. With this in mind, use Process of Elimination on the answers. Eliminate (F) because only Scientist 3 includes a discussion of different colors. Eliminate (G) because all three theories include an example of light behavior that fits the theory. Eliminate (H) because only Scientist 2 mentions propagation through a medium. Scientist 1 states that *when the stream of corpuscles enters the eye, it stimulates the sense of sight*. The correct answer is (J).

ACT Online Science

The Science Test will require a slightly different approach when you are taking the Online Test instead of the paper-and-pencil test. For passages with charts and figures, it is still important to mark the trends in the data to keep track of the relationships between variables. You should write the variables, units, and trends on your whiteboard before answering any questions within the passage. For instance, you can write something like "Length m ↑; Elect. PD volts ↑" for Table 2 on page 188.

As you work the questions in each passage, use the Highlighter tool to highlight words or phrases you saw in the figures, such as "length" and "electric potential difference" in the previous example. This will help you know which figure to use to answer the question. If there are no words in the question that appear directly on the figures, highlight any key words you do see; then look for and highlight them in the passage. This will give you the window to read to find the answer. Although the Highlighter tool is very helpful on the text of the passage and the questions, it is important to note that you will not be able to highlight the figures themselves.

As with the questions in the other sections of the ACT Online Test, use the Answer Eliminator tool on Science questions to keep track of your Process of Elimination. Many Science questions hinge on good POE, so this tool will be very handy. You should also use the Flag tool to keep track of any questions you want to return to Later, and you can see these easily in the Nav window. This can be especially useful if you flag an entire passage as a Later passage to do after you have worked all the Now passages.

The Science Reading passage often comes without figures. If there are any, mark the trends on your whiteboard before reading the theories. Use your whiteboard to group the questions related to each theory. After you read the theory with the most related questions, jot down a few words about the main point. Use your whiteboard as needed to work the questions on the first theory; then move on to reading the next theory. Again, jot down the main idea, as well as any places where the second theory agrees or disagrees with the first. Keeping your notes organized will be the key to tackling the Science Reading passage.

That's It for Science

These strategies will help you tackle any topics you see in the Science Test. Even though the content of that test will look different from test to test, the concepts tested are always the same. And now you have a solid plan to tackle them.

Summary

- Use your Personal Order of Difficulty to find all the Now passages and work them first.

- Now passages feature small tables and graphs, easy to spot consistent trends, and numbers, not words or symbols.

- You will need to be flexible about where to focus your time after completing the Now passages.

  ❑ If you are a strong reader, you may do the Science Reading passage next.

  ❑ If you are better with figures, you may do more complicated charts and graphs or experiments passages next.

- Depending on the make-up of the Science section, you may get your points from answering most questions on most passages or from answering all questions on fewer passages and skipping the worst one or two passages entirely.

- Use your LOTD for any Never questions.

- For passages with figures, follow this approach:

  1. Work the figures—determine the variables in play and the trends in the data.

  2. Work the questions—start with the easier questions first. Look It Up and What If? Questions tend to be easier than Why? Questions.

  3. Work the answers—eliminate answers that don't match the data trends; then compare the remaining answers.

- For passages with multiple experiments, try to spot the similarities and differences between them as you work the figures. Read the text between figures only if you can't find the answer from the figures.

- For the Science Reading passage, follow these steps:

  1. Read the introduction.

  2. Group the questions. Find the hypothesis with the most questions.

  3. Read one hypothesis. Answer the questions about it.

  4. Read another hypothesis. Look for similarities and differences.

  5. Save the questions about two or more hypotheses for last.

ACT Writing

Structure

The Writing Test will provide a paragraph-length prompt with background information and a few considerations related to the topic in question. Don't worry—you won't be asked something specific like, "How does a nuclear reactor work?" You'll be given an issue that anyone can respond to without any particular prior knowledge needed. In addition to the prompt, you'll be given three perspectives related to the issue.

Scoring

Unlike the rest of the ACT, the Writing Test is scored from 2 to 12, and it doesn't factor into your composite score at all. Two graders score your essay on a scale of 1 to 6 in the following areas: **Ideas and Analysis** (your argument and how well you understand the points of view provided), **Development and Support** (how well you support your argument with reasoning or examples), **Organization** (the structure and flow of ideas in your essay), and **Language Use and Conventions** (punctuation, grammar, spelling, etc.). The two scores in each area are added together and averaged to produce a single 2–12 score. Your score report will show both the area scores and the overall score.

Pacing

You'll have 40 minutes to complete the Writing Test. Here's how we recommend you plan your time:

3–5 minutes	Plan what you are going to write (prewrite).
30–35 minutes	Write your essay.
2–3 minutes	Proofread your essay.

Let's take a look at a sample Writing Test.

Planning your essay before you start writing will make the writing process go much faster, and it will also help you produce a much better essay.

Conflict and Social Change

Many societal changes come about as a result of conflict. A single act of persecution or violence towards an individual can spark widespread protests demanding change in an oppressive government. On a smaller scale, students at a school or employees in a workplace may feel dissatisfied with the way things are run and lobby for a change in policies. Many times such conflicts result in positive changes, but is disagreement necessary to evoke change? Given the number of social issues that cause strong emotional reactions from multiple sides, it is worth examining the implications of such conflict.

Read and carefully consider these perspectives. Each suggests a particular way of thinking about the role of conflict in social change.

Essay Task

Write a unified, coherent essay in which you evaluate multiple perspectives on the role of conflict. In your essay, be sure to

- clearly state your own perspective on the issue and analyze the relationship between your perspective and at least one other perspective

- develop and support your ideas with reasoning and examples

- organize your ideas clearly and logically

- communicate your ideas effectively in standard written English

Your perspective may be in full agreement with any of those given, in partial agreement, or completely different.

Perspective One

If people are not in some way dissatisfied with their situations in life, change will never happen. Motivation to act for change can come only from righteous indignation.

Perspective Two

Heated conflicts rarely result in lasting change. On the contrary, those in charge are more likely to respond to civil and constructive conversation than to attacks.

Perspective Three

Much positive change comes about without conflict at all. When people are content, they are better able to work together to further improve society.

Prewriting

Your first step is to plan your essay. Read the prompt and determine the central issue. Then, understand the three perspectives. It may be helpful to categorize each one as "for" or "against" the topic. In our sample prompt, the question asks, *is disagreement necessary to evoke change?* Examine the three perspectives. Perspective 1 is "for" disagreement as a factor in evoking change, Perspective 2 is "against," arguing that peaceful conversations are more effective, and Perspective 3 is also "against" but for a different reason—that being content helps people work toward change. Next, determine your own perspective. You can agree with one of the three Perspectives or another point of view mentioned in the beginning paragraph, or you may take a point of view that blends together multiple Perspectives or is entirely different from any viewpoint provided. **There is no right or wrong answer; you just need to be able to defend your point of view.** Once you have determined your argument, come up with 2–4 examples that can support your point of view. These can be anything you've experienced personally, read in a book, learned about in school, seen on TV, and so on—as long as they help explain your argument.

> Even if you completely agree with one of the Perspectives, you will still need to incorporate multiple points of view into your essay to earn a good score.

Writing

Once you have planned your essay, you'll spend the bulk of the time actually writing it. Your essay must include an introduction and a conclusion as well as multiple body paragraphs. Here is one template you can use if you don't already have an effective structure in mind.

Introduction (3–5 sentences)—Summarize the prompt/issue, clearly state your point of view, and preview the examples you'll be using.

Body Paragraph 1 (5–8 sentences)—Introduce your first example, provide a brief summary, show how the example supports your argument, and restate your point of view.

Body Paragraph 2+ (5–8 sentences)—Provide a transition to move smoothly from the previous paragraph to this one, introduce your example, provide a brief summary, show how the example supports your argument, and restate your point of view.

Conclusion (2–3 sentences)—Restate your argument, recap the examples you used, and end with a concluding thought.

Start with two body paragraphs when you're practicing. Once you get the hang of that, see if you can add a third body paragraph to include more details (it's also okay to do four body paragraphs if you have time). You might decide to write three body paragraphs that support your argument in different ways, two that support and one that explores an exception or limit to your point of view, or three paragraphs each of which shows a different way of looking at the prompt. Regardless, you must have some argument that you mention in the introduction and refer to in each body paragraph. Furthermore, you need to mention the ideas of all three Perspectives—they don't have to be given equal time, but you should include all of those points of view and show how they relate to your argument.

> You can find sample ACT essays with scores and feedback on the ACT website, www.act.org.

Tips for Writing

- Use a formal tone, as you would for a school or college essay. Don't use casual language (like "pretty good") or abbreviations (like "BTW" or "legit").

- Avoid phrases such as "in my opinion" or "I believe." The grader knows that the essay is your opinion. Your essay will be stronger if you make your argument without those phrases. For example, write "Conflict is a necessary component of social change" instead of "I believe conflict is a necessary component of social change."

- Don't reference the Perspectives directly. For instance, instead of saying "Perspective 3 argues…" you can say "Some may argue…" and incorporate the ideas from the Perspective without naming it.

- Spend the majority of the time writing, and don't finish early. Longer essays tend to score higher (because they have more details), so write as many details as you can to support your argument.

- Write neatly if you are taking the test on paper. Essay gradersspend only about a minute reading each essay. If the grader can't easily read your essay, you won't get a good score. Make sure to indent your paragraphs as well so that your structure is clear.

- Don't be afraid to be interesting or let your personality come through. You don't have to write a bland, formulaic essay—but don't neglect the guidelines we provided for the sake of making the essay fun to read.

Proofread

Try to save a few minutes at the end to proofread. One component of your score relates to your writing skills—punctuation, grammar, spelling, and so on. If you have enough errors, they can hurt your score. Go back and look for any mistakes, unclear wording, missing words, or awkward language. However, don't make big changes—your essay will be difficult to read if it has too many cross-outs, arrows, or poor erasures.

STEP 8: Next Steps

Congratulations! You've now developed a list of target schools, determined your goal score, and learned the most efficient and effective ways to reach that goal. You have a plan for how to spend your study time, but you'll likely need some resources beyond what we've included in this book. Let's take a look at what is available to you.

Resources from ACT

In addition to the free, official ACT practice test, ACT also offers some books and free online resources. While these resources do come directly from ACT, remember—ACT is the company that makes the test. It's not really in ACT's interest to provide you with tricks to help you score higher. Advice from ACT will give you some kind of strategy, but for the most part it will simply reinforce what you have learned in school, which may not be enough to improve your score significantly.

Princeton Review Books

You've started to learn our strategies in this book, and there's good news: we teach the same strategies across all of our ACT books. If you're looking for help on all sections of the test, *ACT Premium Prep* is for you. It includes the basic strategies we discussed in this book as well as more detailed strategies for just about every question type on the test, and it also includes plenty of drills and practice sections. If you are focusing on just one or two sections of the test, check out *English Workout for the ACT*, *Math Workout for the ACT*, *Reading Workout for the ACT*, or *Science Workout for the ACT*. If you have mastered the strategies and are looking for even more practice questions,

1,523 ACT Practice Questions will have you covered. You can find these titles wherever books are sold, or at your local or school library.

Courses and Tutoring

Some students find they benefit more from an instructor-led course or tutoring session than from taking charge of prep by themselves. If it's in your budget (or offered by your school!), a prep course or tutor can help keep you on track by meeting at a set time and assigning specific homework. Working actively with an expert instructor, even for only a short amount of time, can help you learn and improve more quickly than working on your own. The Princeton Review offers a variety of online and in-person courses as well as one-on-one tutoring, and by reading this book you already have a good foundation for the strategies we teach in class. You can find more information at www.PrincetonReview.com or by calling us at 1-800-2REVIEW (1-800-273-8439). You can also ask your school counselor about ACT prep that may be offered by your school or in your community.

If you're not sure what prep option is best for you, the following flow chart may help you decide.

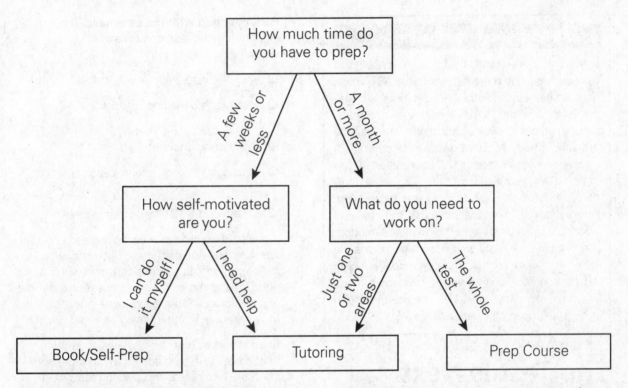

Registering for the ACT

In Step 5, you determined your target test date and made a plan for how you will prep up until that test date. If you haven't already done so, it's a good time to register for the official ACT. This can be done on the ACT website, www.act.org. There you can find a list of upcoming test dates as well as their registration deadlines. The ACT is generally offered on Saturday mornings seven times per year. It's best to register early to ensure that you're able to take the ACT at your preferred location.

To register for the test, you will need to make an account on the ACT website. You'll also need a credit card or other form of payment and a recent photo that shows your face, for security purposes. When you register, you'll select the date and location of your choice. Most students test at their high schools or at other schools nearby. If you are ready to apply to colleges, you'll also be able to select up to four schools to automatically send your ACT scores to for free.

> Your school may also offer a free school-day ACT. Ask your school counselor for more information.

The Test Is Next Week—Now What?

In Step 5, you made a plan for how to prepare for the different sections of the ACT exam. Now, you need a plan for how to approach test day. In the last week before the test, there are a few things you should do in order to be ready for test day.

- **Continue to study every day or every other day, but don't cram.** The work you put in during the weeks and months prior to test day will make a big difference—not what you do in the last few days. Plan accordingly so that you don't feel pressured to stay up late or do anything extreme just before the test.

- **Pack your bag with the essentials.** The night before the test, or even earlier in the week, pack:

  ❑ your calculator with fresh batteries

  ❑ several sharpened non-mechanical #2 pencils

  ❑ your admission ticket

  ❑ some form of photo identification (a school ID is fine)

  ❑ a snack and water bottle for the break

  We also recommend wearing a watch—smartwatches are not permitted, but a digital watch is fine as long as you are certain it won't make noise during the test. Laying out your outfit the night before is also a good idea—one less thing to worry about in the morning.

- **Keep stress at bay.** The best way to avoid test anxiety is to be prepared. By fully preparing in the weeks leading up to the test, you'll help yourself feel more confident and less anxious on test day. If you do find yourself getting stressed out, take a break! Remember, this is just a test, and it's only one component of your college application. Make sure to take time for activities that you find relaxing. If you start to feel burned out on test prep, spend less time working on the ACT. Remember, what you do in the last week isn't as important as the work you have already put in.

- **Focus on areas of strength.** The last week before the test isn't the time to tackle the topics you find the most challenging. Build confidence by practicing your stronger areas—remember, playing to your strengths is key in improving your score.

- **Plan your route.** If you'll be taking the test someplace other than your high school, it's a good idea to take a test drive to the location so that you know how to get there, how long it will take, and where you can park.

'Twas the Night Before the ACT...

The day before the test, stop studying! If 30 minutes of review would help you feel more confident, go for it, but don't do any more than that. The night before the test is your time to relax—whatever that means for you. Keep in mind this is not the time to binge watch a new TV show, go to a party, or play an addictive video game. After the ACT, you have our permission to reward yourself and spend the rest of the day on whatever you find the most fun. But on the night before the test, don't do anything too stimulating or anything that will inadvertently cause you to stay up too late—you won't be able to get that time back. In fact, it's best to stay away from electronics for an hour or two before going to bed. Plan to go to bed about nine hours before you need to get up the next morning.

> If you tend to have trouble falling asleep the night before a big day, it can help if you've gotten a good night of sleep the night before that. That is, if your test is on a Saturday, make sure you go to bed early on Thursday—it will help you be a little more rested even if you don't sleep as well as you'd like on Friday night.

The Big Day

The day has finally arrived to put your ACT skills to the test—literally! Set your alarm early so that you have plenty of time in the morning. This is not the day to roll out of bed and stumble into the test center half asleep. It's a good idea to do 10 minutes of exercise (think jogging around the block or doing some push-ups) and/or take a shower to help yourself fully wake up and get blood and oxygen flowing to your brain.

> We recommend leaving your cell phone at home or in your car if possible. While (completely turned off) phones are permitted at the ACT, bringing one is risky, as you could have your score canceled if it makes a noise or if you accidentally look at it.

Eat a healthy breakfast (no doughnuts!), and eat a good amount—it's going to be about five or six hours before you'll be able to eat lunch. Don't try anything you don't normally do: test day isn't a good time to see what happens if you have coffee or an energy drink. Dress comfortably in layers—regardless of the temperature outside, the classroom could be warm or cold. Remember to take your bag of supplies and leave early, allowing time to park if necessary or to potentially wait in a line of cars dropping off students.

Some Surprising Factors That Can Significantly Affect Your ACT Score

- How confident you feel

- Being too cold or too hot

- The amount of sleep you got

- Wearing uncomfortable clothes

- Being hungry or thirsty

- Whether you are in a good or bad mood

Make sure to consider these other factors in addition to your test preparation when you are getting ready for test day. You don't want to counteract all of the hard work you have put into studying by being hungry, cold, or tired, for example.

What to Expect from the Testing Center

Most likely you will be asked to check in and present your admission ticket in a general area filled with students. You may have to wait for a while, and then you will be directed to the room you have been assigned to take the test. in. Your room will have a proctor, an adult from your community whose job it is to administer the ACT. Your experience with the proctor will vary: some proctors will take the time to read every word of the directions, while others will speed through them. Some will walk around the room, while others will sit the entire time. Some will provide 5-minute warnings when a section is nearing its end, but others won't. Don't count on the proctor to help you out: use your own watch to ensure that you are given the right

amount of time and to keep track of how much time is remaining.

Give Me a Break!

You will be allowed a 10-minute break between the Math and Reading sections as well as a 5-minute break before the essay, if you will be taking that section. Take advantage of this opportunity to leave the testing room, move around, have your snack and drink, and give your brain a break. That way you can come back feeling refreshed and ready to tackle the next portion of the test.

What Could Go Wrong?

If any testing irregularities occur, be sure to inform your proctor if necessary and let ACT know immediately. These irregularities include anything that significantly affects your ability to take the test, like the power going out, the proctor giving you the wrong amount of time or not following instructions, or students around you cheating. Of course, you should let your proctor know right away about anything that can be easily fixed (such as asking another student to stop tapping a pencil).

The Most Important Thing on Test Day

The ACT is a standardized test: that means it's roughly the same every time. By the time you take the test, you will have become very familiar with the structure and content on the ACT, and you'll have learned strategies for the types of questions you can expect to see. Therefore, the most important thing you can do on test day is **stick to the plan**. Don't panic and go back to how you might have approached the ACT prior to prepping for it. Remember that you are well prepared, and execute the plan you have made for how to approach the test.

It's so important, we're going to say it again: *stick to the plan on test day*. If you've prepared, there shouldn't be any surprises—the test should be just as you're expecting.

...Now What?

In most cases, you should receive your ACT scores online about two weeks after taking the test. If, when you registered for the test, you chose to send your scores to colleges, those scores will be sent automatically. If you wish to send your scores to additional schools (or you didn't initially choose to send them), you can do that for a small fee at any time after receiving your score report.

Sending ACT Scores to Colleges

There are two ways to send your ACT scores.

1. As we discussed earlier, one way is to enter the names of up to four colleges when you register for the test. If you will be sending college applications within a few months, you can use this option. The benefit is that these score reports are free to you; the downside is that you'll have to select this option prior to seeing your scores. Even if you're not happy with your scores, they'll be sent anyway.

2. If you're not applying to colleges yet or you'd like to see your scores first, you can choose to send your score report(s) later. The drawback is you'll have to pay for each one; however, if you end up taking the ACT more than once, you'll be able to choose which test date(s) you wish to send. If you take the ACT three times, for example, you could choose to send all three sets of scores, just one date that has the highest composite, or the two best dates. You do have one final option. For colleges that superscore (take your highest score from each section across multiple dates), ACT can send a superscored report with your highest section scores only. As we discussed in Step 1, you must do your research to see what each school requires you to send.

You Did It!

Congratulations! You've found your best-fit colleges, learned how to improve your score, and successfully conquered the ACT. Reward yourself for that accomplishment and wait for the college acceptance letters to come in. Even though you may never have to use some of your ACT skills again (hopefully!), we encourage you to employ the self-confidence you've gained from mastering this test to succeed in your next chapter: higher education at the school of your choice. Now if you can just figure out what you want to major in...

NOTES

NOTES

NOTES

the **ultimate**
sock puppet book

the
ultimate
sock puppet book

●●●

Clever Tips, Tricks, and Techniques
for Creating Imaginative Sock Puppets

TIGER KANDEL
HEATHER SCHLOSS

Creative Publishing
international

Creative Publishing international

First published in the United States of America by
Creative Publishing international, a member of
Quarto Publishing Group USA Inc.
400 First Avenue North
Suite 400
Minneapolis, MN 55401
1-800-328-3895
www.creativepub.com
Visit www.Craftside.Typepad.com for a behind-the-scenes peek at our crafty world!

ISBN: 978-1-58923-793-3

Digital edition published in 2014
eISBN: 978-1-62788-004-6

10 9 8 7 6 5 4 3 2 1

Library of Congress Cataloging-in-Publication Data
available

Copy Editor: Karen Levy
Proofreader:Ron Hampton
Book Design & Page Layout: Sylvia McArdle
Cover Design: Quarto Publishing Group USA Inc.
Illustrations: Tiger Kandel and Heather Schloss
Photographs: Tiger Kandel and Heather Schloss, Kevin Kane, Elizabeth Drews

Printed in China

DEDICATION

To Morley Schloss for his unwavering encouragement and support.

Contents

Introduction

IN TODAY'S WORLD of accelerated technology and "cookie cutter" crafts, our inner creative selves are often overlooked. Art making and imaginative play encourage individuality, independence, hope, and ambition. As communal activities, they reinforce the bonds of family and friendship and open lines of communication. Sock puppets are a fun, fabulous, three-dimensional medium whereby anyone can create wonderfully playful, original artwork regardless of their age, experience, or ability.

Over the past decade, the Sockett® making team of Tigercandy Arts has innovated and perfected techniques that have elevated sock puppet craft to an art form. Moving from the basic to the complex, this book will take you on an instructional journey through the Tigercandy Arts' world of sock puppet design and show you how to make your own one-of-a-kind puppets utilizing the tips, tricks, and original construction methods of the professionals.

Most how-to books are written with preconceived patterns and step-by-step designs intended for the reader to replicate. In *The Ultimate Sock Puppet Book,* you won't be told specifically *what* to make or exactly *how* you *should* make it; rather, you will be given the tools necessary to access your own unique vision and design sense.

This book is a great tool for crafters but is also intended for anyone interested in making original sock puppets or utilizing the medium as a creative outlet, for a performance, or to work with children and adults via the exploration of their own creative potential.

It is not necessary to read this book from cover to cover, although it certainly is an option. This book has been designed for you to select information, as needed, and apply it to your puppet designs as you choose. For example, if you are making a dog sock puppet and want to research how to make tails, you can do so. In this book, you will find multiple tail types, suggestions for materials from which to make them, and application methods. All of the options are laid out for you. In many places, both sewing and gluing techniques are offered, allowing you to make your selections also based on skill level and construction needs.

Part reference guide and part art lesson, this book is intended as an instrument for creativity. Bundling the accumulated knowledge of Tigercandy Arts into an invaluable resource, this book will become an indispensible tool for solving problems, answering construction questions, and overcoming obstacles related to creating elaborate sock puppets. *The Ultimate Sock Puppet Book* is a must-have for every artist and crafter's shelf.

Unearth Your Inner Sock Puppet

SOCK PUPPETS HAVE BEEN part of popular cultural for at least 100 years. They have a quality that appeals to people of all ages and backgrounds. Although part of their charm is in their accessibility, they are often mistakenly thought of as unsophisticated, "throwaway" puppets. In actuality, sock puppets can be beautiful, whimsical, and charming works of art. Unique among puppets for its close fit on the hand, the sock puppet is, by its very nature, more expressive than other types of hand puppets and more intimately an extension of its user.

At one time or another, nearly every parent or child has put a sock on his or her hand and pretended to make it speak. For children, there is an allure to seeing a familiar, inanimate object suddenly transform into something exciting and alive. In adults, sock puppets give rise to a sense of nostalgia for childhood and simpler, more playful times as well as the basic act of spontaneous creation from which we have become so far removed.

There are many concrete reasons why people are inspired to make sock puppets. A teacher may want to make a set of puppets to tell a story. Parents may use a sock puppet to get their child through a violin lesson. Therapists use sock puppets to assist with communication. At times, children will confide in a puppet, telling secrets that they will not share with a human being. Sock puppets are the answer if you are looking for a fun activity to do with your kids, want to put on a puppet show on a rainy afternoon, or wish to give an original gift to someone you love.

Then there are the indefinable variables that serve as inspiration for creation: a feeling evoked by a photograph, the sensation of a luxurious faux fur on your fingertips, a scent in the air, the natural world around us. If you are interested in exploring your own creativity, puppetry can be extremely rewarding. Let the things that inspire you bring you back to that nostalgic place of play. This is where you will find your most interesting designs.

CONTEMPLATING YOUR DESIGN

A sock puppet at its essence is a caricature, a soft sculpture created within the dimensions of a sock while simultaneously reaching beyond those boundaries to capture the appearance and personality of a character.

Designing a sock puppet is different from making a doll or a stuffed animal. When you make a sock puppet, you are transforming one complete, preexisting form into another. The look of a sock puppet is affected not only by the elements from which it is made but also by the way it fits the puppeteer's hand. With each new hand, there is a unique fit, turning the shape of the hand into an integral part of the design.

The second way is to let the *materials* inspire you. Choose a sock you love and gather an assortment of puppet-making goodies, such as felt, pompoms, or faux fur, that interest you for their color or texture or both. Holding these materials next to the sock body allows intuition and your natural creativity to be your guide.

Even if an idea comes easily, knowing where or how to begin can sometimes be difficult. If this happens, start with the basics. If you are using a picture or a real-life example as a model, study the face of your subject. Identify the basic shapes within its features. Are the ears elongated ovals or short triangles? What shape are the eyes? Shapes can be turned into the felt or fabric features of your sock puppet. If you are working from your imagination, there are a couple of ways to approach a new design. Try drawing a rough sketch of what your character looks like in your mind. Then identify the simple shapes within your drawing. Another approach is to begin with an assortment of small, precut, felt shapes and experiment by piecing them together. Overlap and layer the shapes in different configurations to arrive at interesting features for your puppet.

In the act of making a sock puppet, you are doing two things. First, you are illustrating what the sock is going to be (e.g., a cat, a dog, a donkey). Second, through individual, sometimes subtle design choices, you are creating the puppet's personality (e.g., an old mouse, a pirate dog, a sleepy donkey).

There are two general ways to approach designing your sock puppet. The first way is to begin with a concrete idea like a cat or a dog, a mermaid or a princess. Look at images of your subject and then choose materials that communicate the character's personality to you.

DESIGNING WITH CHILDREN

Making sock puppets is a great project to do with children. Socks are relatively easy to come by, you can utilize many different craft materials (even scraps), and inspiration is everywhere. With some basic guidance and a quick lesson in shapes, every child can create a great sock puppet.

When beginning a sock puppet project with kids, it is usually best to have them choose a subject before they start working. Their design will most likely evolve as they go, but choosing ahead of time will give them a goal and keep them focused. This is especially helpful for children who aren't artistically adventurous or who get frustrated easily.

If a child is having difficulty selecting a subject, it is okay to make suggestions. Sometimes, setting parameters is helpful. For example, if you are working in a classroom, tell everyone to choose an animal. Follow up with a discussion about what their animals looks like. Show pictures if you can, and ask them to identify the animals' basic attributes. You may choose to begin a project with a variety of shapes cut from paper or felt. Discussing the differences among the shapes, ask the children which shapes they detect in their physical environment. Then show them the images of animals and ask them to do the same thing. Holding the shapes they identify up to a sock, illustrate how they will apply shapes to create their own animal sock puppets. Basic shapes like triangles, ovals, circles, and rectangles are easy for kids to make and will help them pull off their designs effectively. Once the faces have been built, they can detail their puppet with manes, tails, teeth, feathers, and so on.

Although a child may be developmentally ready for the next step, sometimes the best method does not imme-

diately occur to him or her. For example, one particularly bright eight-year-old girl was making a dolphin sock puppet. After studying the features, she saw that she would need to give it a fairly large nose with an unusual shape. She reached for a handful of acrylic pompoms, a material she enjoyed and was familiar with. Her intention was to glue a row of pompoms together to create the long nose. The instructor acknowledged the child's ingenuity but also knew it was an impractical solution because the structure would be too unstable. Using the opportunity to teach a new skill, she showed the girl how to make a stencil by sketching the shape of the dolphin's nose onto paper, cutting it out, and then tracing it onto stiff felt, effectively creating the nose as one single piece. The little girl was quite impressed and took to the method rather quickly, making stencils for other features she saw, as well.

Although it is important to work with children at their level and to allow them to explore and discover things on their own, it is also necessary to expose them to new ideas in order for them to learn and build skills. Take some time to study the techniques in this book before embarking on a sock puppet project with kids. You will be better prepared to instruct and guide them toward selecting the best methods necessary to realize their vision.

SELECTING SOCKS

You may have a specific idea about the character you want to make and choose a sock with a personality to match, or you may have a cool sock that inspires your design, such as a striped sock to make a zany snake or a fluffy pink chenille sock to turn into a pig.

If you are using a sewing machine, then choose a sock with a fairly tight knit. Tacky glue will run through a loosely knit sock. If you are using hot glue, then the knit is not as important. When selecting a sock, consider the puppeteer. Choose one that suits his or her tastes and requirements. For example, a sock puppet for a small child should be made on a child's sock. He or she is more likely to use and enjoy a puppet that fits well. If your user has any tactile sensitivities, choose a sock that is very soft. Consider the puppet's purpose. For instance, if you are making a puppet for a show, then you may want to choose a sock with a long cuff to hide the performer's arm.

SELECTING MATERIALS

You don't need a lot of different materials to make amazing sock puppets. Most of the sock puppets shown in this book are made with four primary ingredients: ecofriendly felt, faux fur, yarn, and acrylic pompoms. Additional materials used for trim and stuffing include nylon fishing line, ribbon, and polyester fiberfill. Of course, if ever there were a time to be creative, it is when you are designing sock puppets! Their very name suggests a toy born from ingenuity. Depending upon whether you are gluing, sewing, or using a combination of the two methods, there are numerous materials and fabrics that can be incorporated into your construction. Nothing is off-limits. Even the hardware store can be a good place to find puppet-making elements. Here is a list of the most common, easy-to-use, and readily available materials. If you are a crafter, many of these items may already be in your closet. If not, they can be found at your local craft store. For a more diverse selection, check specialty stores and independent online providers.

1. Felt is the perfect material for making sock puppets in terms of both cost and functionality. The two most popular types are wool and synthetic, or ecofriendly, felt. Felt is available in myriad colors and prints. It can be easily cut into any shape. It can be quilted. It can be glued or sewn and does not fray. It can be marked with pen, marker, pencil, or chalk. Synthetic felt is washable, as is some wool felt. Felt is great for making sock puppet ears, eyes, noses, limbs, tails, spots, stripes, teeth, and clothing.

2. Stiff felt is acrylic felt that has been factory treated with a fabric stiffener. It is easy to cut but is not malleable the way soft felt is. If it gets bent, it will crease irreversibly and lose its stiffness. It is better glued than sewn. Stiff felt is best used as a second or inner layer to make ears stand up straighter or tongues stick out farther. It can also be used to make animal whiskers, teeth, and props such as swords.

3. Fabrics that cut easily and don't fray are recommended. Among these are anti-pill fleece, cotton jersey knit, suede, leather, and vinyl. You will want to test your fabric to make sure that it adheres or sews easily depending upon the method you are using. Common uses for these materials are puppet clothing, and they can also be used creatively as ears and limbs.

4. Faux fur can be glued or sewn. It is available in hundreds of colors, textures, and pile lengths. Pile refers to the individual fur strands. Thickness of pile refers to the distance between the strands. The quality and softness of faux fur varies a great deal. Lower quality faux fur tends to shed and has a rougher texture. Higher quality fur is often softer, denser, and more luxurious, but also more expensive. Faux fur can be used for making animal fur, manes, and tails.

(Continued)

5. Yarn can be made from natural or synthetic fibers. It comes in a wide spectrum of colors, textures, and qualities, ranging from basic acrylic to cotton to specialty wools and silk. A related material, wool roving, closely resembles actual human hair and comes in every natural shade as well as an abundance of colors. Yarn can be sewn, but it can be difficult to attach with cold glue; a glue gun makes things a bit easier. Yarn can be used as tails, manes, whiskers, and hair.

6. Pompoms are available in both wool and acrylic. Acrylic is the most common and readily available as well as very inexpensive. Pompoms come in many different colors and about ten standard sizes. They can be sewn with practice but are extremely easy to glue with either tacky or hot glue. Their round, fluffy shape makes them particularly ideal for noses, pop-up eyes, and bunny tails.

7. Craft foam, aka fun foam, is a synthetic material with a soft smooth, texture. Packaged as sheets or precut shapes, it is available in a wide variety of colors and patterns. Craft foam can be marked with ink and easily cut with scissors, a hole puncher, or a leather punch. Craft foam cannot be sewn, but it can be easily adhered with cold or hot glue. Craft foam can be used as eyes, noses, teeth, spots, and whiskers.

8. Feathers are attractive for their color and texture, particularly with kids, but they are not the easiest material to use in sock puppet construction. They are difficult to sew and messy to glue. Their delicate nature makes them a poor choice for a permanent design. If using feathers, hot glue is recommended. Popular uses for feathers are as bird wings, tail feathers, and headdresses. These features can also be achieved with soft felt.

9. Fiberfill stuffing is cotton or synthetic filling generally used for making pillows and stuffed animals. For sock puppets, it is good for stuffing things like horns, tusks, and tails.

10. Found materials such as buttons, beads, baubles, ribbons, and nylon fishing line can all be useful in sock puppet design. Buttons can be sewn or glued and make terrific eyes. Pieces of broken jewelry can be added as embellishments. Fishing line is particularly good for making whiskers. Most of these materials can be found at your local craft store, but for fancier and more diverse choices, check your local specialty stores and independent online providers.

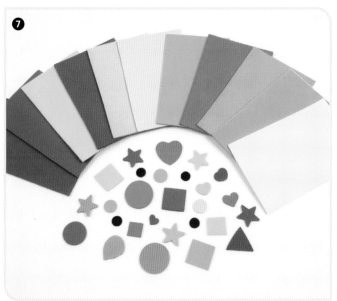

GLUING VS. SEWING

Whether to glue or sew your sock puppet or combine the two methods is one of the most important design decisions you will make. It needs to be made early on in your process because it will affect most of your other choices. In this book, we will be showing you sock puppets made using both gluing and sewing techniques. For expediency, we will be using a glue gun.

GLUING

Glue is a popular choice because it is accessible to everyone. You don't need sewing skills. It is probably the better choice for a classroom or when working with small children. Glue lets you use a wider variety of craft materials because not everything can be sewn. Using glue makes construction time shorter. On the flip side, a glued sock puppet will have a limited choice of mouths (stiff only). Glue will also give your sock puppet a more rigid feel and appearance. Glued puppets cannot be washed. The life of a glued puppet may ultimately be shorter.

Recommended Glues

If your situation allows and using hot glue is not a safety concern, a glue gun is the best method for gluing sock puppets. Hot glue not only provides the strongest and longest lasting bond but also has the fastest drying time. It cools in a matter of seconds and is instantly secure. A glue gun and glue sticks are relatively inexpensive and can be purchased at a craft store. Use caution when using a glue gun. It is extremely hot, as is the glue when it is in a liquid state. A hot glue gun is not recommended for use around children without close supervision.

If hot glue is not an option, tacky glue is the most reliable nontoxic, cold glue. It adheres to a wide variety of natural and synthetic materials and creates a strong, long-lasting bond when completely dry. Tacky glue has a very long drying time (minimum 24 hours) and needs to be applied liberally to work well. It is water-soluble, so puppets constructed with tacky glue should not be washed.

TIP

"School" glue is not recommended for making sock puppets. It will not effectively adhere most craft materials to each other or to a sock and may result in a frustrating experience.

SEWING

There are some definite benefits to sewing your sock puppet. If you have basic sewing skills, then you may want to incorporate them into your construction process. You can use a sewing machine or sew by hand. As long as you use washable materials (e.g., felt or faux fur), a sewn sock puppet will be washable. A sewn sock puppet will have a neater, softer look and feel and the option of a soft mouth. Because sewing (particularly machine sewing) is stronger than glue, the life of the puppet will be longer. On the flip side, sewing sock puppets can be time consuming. Small parts require you to sew very slowly and carefully, and sewing will limit your choice of materials.

GLUING AND SEWING TOGETHER

A flatbed sewing machine can be perfect for sewing puppet parts, such as ears, face patches, limbs, and clothing. The closed-up, tubelike nature of the sock, however, makes it tricky to use the flatbed for attaching those parts. Although they can be hand sewn, this is difficult due to the limited visibility and the tendency of the needle to get tangled or caught in the knit. If you have sewing skills, combining gluing and sewing may be the best option for speed and ease. Sew the puppet's mouth, limbs, clothing, and most features separately, and then use a hot glue gun to attach them to the sock puppet's body.

Tricks of the Trade

MAKING SOCK PUPPETS is a diverting and enjoyable project, even at the most basic level. If you are interested however in more than an activity; in excelling past the beginning stages of the used sock, button eyes, and pompom nose then this chapter will teach you well-developed, time-tested, and routinely perfected tricks of the trade that will turn your sock puppet craft into an art form.

DYEING SOCKS

Chances are, if you are making a sock puppet or two, that you will be able to find a sock in a color that makes you happy and suits your needs. If not, you can always dye your own. Just about any color that you can conceive can be found in a basic, colorfast dye for home use or can be created by mixing two or more colors. Dyeing your own socks is also a creative way to add patterns and flair to your puppet. For instance, you can tie-dye spots on the skin of a frog or an asymmetrical striped pattern onto a tiger.

When dyeing socks at home, always follow the directions on the package you are using. Here are some basic tips for a more successful dyeing experience.

▶ Use a sock with as high a cotton content as possible; 80 percent or more is best. The other material should be nylon, not polyester. Polyester and other synthetics do *not* dye well and will leave your sock looking faded or blotchy.

▶ Use a fixative whenever possible. A fixative will preserve the color and, if you are sewing, make your puppet more washable.

▶ If using your dryer, add a piece of clean cotton towel as a dye catcher to help prevent the dye from staining your dryer.

TIE-DYE

MATERIALS

- 1 white or light-color sock
- 15 narrow rubber bands
- 10 wide rubber bands
- rubber or latex gloves
- 1 package dark-color dye
- 1 package fixative

Directions for Tie-Dyeing Spots

1 Gather small bunches of the sock, and tie them tightly with narrow rubber bands.

2 Wet the sock and squeeze out all the excess water.

3 Put on rubber gloves. Soak the sock in dark dye, following the directions on the package.

4 Rinse in clean water, use a fixative, and rinse again.

5 Dry completely in the dryer or on the line.

6 Remove the rubber bands.

7 Briefly return the sock to the dryer or air dry if the sock is still damp where the bands have been removed.

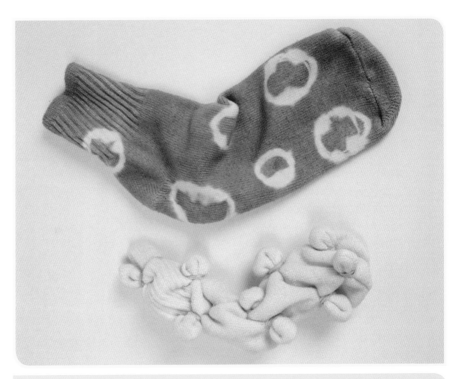

TIP

To make *symmetrical* stripes, fold the sock in half lengthwise and wind the rubber bands tightly and evenly, spacing them 1" (2.5 cm) apart. Repeat this process until the sock is tied.

Directions for Tie-Dyeing Asymmetrical Stripes

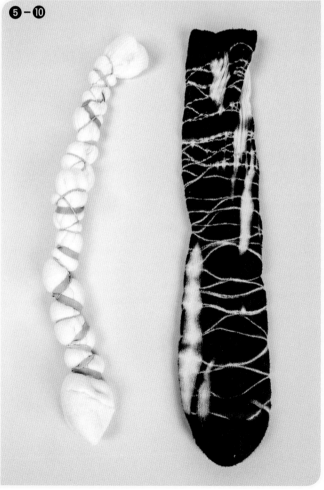

❶ Fold the sock in half lengthwise with the top of the sock facing out (or bottom, depending upon which side you want the stripes to appear on).

❷ Beginning with wide rubber bands, wind them unevenly one at a time around the sock.

❸ One-third of the way up the sock, reverse the fold.

❹ Tie one or two more wide rubber bands. Reverse the fold again and tie more rubber bands until you run out of room.

❺ Fill spaces in between with narrow rubber bands.

❻ Wet the sock and squeeze out all the excess water.

❼ Put on rubber gloves. Soak the sock in dark dye, following the directions on the package.

❽ Rinse sock in clean water, use a fixative, and rinse again.

❾ Dry completely in the dryer or on the line.

❿ Remove the rubber bands.

⓫ Briefly return the sock to the dryer or air dry if the sock is still damp where the bands have been removed.

CREATING THE MOUTH

Mouth, maw, piehole, or kisser—no matter what you call it, every sock puppet needs one to communicate! This very important feature comes in two basic styles: soft and stiff. The one you choose may in part depend upon whether you are gluing or sewing.

SEWN SOFT MOUTH

Best achieved with sewing, a soft mouth will give your sock puppet a round, gentle, seamless look. It allows for a wide range of motion and gives your puppet the ability to make different facial expressions.

- 1 sock
- ruler or tape measure
- chalk, pen, or fine marker
- sharp craft scissors
- 5¹/₂" (14 cm) circle in felt color of choice
- Soft Mouth stencil, page 132 or 133
- stickpins
- sewing materials

Directions

❶ Place the sock flat (vertically) with the underside facing up.

❷ Approximately 1¹/₂" (3.8 cm) from the top, draw a thin, vertical line approximately 1¹/₄" (3.1 cm) long in the center of the sock and equidistant from both edges.

❸ Using sharp scissors, cut along that line, creating a small slit in the sock. Turn the sock inside out.

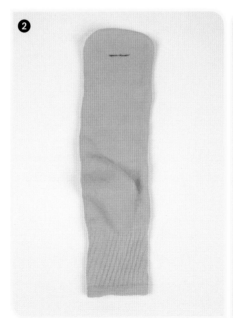

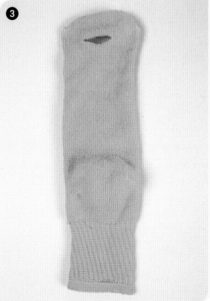

Steps 4 through 8 may take practice. Do not get discouraged if you have to repeat the steps a few times to get them right.

4 Holding the felt circle, carefully fold the felt in on itself twice, making a fan fold approximately 1¼" (3.1 cm) wide (leave enough felt to make three more folds).

5 Beginning at the top of the sock slit, carefully pin the fold to one side. Make sure the edges of the felt line up neatly with the edge of the sock slit.

6 Make another fan fold in the felt and pin that next to the first fold, completely filling the top of the slit.

7 Turn the sock around (not over) so the bottom, unpinned portion of the slit is on top.

8 Make two more fan folds and attach them to the unpinned portion of the sock slit. When finished, there should be four folds in total. The felt circle will be completely pinned in and resemble a small cup.

9 If there is a gap, add an extra pin to close it up or re-pin the entire circle as necessary.

10 **For hand sewing (A)** use a tight whipstitch to secure the mouth to the sock. Take care to sew completely through the felt and the sock, preserving the fan folds. Remove the pins.

For sewing by machine (B) use a topstitch (leave ³⁄₁₆-inch [5 mm] seam allowance) to secure mouth to the sock. Take care to sew completely through the felt, preserving the fan folds. Remove the pins as you go. Check your work and sew over any missed areas.

11 Turn the sock right side out. Tuck the mouth in. Ta da!

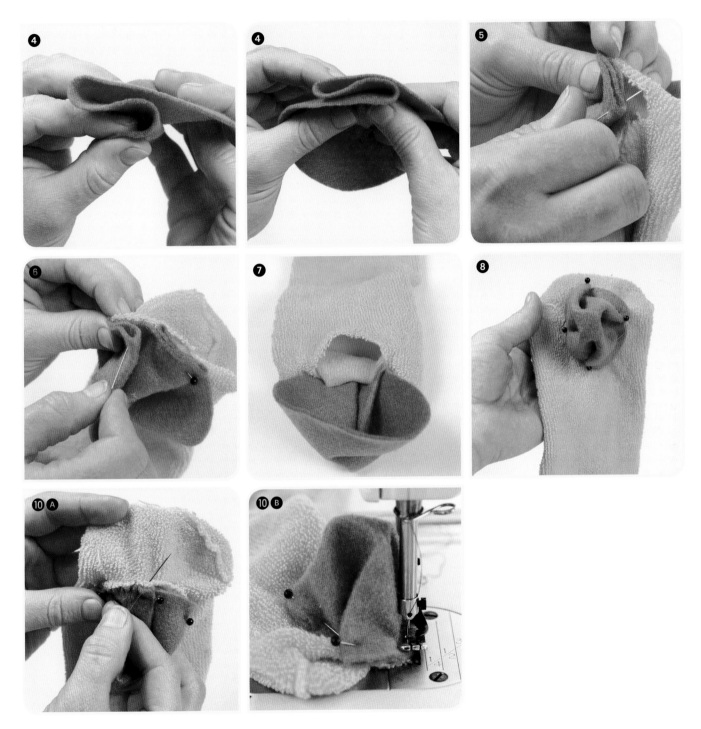

GLUED STIFF MOUTH

Easily attached with glue, the traditional stiff mouth is fast and simple to make. Hot glue is recommended, but tacky glue will also work. A stiff mouth will give your sock puppet a more angular expression than a soft mouth. The mouth will be larger and will open wider, but it will not be as flexible or able to make different facial expressions.

- Stiff Mouth stencil A (page 134)
- Stiff Mouth stencil B (page 134)
- 1 sheet 9" × 12" (23 × 30.5 cm) soft felt in color of choice
- 1 sheet 9" × 12" (23 × 30.5 cm) stiff felt in color of choice (or craft foam or cardboard)
- sharp craft scissors
- chalk, pen, or fine marker
- hot glue gun and glue sticks
- 1 sock
- ruler or tape measure

Directions

1 Trace stencil A onto soft felt and cut out shape.

2 Cut stencil B along cut line. Trace both top and bottom halves onto stiff felt with chalk. Cut out shapes.

3 Align the top half of the stiff felt shape with the top edge of the soft felt shape. Glue down.

4 Align the bottom half of the stiff felt shape with the bottom edge of the soft felt shape. Glue down. Let dry. The center fold will be the mouth hinge.

5 Place the sock flat (vertically) with the underside facing up. Make a small mark in the center of the sock approximately ½" (1.3 cm) from the top.

6 Place the top edge of the felt mouth over the mark. Glue the top half completely to the sock. Then glue the bottom. If using tacky glue, weigh down the mouthpiece while it dries to ensure a secure bond.

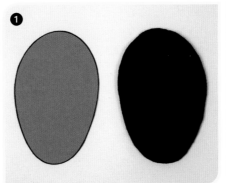

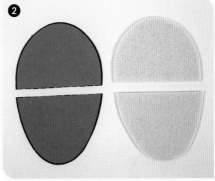

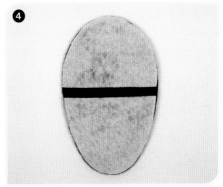

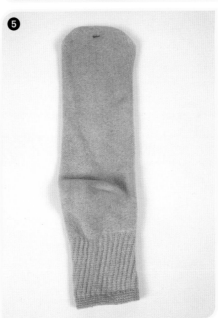

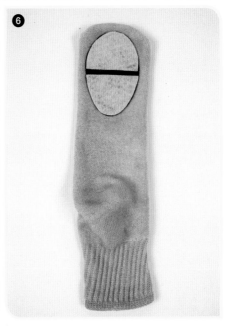

MAKING STENCILS

Once you have figured out the design, shape, and size of a part, stencils can be an invaluable tool and a great time-saving device. Stencils are useful for achieving symmetry between features such as ears, and they will help you avoid making mistakes and wasting materials. Stencils can also give you the opportunity to try different features before attaching them to your sock puppet permanently. Creating stencils is quite easy; they can be made from shapes you sketch by hand. Programs such as Photoshop and Illustrator can also be useful for stencil design. They are well stocked with symmet-

rical versions of standard shapes, such as hearts, stars, squares, and circles, and easy-to-use tools with which to design your own custom shapes.

Store all of your stencils for future use. They are a great way to keep records. Stencils can be used for making multiple puppets of the same design, and they can be altered when necessary to make something similar. You never know when you might have a sock puppet emergency!

MATERIALS

- pencil and eraser
- sketch paper
- dark pen or thin marker
- scissors
- cardstock (or cardboard or stencil plastic)

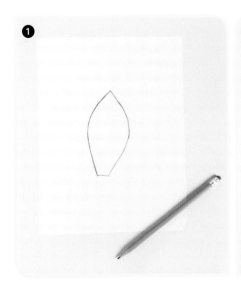

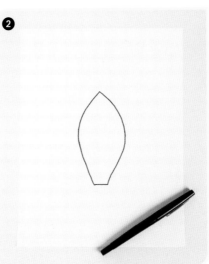

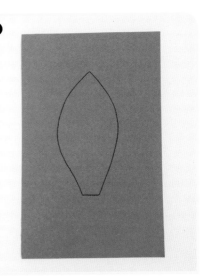

Directions

- -

❶ With pencil on sketch paper, sketch the shape you want.

❷ Give it a dark ink outline. Cut it out.

❸ Use your printer to copy the shape onto cardstock or carefully trace it onto cardboard or stencil plastic.

❹ Cut the stencil out. Voilà, a stencil is born!

TIP

- -

Assorted stencils can be found in the back of this book on pages 132–143. You are encouraged to modify them as necessary.

SEWING TIPS

Sewing sock puppets is more difficult than sewing a doll or a stuffed animal because you are sewing onto a premade, closed-up, tube-shaped item, which allows you less maneuverability and limited visibility. Additionally, the stretchiness and tightness of the knit can vary quite a bit from sock to sock. Another important issue is that many of the parts you will be sewing are quite small, so you have to sew very slowly and carefully. Here are some helpful tips to guide you through the complexities of sewing sock puppets.

▶ For most applications presented in this book, use a topstitch with a sewing machine and a tight, straight stitch for hand sewing *unless otherwise indicated.*

▶ It is possible to utilize a flatbed sewing machine for most, but not all, applications; however, a free arm or post machine is recommended because it will reduce the need to be constantly pulling your sock out of the way of the needle. Hand sewing is also a good method, albeit much slower going.

▶ Due to the unusual sewing process, the sock often has to be pulled or contorted, at times making traditional stickpins slip out of place. Should you experience this, use a *small* dab of hot glue in place of pins to lightly tack parts together and to the sock before sewing them down.

▶ Because of the limited visibility you have when sewing parts onto a sock, you should routinely check to make sure you are not accidentally sewing the sock to itself.

▶ For sewing very small parts, it will be necessary to utilize the hand crank rather than the foot pedal of your sewing machine in order to control the speed.

▶ Due to the small and, at times, irregular shapes you will be sewing, it can be difficult to maintain a constant, even seam allowance. A presser foot and guide is an invaluable tool. Place the presser foot guide along the edge of the felt as you sew around the shape using a topstitch. If you keep the guide hugging the edge, you will have a neat, even, professional-looking seam when you are done.

▶ Thread color can be a fun, creative component of your design. When utilizing the doubled and appliquéd techniques, in particular, experiment by using one color for the top thread, which will appear on the front of your piece, and a different color for the bobbin thread, which will show on the back.

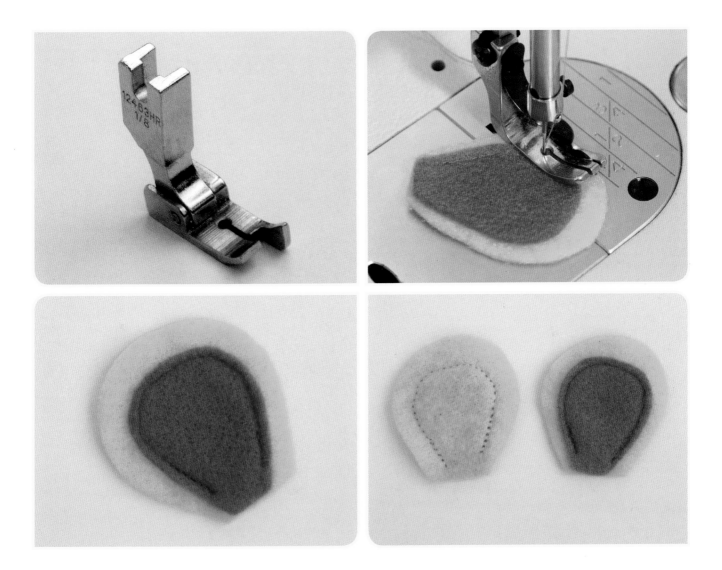

DOUBLED AND APPLIQUÉ TECHNIQUES FOR MAKING APPENDAGES

Regardless of the style of the feature or appendage you are constructing, using a *doubled* or an appliquéd layer of felt will add beauty and strength and enforce the illusion of depth. For example, on an ear, this is achieved by making both an outer and an inner ear. On a *doubled* ear, the outer and inner ears are the same size. For an appliquéd look, the inner ear is the same shape as the outer ear but ¼" to 1" (6 mm to 2.5 cm) smaller, depending upon your design. Most people use the same color for the outer and inner ears when they use the doubled technique and contrasting colors or shades when they use the appliquéd technique.

- Ear stencil(s) (page 134–136) *or make your own*
- 2 sheets 9" × 12" (23 × 30.5 cm) soft felt in color of choice
- 1 sheet 9" × 12" (23 × 30.5 cm) soft felt in a contrasting color (optional)
- faux fur (optional)
- chalk, pen, or fine marker
- sharp craft scissors
- hot glue gun and glue sticks
- sewing materials
- stickpins

DOUBLED APPENDAGES

Directions

1 Trace the Ear stencil onto felt (or faux fur, depending on your animal). Flip the stencil and trace again. Cut out the parts.

2 If gluing: *Double* the ear by gluing to an unused portion of felt **(A)**. Cut out the shape **(B)**. Repeat for the second ear.

If sewing: *Double* the ear by pining to an unused portion of felt **(C)**. Sew around the outer edge to secure. Trim excess. Repeat with the second ear **(D)**.

Note: For convenience, the doubled and appliquéd techniques are being demonstrated on ears; however, they can be applied to most appendages, including legs, beaks, wings, fins, teeth, tongues, and more.

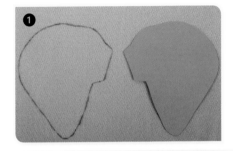

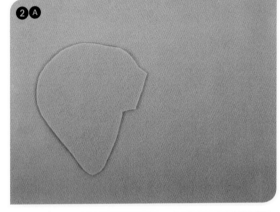

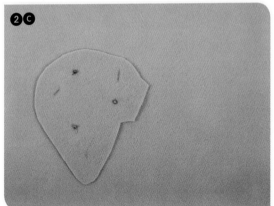

APPLIQUÉD APPENDAGES

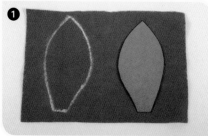

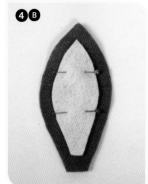

Directions

1 Trace the outer ear stencil onto your felt (or faux fur, depending on your animal). Flip the stencil over and trace another ear next to it. Cut out both ears.

2 Repeat step 1 with the inner ear stencil on the contrasting felt.

3 Place the inner ear in the center of the outer ear, leaving some felt showing on all sides (except when making a *split* ear [page 54]).

4 **If gluing:** Carefully glue the inner ear to the outer ear. Let dry completely **(A)**.

If sewing: Use either stickpins or a few drops of hot glue to secure the inner ear in place **(B)**. Sew around the outer edge of the inner ear to attach the two pieces together **(C)**.

ATTACHING APPENDAGES

Attaching appendages such as ears, tails, horns, and limbs to a sock puppet can be awkward and messy. If you want ears to stand up straight, this can also be difficult. Felt *buttons* are a great way to solve these issues and are one of the best tricks in sock puppet design.

A *button* is a simple, circular shape that will help securely attach many features, limbs, and appendages. *Buttons* lend your sock puppet a clean, professional look by making features appear as though they are truly attached to the body rather than simply "stuck on." A button is usually made from the same material as the appendage it is attaching, except in the case of yarn or fur. The button should be as small as possible but still large enough to accommodate what has to pass through it.

Note: For convenience, the *button* technique is being demonstrated on an ear; however, it can be applied to nearly all appendages that extend from the body. For appendages other than ears, disregard the word

stem in the directions and instead pull the end of the appendage through the *button*. Follow the rest of the directions accordingly. Feel free to combine gluing and sewing methods to suit your needs.

TIP

Chalk is a good tracing medium because it won't leave a permanent mark on your fabric.

- *Button* stencil (small, medium, or large, page 135)
- 1 sheet 9" × 6" (23 × 15.2 cm) felt in same color as ear
- chalk, pen, or fine marker
- sharp craft scissors
- hot glue gun and glue sticks
- sewing materials

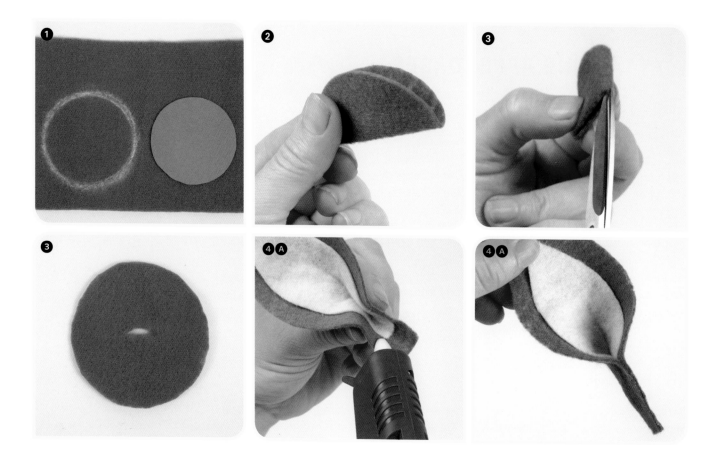

Directions

① Trace the *Button* stencil onto the same color felt as the ear. Cut it out.

② Locate the center and fold the *button* in half twice.

③ Make a very small incision in the center of the fold.

④ **If gluing:** Glue the base of the ear and pinch together while it dries, creating a stem **(A)**. Pull the stem through the incision. Trim the stem if it is too long but leave enough to glue to the sock **(B)**. Add a little glue to the end of the stem and all the way around the underside of the button **(C)**. Firmly press the *button* to the desired place on the sock. Add more glue if needed **(D)**.

If sewing: Pinch the ear base together, creating a stem. Pull the stem through the incision **(E)**. Fold the *button* in half *toward the ear* and sew the *button* to the stem. Be sure to pass through all three layers. After sewing, trim the stem if it is too long but leave a little sticking out **(F)**. Put a small amount of hot glue on the end of the ear stem and

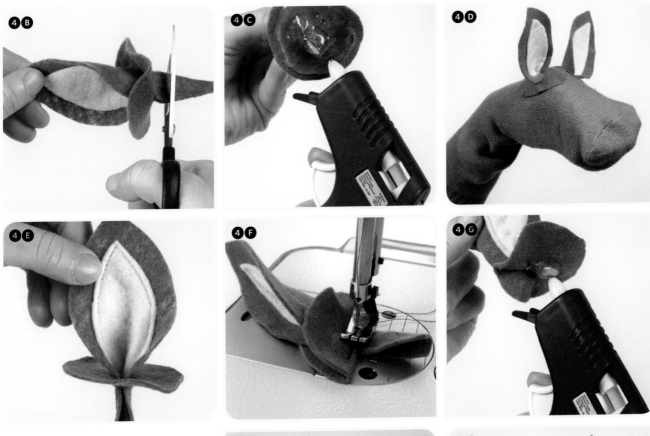

4 B

4 C

4 D

4 E

4 F

4 G

4 G

4 H

stick it to the desired location on the sock. This will do two things: It will make the ear stand up straight, if desired, and it will hold the ear in place **(G)**. Sew around the outer edge of the *button*, fully attaching it to the sock **(H)**.

Keep it short! The appearance of a head and body are illusions created by careful proportion and placement of facial features. Short faces are cuter and help define where the head ends and the body begins. A short face will animate your puppet and facilitate eye contact with the audience. Once the mouth has been put in, you can determine the ideal facial feature placement by following these rules.

GUIDELINES FOR PERFECT FEATURE PLACEMENT

▶ Whenever possible, assemble and complete *all* of your sock puppet's parts *before* attaching them to the sock. It is easier to add than to remove.

▶ Always determine placement with the sock on your hand, never with it lying flat on the table, because the sock puppet will change shape when it is worn.

▶ The ears and hairline should always be placed on or just below your knuckles.

▶ Eye placement is extremely important. The eyes should be placed directly on or slightly above the center finger joints and very close together. Eyes should be touching or very nearly.

▶ The pupils, if you are using them, should be placed slightly off center and close to the bottom inner corner or edge of the eye while still leaving the underlying layer visible on all sides.

▶ The nose should be centered below the eyes. Size, shape, and proximity will vary greatly with each design.

Making Animal Faces

THE SECRET TO CONSTRUCTING a successful sock puppet animal is to capture the spirit of the animal without completely losing the essence of the sock. With a focus on heads and faces, this chapter is filled with possibilities for actualizing your original animal designs. You will learn professional techniques for identifying the key features unique to your subject and rendering them in sock puppet form.

WORKING FROM LIFE AND PICTURES

The easiest way to explore an animal's features is to look at pictures. You can also use a real-life model such as your dog or cat. Ask yourself what characteristics specifically make an animal look like that animal and what makes it look different from other animals. Remember, less is more. Start small and try not to get bogged down by too many details. These can be added as you go. Keep in mind that you are working within the confines of a sock. A sock that is overloaded with material will lose flexibility and make your puppet more difficult to manipulate.

▶ The focus is on the most obvious features—the neck and head—rather than the whole body.

▶ Tie-dye has been used to suggest the giraffe's pattern and to keep the sock flexible and free of extra material.

▶ The size and shape of the ears, the long mane, small horns, and the brush lashes communicate "giraffe" immediately.

▶ This design is very effective while using relatively few parts.

FACIAL STRUCTURE

In addition to the placement of features, altering the appearance of facial structure may be necessary to effectively represent your animal. Because socks have no angles or naturally occurring hard edges they do not easily communicate bone structure (i.e., the bridge of the nose, skull, muzzle, or jawline). Incorporating a felt face patch can change the contour of the animal's face. Face patches are often the same color as the sock but can also be used to represent bicolored animals, such as cows. Face patches are frequently placed beneath more prominent features, such as the eyes and nose.

- Face Patch stencil (page 135) *or make your own*
- 1 sheet 9" × 12" (23 × 30.5 cm) soft felt in color of choice
- chalk, pen, or fine marker
- sharp craft scissors
- hot glue gun and glue sticks
- stickpins
- sewing materials

Directions

❶ Trace the Face Patch stencil onto the felt and cut out the shape.

❷ Put the sock on your hand to determine placement (page 45). Secure the face patch to the sock by placing a few drops of hot glue on the back center or by using stickpins.

❸ **If Gluing:** Slowly add hot glue around the edges a little at time to completely secure face patch to sock **(A)**.

If Sewing: Using hand or machine, sew around the edges of the patch, completely securing it to the sock **(B)**.

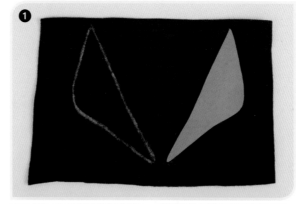

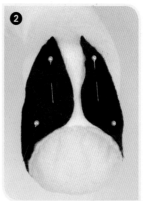

EARS

The ears are one of an animal's most distinctive attributes. Exaggerating or elaborating on these features will bring forth the spirit of the animal and play on the caricature-like style of the sock puppet.

Animal ears come in many shapes and sizes, and for each one there is an ideal way to create it and attach it to your sock puppet. Although there are endless design possibilities, nearly every type of sock puppet animal ear can be placed into one of three categories pertaining to its method of attachment: *button*, *floppy*, and *split*. For best results, read this entire section before beginning work because ear construction and ear attachment methods are frequently interconnected. All of the felt ears being presented in this chapter will be constructed using either the doubled or appliquéd technique.

- Ear stencil (Button, page 135; Floppy, page 136; or Split, page 136) or *make your own*
- 1 or 2 sheets 9" × 12" (23 × 30.5 cm) soft felt in color of choice
- 1 or 2 sheets 9" × 12" (23 × 30.5 cm) soft felt in contrasting color
- faux fur (optional)
- pen or fine marker
- sharp craft scissors
- hot glue gun and glue sticks
- sewing materials
- stickpins

BUTTON EARS

The *button* ear is named for its *button* attachment (page 41). This style is most effective when used on large ears that stand up or out, away from the animal's head (e.g., bunny, horse, giraffe, cow).

Directions

❶ Follow directions for Doubled Appendage (page 38) or Appliquéd Appendage (page 38).

❷ Attach ears using buttons (page 41).

FLOPPY EARS

A *floppy* ear is an ear that hangs down (e.g., many types of dogs and floppy-eared bunnies) and gets attached directly to the animal's head in one place. A *floppy* ear can be easily modified to include faux fur, if desired.

Directions

❶ Follow directions for Doubled Appendage or Appliquéd Appendage (page 38).

❷ If you are not adding faux fur, skip to step ❹. If adding faux fur, cut a piece of faux fur slightly larger than the ear.

❸ **If gluing:** Add glue to the back of the felt ear everywhere you wish the fur to attach. Add fur. Let dry **(A)**.

Trim excess fur carefully, following the shape of the ear. Retain the pile length **(B)**.

If sewing: Add a few drops of hot glue to the back of the felt ear. Secure the faux fur in place. Let dry. Trim excess fur carefully, following the shape of the ear **(C)**.

Sew around outer edge to attach the felt ear and the faux fur layer together **(D)**.

❹ To attach ears to sock, put the sock on your hand and find the knuckle line. Place a mark (or pin) approximately 1" (2.5 cm) in from both edges of the hand.

❺ **If gluing:** Place a line of glue along the top edge of inside ear. Press firmly to secure it to the sock **(A)**.

If sewing: Pin the ears to the sock to hold in place. Sew the ears to sock along their top edge, following their natural shape **(B)**.

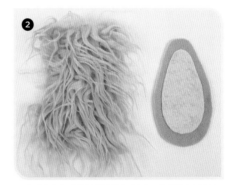

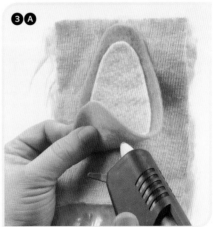

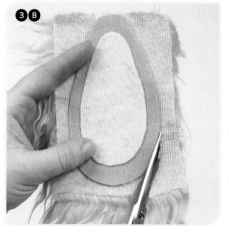

3 B

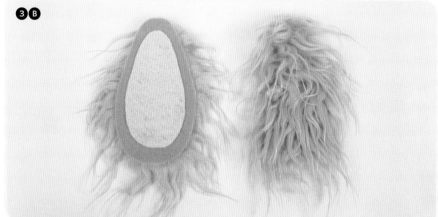

3 B

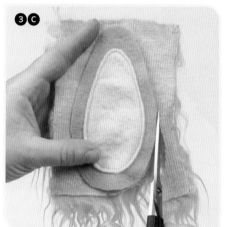

3 C

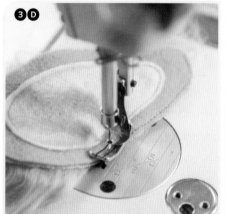

3 D

5 A

5 B

SPLIT EARS

A *split* ear is an ear whose size or shape may not easily accommodate a *button* (e.g., cats, tigers, lions, and elephants). A *split* ear attaches to the head in two places. The bottom of the inner ear folds and attaches forward while the bottom of the outer ear folds and attaches back.

Directions

- -

1 Follow steps 1 and 2 for Doubled Appendage or Appliquéd Appendage (page 38).

2 Place the inner ear on top of the outer ear and line up their bottom edges.

3 **If gluing:** Leaving ¼" (6 mm) unglued at the bottom, add hot glue to the back of the inner ear. Firmly attach the inner ear to the outer ear **(A)**.

If sewing: Using stickpins or a few drops of hot glue, secure the inner ear to the outer ear **(B)**. Sewing around the outer edge of the inner ear, attach the two layers together. Leave ¼" (6 mm) seam allowance *unsewn* at the bottom to be used later to attach the ear to the sock **(C)**. Repeat with the second ear.

4 Put the sock on your hand and find the knuckle line. Approximately ½" (1.3 cm) in from either side, place a pen mark or a straight pin where you will put your ears.

5 **If gluing:** Fold the unglued edge of the inner ear forward and the unglued edge of the outer ear backward. Place a line of glue on the underside of folded front edge and glue to the sock in the desired place **(A)**. Gently lift the folded back edge, place a line of glue, and adhere it to the sock **(B)**.

If sewing: Fold the unsewn edge of the inner ear forward and pin it to the sock in the desired place **(C)**. Fold the unsewn edge of the outer ear backward and pin it to the sock **(D)**. Remove the sock from your hand and sew a seam, attaching the front fold to the sock. Repeat with the back fold. Remove pins **(E)**.

6 Trim threads and excess fabric as needed.

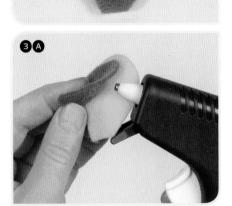

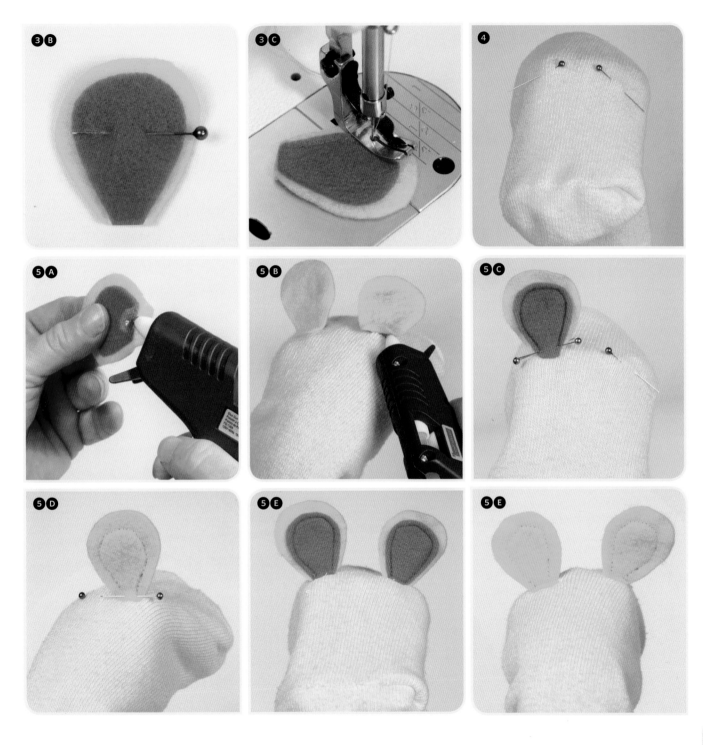

EYES

Puppets are meant to engage an audience, and their eyes are the means by which they make contact. In some ways, the sock puppet's eyes are the most important feature. You may choose to represent the shape and color of your animal's eyes realistically, or you may aim for something more fantastical. Some eyes are made from stacking flat felt or fabric pieces. Others utilize three-dimensional elements. They can be as simple as a pair of buttons, or you can create more complicated versions by combining felt or foam with pompoms to make eyes that pop up. Whatever style you choose, for optimal eye contact, certain guidelines universally apply (page 45).

STACKED EYES

There are many ways to create a sock puppet's eyes. If you begin with a flat eye base, you can build it up by stacking layers on top to add depth. This generally means adding at least an iris and a pupil. Strong, contrasting colors will add light and sparkle and enhance their liveliness.

When making animals, there is no reason to stick to conventional eye shapes. By making stencils, you can design and cut out your own unique eye bases. Both felt and craft foam are available in a wide, colorful assortment of precut shapes and sizes. Squares, hearts, triangles, and stars all make interesting eyes. Hole punchers work particularly well on craft foam.

Gluing Stacked Eyes

The small size of eye parts can make sewing them difficult. Using glue is a practical solution. The advantage to glued eyes is that you can use foam or felt and you can assemble them faster. It also allows you to create a variety of sets to try on your puppet without having to attach them first. Note that foam eyes will appear very three-dimensional while felt eyes will be more compressed.

> **TIP**
>
> Once the first eye layer is glued to the sock, you cannot make any changes, so it is best to construct an entire stacked eye *before* attaching it to the sock.

Sewing Stacked Eyes

Sewing the eyes may be challenging, but it does have its benefits, including a beautiful appliquéd look and a permanence not typical of glued parts.

Directions

1. Sewing carefully around the perimeter of each piece, attach the eye parts to the sock *one at a time*.

2. If you are sewing by machine, to accommodate the small parts, sew *very slowly* using the handwheel.

EYES WITH HEAVY LIDS AND LASHES

Eyes can be made even more expressive by adding eyelids and eyelashes. Something as simple as changing the size of an eyelid can alter the personality of your puppet. Large brush lashes and heavy lids will make your puppet appear sleepy or grumpy, while shorter lids will make the eye appear more open and lively.

MATERIALS

- two ⁵/₈" (1.5 cm) circles in white or light color (for iris)
- two 1" (2.5 cm) circles in a dark color (for eye bases)
- two ⁹/₁₆" (1.3 cm) circles in black (for pupils)
- 1" (2.5 cm) circle in black (for lids)
- 3" × 4¹/₂" (7.5 × 11.4 cm) piece black felt (for sewing)
- sharp craft scissors
- hot glue gun and glue sticks
- sewing materials
- stickpins

Directions for Gluing

① Trim the tops off ⅝" (1.5 cm) circles. Make both circles match.

② Carefully glue ⅝" (1.5 cm) circles to 1" (2.5 cm) circles. Position them slightly off center toward the inner edge.

③ Trim the tops off of ⁹⁄₁₆" (1.3 cm) circles. Glue the ⁹⁄₁₆" (1.3 cm) circles to the ⅝" (1.5 cm) circles, lining up the top edges.

④ Cut a 1" (2.5 cm) black circle in half. Glue a half circle to the top of each eye.

⑤ Cut two strips from black felt for lashes, making them approximately ¼" (6 mm) wide by 1¼" (3.1 cm) long.

⑥ Place a line of hot glue on the edge of the eyelid and glue the lash strip down.

⑦ Once the glue has dried completely, fringe the felt strip to create eyelashes. Trim excess felt on either end.

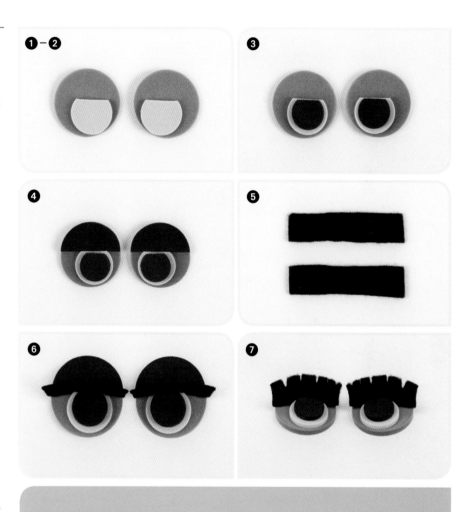

TIP

You can substitute your own sizes for the eye base, iris, and pupil. The lid should always be the same shape and size as the eye base.

Directions for Sewing

1 Using a *small dab* of hot glue, tack 1" (2.5 cm) circles to the puppet in the desired location. Sew them down.

2 Using a *small dab* of hot glue, lightly tack ⅝" (1.5 cm) circles on top of the 1" (2.5 cm) circles. Place them slightly off center toward the inner edge. Don't sew them down.

3 Using a *small dab* of hot glue, tack ⁹⁄₁₆" (1.3 cm) circles on top of the ⅝" (1.5 cm) circles. Sew them down.

4 Cut two strips from black felt 1" (2.5 cm) wide by 1½" (3.8 cm) long.

5 Cut a 1" (2.5 cm) black circle in half. These will be the eyelids.

6 Place one lid near the top of a black strip. Sew them together through the bottom edge of the lid. Repeat with the other eyelid.

7 Trim excess felt on the left and right sides of the eyelid. Repeat with the other eyelid.

8 Use a stickpin to tack the lid in place over the eye (the eyelash felt will temporarily cover the eye). Sew all the way around the perimeter of the eyelid. Repeat with the other eye.

9 Push the eyelash felt up with your finger. Trim it to the desired width and length. Fringe the lash. Repeat with other eye.

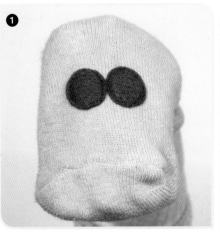

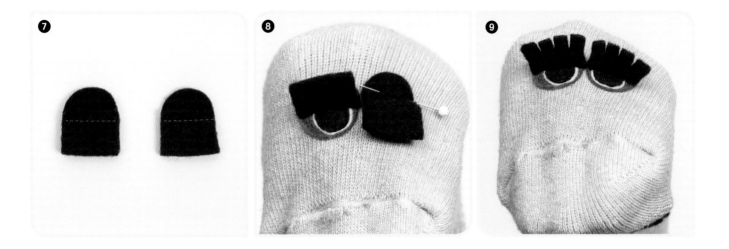

POP-UP EYES

An example of a three-dimensional eye is the *pop-up* eye. A *pop-up* eye is a stacked eye made from felt or foam and then backed by a pompom. This type of eye is particularly good for achieving eye contact because it sits high on the puppet's head. Some examples of animals that might use a *pop-up* eye are frogs and fish; however, your puppet design is entirely your own. The simplest way to create a *pop-up* eye is to glue a stacked eye directly onto a pompom. For a more elaborate method, use sewing to incorporate the pompom into the *stacked* eye.

- Pop-Up Eye stencil (page 136)
- two 3" × 4½" (7.5 × 11.4 cm) pieces felt in dark color
- two 1" (2.5 cm) felt circles in light color
- two ¼" (6 mm) black pompoms
- two 1" (2.5 cm) pompoms matching felt color
- chalk, pen, or fine marker
- sharp craft scissors
- hot glue gun and glue sticks
- sewing materials
- stickpins

Directions for *Sewn* Pop-Up Eyes

❶ Trace the Pop-Up Eye stencil onto a 3" by 4½" felt sheet. Flip the stencil over and trace another eye next to the first one. Cut out both shapes.

❷ Sew the cut-out eye base shapes to a second sheet of 3" by 4½" felt. Neatly cut both shapes out.

❸ Use a *tiny* dab of hot glue to tack a 1" (2.5 cm) felt circle to an eye base. Position it *slightly* toward the inner edge. Repeat with other eye.

❹ Sew around the perimeter of the circles, attaching them to the eye bases.

❺ Sew or glue the ¼" (6 mm) black pompoms to the 1" (2.5 cm) felt circles. Position them *slightly* toward the inner edge.

❻ Put the sock on your hand. Find the middle finger joints. Just above the joint line, pin the eyes to the sock in the desired location (page 45).

❼ Sew the eye base to the sock along the flat edge. Repeat with other eye. Trim excess thread.

❽ Push eyes forward. Glue 1" (2.5 cm) pompoms to the sock, directly behind the eyes.

❾ Add glue to back of the felt eyes and secure them to the pompoms.

①

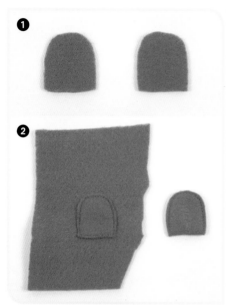

②

③

④

⑤

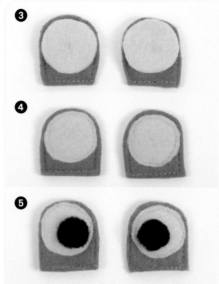

⑥

⑦

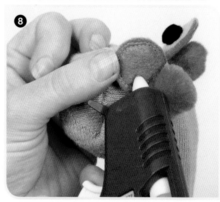

⑧

⑨

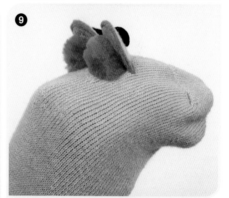

TIP
- -

When sewing pompom eyes,

▶ Change the shape and size of the eyes by adjusting the stencils
and using smaller or larger pompoms.

▶ You may substitute ¼" (6 mm) circles for ¼" (6 mm) pompoms.

Making Animal Faces

63

WHISKERS

Many animals have whiskers. The material you choose for your whiskers can have an effect on the personality of your animal. For instance, whiskers made of yarn will droop; therefore, they would be a good choice if you want your animal to appear sick, sleepy, or old. Some materials, such as stiff felt or craft foam, can be bulky but fun and may be a good choice for children because they are easy to handle. If you are using tacky glue, which has a slow drying time, thicker whisker materials will hold their place better. Nylon fishing line is the most popular choice for whiskers. It looks real, holds its shape well, and is fairly simple to attach with hot glue.

TIP

If using yarn or fishing line for your whiskers, tie the strips together to prevent them from slipping out of place while gluing.

- whisker material of choice (fishing line, yarn, foam, etc)
- sharp craft scissors
- hot glue gun and glue sticks

Directions

❶ Cut three or four thin strips approximately 4" (10.2 cm) long.

❷ Line up whiskers and find the center (strips should be equal length on either side). Using as *little glue as possible*, attach whiskers to the sock where the nose will go.

❸ Center and glue or sew the nose over the whiskers.

❹ Once the nose is attached and glue is completely dry, trim the whiskers to the desired length or leave them as they are.

❶

❷

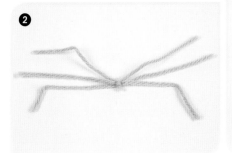

❸-❹

NOSES

Animal noses come in a wide variety of shapes and sizes. Nearly as varied are the ways they can be represented and the selection of materials available with which to do this; felt, foam, and pompoms all make great noses.

Sock puppet animal noses fall into two categories: two dimensional and three dimensional. By examining your animal's face, you can determine which nose is appropriate. In some instances, a combination of the two is the correct choice. For example, you might decide to make a face patch (two dimensional) to indicate the bridge of the nose and add a pompom (three dimensional) on top to represent the nose itself.

TWO-DIMENSIONAL NOSES

The two-dimensional nose is essentially a flat nose that sits close to the face rather than being built or sculpted outward. Any type of material that can be cut into the desired shape (e.g., felt, fabric, or foam) will work. A

two-dimensional nose is made by creating a stencil in the desired shape and tracing it onto your material (page 34).

Sometimes, a two-dimensional nose is best combined with a face patch. For instance, to depict an animal with a broad face, such as a lion, you might make a long, wide, rectangular face patch to form the bridge of the nose and then add a smaller felt piece at the end for the nose itself. For a cat or tiger, for example, you might use a face patch that is more slender and curved.

To create the illusion of a wide, round snout such as on a cow or pig, you can use an oval or circular-shaped two-dimensional nose.

Some animals may require only nostrils to represent the presence of a nose such as on a reptile, horse or giraffe. In this case, the flat shapes would be separate pieces and much smaller. Nostrils can also be layered on top of two-dimensional noses for greater effect. For directions on securing a two-dimensional nose, see page 49.

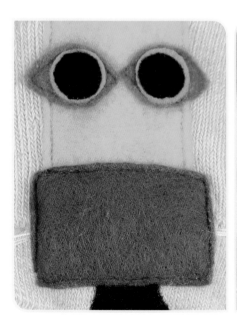

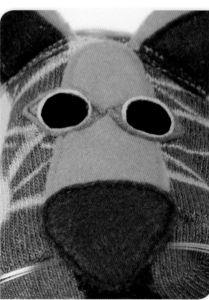

THREE-DIMENSIONAL NOSES

The three-dimensional nose stands out away from the face. This nose can be represented simply with the use of an acrylic pompom, a foam shape, a button, or a bead.

Pompom Noses

Pompoms are good for representing many types of animal noses. They come in a wide variety of colors and sizes that can radically alter the personality of your puppet. For example, if a pompom is used for a dog's nose, a change in size can help define the look of a particular breed. The simplest way to attach a pompom nose is with hot glue, but there are also sewing methods (see opposite page). This method is for hand or machine sewing only.

MATERIALS

- pompom
- sharp craft scissors
- SEWING MATERIALS:
    - sewing machine (use medium- to heavy-weight needle)
    - hand sewing (use heavy-weight thread)

TIP

- -

Sewing machines will have different tolerances for this particular application. To avoid needle breakage, try slowing the speed or using the handwheel when sewing on pompoms.

Directions for Hand Sewing

- -

❶ Double the thread. Tie a large knot at the end to prevent slipping.

❷ Starting from underneath, attach the pompom to the thread by pushing the needle up through the center of the pompom. Reverse direction and sew through the pompom again, pushing the needle down.

❸ Once the thread is attached, place the pompom in the spot on the sock where you want the nose to go. Using four or five stitches, sew the pompom to the sock, not unlike sewing a button to a shirt.

❹ Turn the sock inside out. Knot the thread. Trim excess.

Directions for Machine Sewing

- -

❶ Tack the pompom on the sock where the nose will go using a *small dot* of hot glue.

❷ Place the sewing machine foot directly over the top of the pompom.

❸ Create a short seam down the center of the pompom. Forward and backstitch a couple of times to firmly attach and secure stitches.

Sculpted Noses

A three-dimensional nose can also be achieved through more complex methods such as the layering and sculpting of felt. For this example of a sculpted nose, we will use an elephant's trunk. This method is for hand or machine sewing only.

MATERIALS

- Elephant Trunk stencil (page 137)
- 2 sheets 9" × 12" (23 × 30.5 cm) gray felt
- pen or fine marker
- sharp craft scissors
- sewing materials
- stickpins

Directions

❶ Trace the stencil onto a sheet of gray felt. Cut it out.

❷ In pencil, draw four horizontal lines 1½" (3.8 cm) apart on the cut-out trunk.

❸ Place the felt trunk on top of a second sheet of gray felt. Sew all the way around the outer edge.

❹ Neatly cut out the doubled trunk shape.

(Continued)

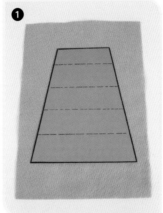

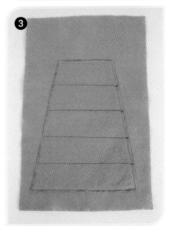

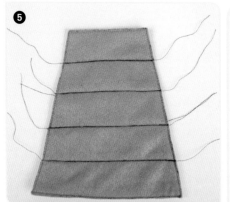

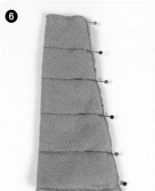

❺ Sew directly over each of the horizontal pencil lines. Trim any hanging threads.

❻ Fold the trunk in half, inside out and lengthwise (the long way), lining up the stitches on both edges. Pin it in place.

❼ Sew the two aligned edges together. Remove pins.

❽ Turn the trunk right side out. Puff it out to form a cylinder.

❾ Put the sock on your hand with seam facing down. Center and pin the trunk in place directly above the puppet's top lip. Maintain the cylindrical shape while pinning (this may take a few tries).

❿ **For hand sewing:** Leaving a very small seam allowance, hand-sew the trunk to the sock. Remove pins.

For machine sewing: Use a sewing machine only if it allows for a wide enough range of motion.

TEETH, TONGUES, TUSKS, AND HORNS

It can be fun to add extra elements such as teeth and tongues to further enhance your animal's appearance. In this instance, it is important to utilize *selective placement* to avoid overloading your sock puppet's mouth with unnecessary material. One way to determine what to add is to decide what emotions or presence you want to elicit from your character. For example, if you are making a dog that is happy go lucky, friendly, or goofy, a long tongue for giving wet sloppy kisses could be perfect. On the other hand, if you are creating a wild, ferocious dog or a wolf, then adding pointy canines would be a better option. Sometimes, you may feel that the addition of teeth is essential to your character, such as tusks on an elephant or walrus. In this case, you may choose to make that the only extra you add to the mouth.

TEETH

Craft foam, felt, and stiff felt are the easiest materials to use for teeth because they can be cut into any shape. It is essential to use selective placement in the application of teeth. Too many teeth or teeth that are too long will interfere with the way your puppet's mouth opens and closes. The object is to create the *suggestion* of teeth. When making a tiger, for example, two triangular-shaped canines strategically placed should be enough to say "ferocious teeth!"

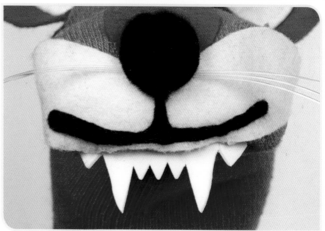

Square Felt Teeth

This technique is being demonstrated with square teeth; however; it can be used with any shape teeth.

- 9" × 12" (23 × 30.5 cm) sheet white or off-white soft felt
- ruler
- pen or thin marker
- sharp craft scissors
- hot glue gun and glue sticks
- sewing materials
- stickpins

Directions

❶ Determine the size of rectangle or square needed for your teeth: large for horse, small for rodent, and so on. Measure and draw the shape onto the felt. Cut it out.

❷ **If gluing:** *Double* the teeth by gluing them to an unused portion of felt. Cut out the doubled teeth **(A)**. Cut slits in the felt to form teeth **(B)**. For a soft mouth, glue the uncut edge directly beneath the top seam inside the mouth. For a stiff mouth, glue directly *in front* of the mouthparts **(C)**.

If sewing: *Double* the teeth by sewing them to an unused portion of felt **(D)**. Sew multiple, short seams to create individual teeth **(E)**. Pin teeth into place. Sew the first seam along the top edge. Sew a second seam parallel to the first, directly across the individual teeth **(F)**.

❶

❷Ⓐ
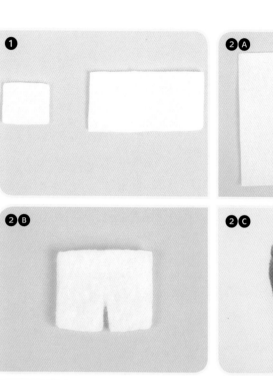

❷Ⓑ

❷Ⓒ

❷Ⓓ

❷Ⓔ
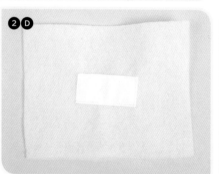

❷Ⓕ

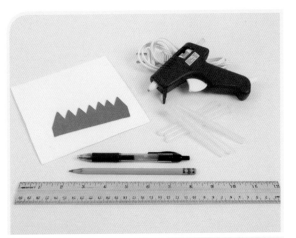

- Shark Tooth stencil (page 136) *or make your own*
- 6" × 6" (15.2 × 15.2 cm) square white or off-white craft foam
- pen or fine marker
- sharp craft scissors
- hot glue gun and glue sticks

TIP

Whenever possible, create the teeth stencil as one piece with a flat top edge. This will make it easier to attach them to your puppet.

Pointy Craft Foam Teeth

This technique can be used with any shape teeth. Craft foam can be applied only with glue.

Directions

❶ Trace the stencil onto the craft foam. Cut out teeth.

❷ **For a stiff mouth:** Glue the flat edge of the teeth directly onto the gum line.

For a soft mouth: Glue the flat edge of the teeth directly *beneath* the top seam inside the mouth.

TONGUES

While not a necessary attribute, tongues add flair to a sock puppet and they are always an unexpected surprise when the puppet opens his mouth. In some instances, a tongue can help develop your character. For example, a long, fly-catching tongue is a great feature to add to a frog puppet. A punk rock pig puppet might have a pierced tongue. If you want to make a character appear sickly, then a green tongue is the way to go.

Directions

❶ Design a tongue shape for your character. Make a stencil (page 34).

❷ Follow the directions for the *doubled* technique (page 38).

❸ **If sewing:** You can enhance the tongue by sewing a seam down the middle.

❹ Attach the tongue by gluing it or sewing it inside the puppet's mouth.

TUSKS

The stuffed, felt tusk method is for hand or machine sewing only.

MATERIALS

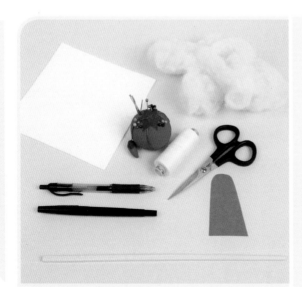

- Tusk or Horn stencil (page 138 or 143) *or create your own*
- 6" × 6" (15.2 × 15.2 cm) square white or off-white felt
- fiberfill stuffing
- pen or fine marker
- sharp craft scissors
- stickpins
- sewing materials
- chopstick or ¼" (6 mm) wooden dowel
- hot glue gun and glue sticks

HORNS

Horns are made in the same way as tusks. It is merely the size and placement that change. For a large horn, use the Horn stencil. For a small horn, use the Tusk stencil. Horns can be attached using the *button* technique or, when appropriate, substitute a round *button* for a section of faux fur or a body part.

Directions for Hand or Machine Sewing

- - - - - - - - - - - - - - - - - - -

❶ Trace the Tusk or Horn stencil twice onto a felt square.

❷ Cut pieces out.

❸ Fold one tusk (or horn) in half. Pin if needed. Sew the edges together. Repeat with the second tusk (or horn).

❹ Using the chopstick (or dowel), firmly push on the wide end, slowly rolling the felt down until the piece is completely right side out. Repeat with the second piece.

❺ Use the chopstick to densely pack the tusks or horns with small pieces of stuffing.

❻ Attach the tusks or horns to your puppet using small felt *buttons* (page 41).

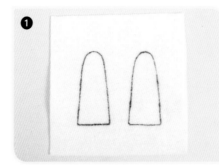

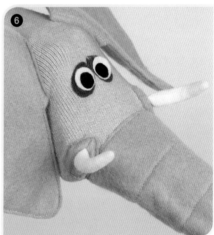

DIRECTIONS FOR GLUING

- -

1. Create a tusk or horn shape and make a stencil.

2. Trace the stencil onto felt. Cut it out.

3. Follow directions for the *doubled* technique to make tusks or horns (page 39). Glue directly to your puppet in the desired location.

BEAKS

- Triangular Beak stencil (page 139) *or design your own*
- 9" × 12" (23 × 30.5 cm) sheet soft felt in color of choice
- 9" × 12" (23 × 30.5 cm) sheet stiff felt in color of choice (optional)
- pen or fine marker
- sharp craft scissors
- ruler
- hot glue gun and glue sticks
- sewing materials
- stickpins

If you are making a bird, a beak is essential for defining the look of your puppet. Other animals such as a platypus, an octopus, and even some dinosaurs also have beaks. Beaks can be applied in one of two ways: inside the mouth or outside the mouth. The method you choose will largely depend upon what animal you are making, which materials you are using, and whether your sock puppet has a soft or a stiff mouth.

BEAK ATTACHED INSIDE THE MOUTH

Feel free to create your own beak shape to use with this technique.

TIP

To make a craft foam beak, use craft foam in place of felt and follow the directions for gluing the beak. Disregard step ③

Directions

① Trace the stencil onto soft felt. Flip the stencil. Trace it again.

② Cut out both beak shapes (bottom and top).

③ *Double* the beaks by gluing or sewing each one to an unused portion of the felt (you may use stiff felt for this second layer if you like). Trim excess felt.

④ Put the puppet on your hand with the mouth open. Make sure the sock is centered. Insert the beak evenly.

⑤ **If gluing:** Place a line of hot glue along the flat edge of top beak. Glue it to the roof of the mouth approximately ½" (1.3 cm) from the opening **(A)**. When glue dries,

add more glue where needed to secure **(B)**. Repeat steps A and B with the bottom beak. Make sure that the top and bottom beaks align before gluing **(C)**.

If sewing: (for soft mouth puppets only) Pin the top beak into place approximately ½" (1.3 cm) from the opening of the mouth. Sew one seam along the flat edge of the top beak, attaching it to the roof of the mouth **(D)**. Sew a second seam approximately ½" (1.3 cm) from the first, securing the beak to the "lip" of the sock just outside the mouth **(E)**. Repeat steps D and E for the bottom beak. Make sure that the top and bottom beaks align before sewing **(F)**.

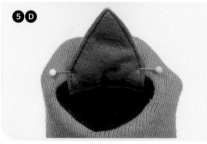

DUCKBILL ATTACHED OUTSIDE THE MOUTH

Feel free to create your own beak shape to use with this technique.

TIP

To make a craft foam duckbill, use craft foam in place of felt and follow the directions for gluing the duckbill. Disregard step ❸

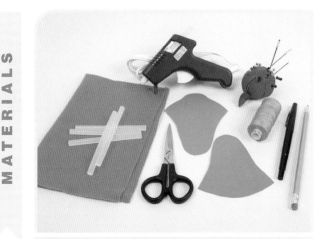

MATERIALS

- Duckbill stencils (page 138) *or design your own*
- 9" × 12" (23 × 30.5 cm) sheet soft felt in color of choice
- pencil, pen, or fine marker
- sharp craft scissors
- ruler
- hot glue gun and glue sticks
- sewing materials
- stickpins

Directions

❶ Trace both stencils onto the felt.

❷ Cut out the shapes.

❸ *Double* the bill shapes by gluing or sewing each one to an unused portion of the felt. Trim excess felt.

❹ Center the puppet on your hand with the mouth open to make sure the bill is applied evenly.

❺ **If gluing:** Place a line of hot glue along the top edge of the upper bill. Glue to the sock approximately midway between first and second finger joints **(A)**. Place a line of hot glue along the top edge of lower bill. Glue under the mouth, just beneath where your thumb extends forward when the mouth is open **(B)**. Add more glue as needed to secure.

If sewing: (for soft mouth puppets only) Pin upper bill to the sock just above the sock seam (approximately midway between first and second finger joints) **(C)**. Remove the sock from your hand. Sew the beak down, removing pins as you go **(D)**. Pin the bill to the sock under the mouth, just beneath where your thumb extends forward when the mouth is open. Remove the sock from your hand. Sew the bill down, removing pins as you go **(E)**.

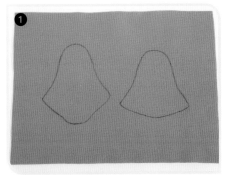

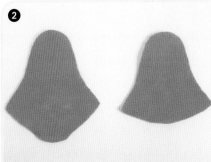

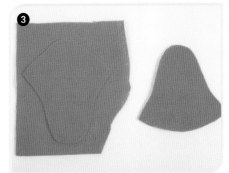

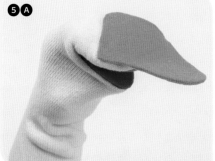

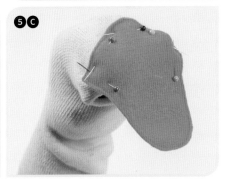

Making Animal Bodies

THE UNIQUE LOOK of most animals extends past the head and face to the body. Such characteristics include, but are not limited to, distinctive markings, furry manes, and interesting tails. With a focus on animal bodies, this chapter explores the different ways to execute these individual attributes and fully realize your sock puppet design.

MARKINGS, MANES, AND FUR

Adding decorative elements such as markings and fur will bring out the unique qualities of your animal. The abundance of colors, styles, and textures available makes faux fur hard to resist and, in many instances, the easiest to use; however, faux fur can weigh a sock puppet down. Therefore, when using fur, it is best to aim for *selective placement*. Small patches added to the top of the head, between the ears, or on the chest can be very effective. For example, by backing floppy ears with faux fur, you will represent a shaggy dog without actually having to cover the entire sock with fur. Similarly, markings should be used sparingly. Keep in mind that the object is to capture the characteristics of the animal without completely losing the essence of the sock or the flexibility of the puppet.

MARKINGS

Animal markings such as tiger stripes and leopard spots can be created through the application of small felt or fabric pieces. Creative dyeing is another way to represent these markings. Dyeing the pattern offers the distinct advantage of using less material on the sock and thereby retaining more of the puppet's flexibility.

MANES

If you are making an animal that has a mane, such as a lion or a giraffe, there are a number of different materials that can be used. Selecting a material for its texture as well as color will help you create an accurate representation of your animal. Manes can be placed horizontally, vertically, or curving around the contours of the sock. Yarn and faux fur are the most obvious materials, but felt can also be used to create the look of fur.

Faux Fur Manes

When using faux fur, it is important to observe the direction in which the pile naturally falls, so you can use it to your advantage within your design. Take care to cut along the fabric base in order to preserve the length and integrity of the pile. The easiest way to form a mane is by cutting a rectangle out of the fur. The width and length of the rectangle, along with the placement, will vary according to the animal you are creating.

MATERIALS

- 12" × 6" (30.5 × 15.2 cm) piece faux fur
- ruler
- chalk, pen, or fine marker
- sharp craft scissors
- hot glue gun and glue sticks
- sewing materials
- stickpins

Directions

① Using a ruler, measure and trace a rectangular mane onto the wrong side of the faux fur. Take care to place the pile in the direction you desire *before* tracing.

② With fur side down, carefully cut out your shape along the traced line. Take care to keep the scissors blade on the fabric backing. *Avoid cutting the actual pile.*

③ Choose the desired location for the mane. For manes that follow the contours of the face, such as lions, tack the mane in place with the sock on your hand.

④ Apply a few drops of hot glue to the fabric backing and lightly tack the mane in place on the puppet.

⑤ **If gluing:** Slowly apply hot glue around the underside edges of the fabric backing to completely secure the mane to sock (keep in mind that the more glue you use, the stiffer and less flexible the puppet will be). Firmly press the mane into place as you go. Take care not to get any glue on the actual fur **(A)**.

If sewing: Sew around the edges of the mane, completely securing it to the sock **(B)**.

Felt Manes

Looping, doubling, and fringing felt are some of the methods that can give it the look of fur. These techniques can be easily executed by either gluing or sewing.

Looped Felt Mane

- 9" × 12" (23 × 30.5 cm) sheet felt in color of choice
- ruler
- chalk, pen, or fine marker
- sharp craft scissors
- hot glue gun and glue sticks
- sewing materials
- stickpins

Directions for Looped Felt Mane

1. With a ruler, measure and trace a rectangle onto the felt 6" (15.2 cm) long by 4" (10.2 cm) wide. If using a child's sock, make it 5" (12.7 cm) long by 4" (10.2 cm) wide.

2. Cut it out.

3. Fold the rectangle in half lengthwise. Pin if desired.

4. Glue or sew the edges together, removing pins as you go.

5. On the folded edge, make several cuts into the felt about ½" (1.3 cm) apart and 1½" (3.8 cm) deep.

6. Choose the direction of the mane (vertical, horizontal, or curved).

7. Place the sock on your hand. Using a small amount of hot glue, tack the mane into place.

8. **If gluing:** Add more hot glue to secure the mane in place.

   If sewing: Create a seam by sewing the flat edge to the sock **(A)**. Further secure the mane to the sock by sewing a second seam just beneath the loops (approximately ¾" [2 cm] from first) **(B)**. Close up the sides, if desired.

Directions for Fringed Felt Mane

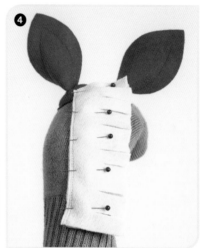

❶ Follow steps 1 through 4 for Looped Felt Mane.

❷ Cut along *folded edge only*, separating the mane into two halves but leaving it connected on one side.

❸ Using sharp scissors, make multiple cuts on the open side about 1½" (3.8 cm) deep. For fewer fringes, leave more space between cuts; for more fringes, leave less space. Take care not to cut through the attached side.

❹ Follow steps 6 through 8 for Looped Felt Mane.

TAILS

Adding a tail to your animal sock puppet will make your character more recognizable and will extend the parameters of the body by giving it a back side. In nature, tails come in thousands of interesting shapes and sizes. In sock puppet design, there are nearly as many fun ways to represent them. By incorporating one or a combination of techniques you will be able to approximate the look of your animal's unique tail. Common materials used for tails are yarn, faux fur, and felt.

YARN TAIL

The two best ways to make a yarn tail are loose and braided. A loose yarn tail creates a flowing look (e.g., horse). Knotting the ends of the individual strands will prevent the yarn from unraveling. To create a yarn tail with a tighter, sleeker look (e.g., lion), you may want to braid the yarn. Try combining different colors to enhance the effect. For example, you can create a realistic-looking zebra tail by braiding black and white yarn together.

MATERIALS

- yarn
- ruler
- sharp craft scissors

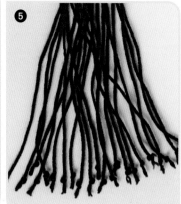

Directions

- -

❶ Determine the length of your tail.

❷ Cut approximately 21 strands of yarn.

❸ Gather and tie them together at one end using another piece of yarn.

❹ For a braided tail, braid the yarn and tie the end tightly. Trim excess.

❺ For a loose tail, knot the individual strands at the ends to prevent unraveling.

❻ Use a *button* to attach the tail to your puppet (page 41).

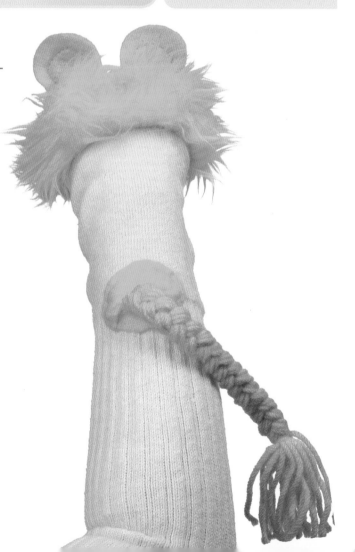

FAUX FUR TAIL

Making a fur tail is a good example of *selective placement*. It will communicate that your animal is furry without you having to overuse the fur or cover the entire

sock, which can restrict movement. Fur tail techniques are for hand or machine sewing only and are not for use with glue.

- 8" × 8" (20.3 × 20.3 cm) square faux fur
- ruler
- pen or finer marker
- sharp craft scissors
- stickpins
- sewing materials
- chopstick or ¼" (6 mm) wooden dowel

TIP

When measuring faux fur, the word *length* refers to the direction of the pile.

Directions

❶ Place your fur piece with the fabric underside facing up and with pile facing down.

❷ Using your ruler, draw a rectangle 8" (20.3 cm) long by 4" (10.2 cm) wide on the fabric underside.

❸ With fur side down, carefully cut out your rectangle along the drawn line. Keep the scissors blade on the fabric backing and *avoid cutting the actual pile.*

❹ Fold the fur rectangle in half with right sides (fur) together and pin in place.

❺ Sew the edges together. Remove pins.

❻ Using the chopstick or dowel, firmly push on the wide end, slowly rolling the fur down until the tail is completely right side out.

❼ Sew the tip of the tail closed.

❽ Use a large *button* to attach the fur tail to your puppet (page 41).

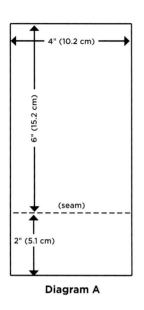

Diagram A

Diagram B

Tipped Faux Fur Tail

❶ Choose two colors of faux fur: one for the tail and one for making a tip.

❷ Follow the directions for Faux Fur Tail (page 95) with these changes to step 2: Using your ruler, draw one rectangle 6" (15.2 cm) long by 4" (10.2 cm) wide on the fabric underside of the main color fur. Draw another rectangle 2" (5.1 cm) long by 4" (10.2 cm) wide on the fabric underside of the tipped color fur. Cut out and sew together (diagram A).

Striped Faux Fur Tail

❶ Choose two to four colors of faux fur.

❷ Follow the directions for making a Faux Fur Tail (page 95) with these changes to Step 2: Using your ruler, draw five rectangles 2" (5.1 cm) long by 4" (10.2 cm) wide on the fabric undersides of the faux fur. Cut out and sew together (diagram B).

FELT TAIL

Felt tails can be made in any number of ways simply by changing the length and shape of your stencil, adding stuffing, rolling the felt, or attaching faux fur.

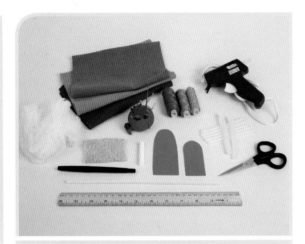

- **Tail stencil** (small or large, page 139) *or create your own*
- **9" × 12" (23 × 30.5 cm) sheet felt** in color of choice
- **fiberfill stuffing** (optional)
- **2" × 2½" (5.1 × 6.4 cm) faux fur** (optional)
- **pen or fine marker**
- **sharp craft scissors**
- **hot glue gun and glue sticks**
- **sewing materials**
- **stickpins**
- **chopstick or ¼" (6 mm) wooden dowel** (optional)

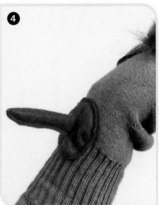

Directions

❶ Trace the Tail stencil onto felt.

❷ Cut out the tail shape.

❸ Fold the tail in half. Glue or sew the edges together.

❹ Use a medium *button* (page 41) to attach the tail to your puppet.

Stuffed Felt Tail

The longer and more densely packed a stuffed appendage, the more curve it will have. Stuffed felt tail methods are for hand or machine sewing only.

Directions

- - - - - - - - - - - - - - - - - -

❶ Trace the tail stencil onto felt. Cut out the shape.

❷ Fold the tail in half, pin, and sew both halves together along the edge.

❸ Using the chopstick or dowel, firmly push on the wide end, slowly rolling the felt down until the tail is completely right side out.

❹ Starting with small pieces of stuffing, use the chopstick to fill the tail.

❺ Use a medium *button* to attach the tail to your puppet (page 41).

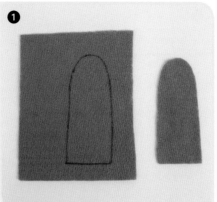

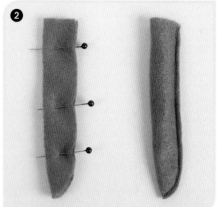

Rolled Felt Tail

Rolled felt tails can be easily made from a rectangle. Adjust the size to accommodate your specific animal. Add a fringe or faux fur tip to complete the look.

Directions

----

1 Measure a rectangle onto the felt. For example, a long tail might be 5" (12.7 cm) long by 3½" (8.9 cm) wide; a medium tail might be 4" (10.2 cm) long by 1½" (3.8 cm) wide; and a short tail might be 3" (7.6 cm) long by 2½" (6.4 cm) wide.

2 Cut out the rectangle.

3 Fold or roll the tail three or four times. Pin in place.

4 Glue or sew the edge down. Stop 1" (2.5 cm) *before* the end.

5 *Optional:* To add fringe, make multiple small cuts in the remaining, unglued/unsewn end of the tail.

6 *Optional:* To add fur:

If gluing: Adding hot glue as you go, wrap the remaining 1" (2.5 cm) of the felt tail in faux fur. Trim fur piece if necessary **(A)**.

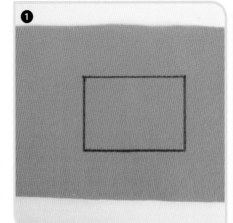

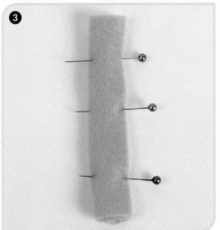

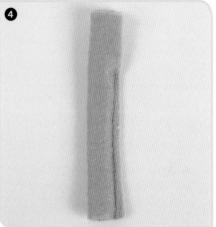

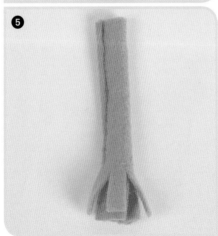

If sewing: Fold fur in half with right sides together (fur facing in) and pin **(B)**. Sew along the edge **(C)**. Turn the fur right side out **(D)**. Insert the unsewn end of the tail into the sewn fur piece. Sew along the connecting edge to secure **(E)**.

7 Use a medium *button* to attach the tail to your puppet (page 41).

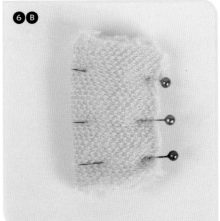

6 B

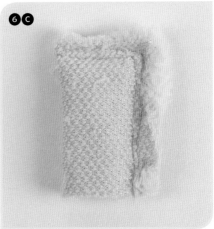

6 C

6 D

6 E

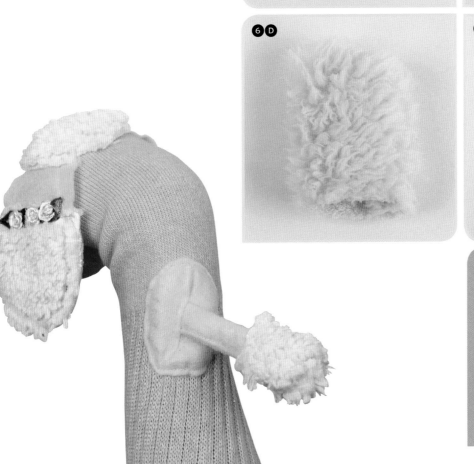

TIP

Experiment with the rolled tail technique by designing your own stencils. To make a rodent's tail, create a stencil that is 9 inches (23 cm) long and gets narrower toward one end.

WINGS AND FEATHERS

You have a number of options when it comes to adding wings and feathers to your sock puppet. First, of course, are *actua*l feathers. These are commonly available in craft stores and in catalogs. They come in many different sizes and colors and originate primarily from chickens and turkeys. The advantage to using real feathers is that they look, well, *real*, adding an authenticity to the design. This can work just fine for a puppet that will be used as an art piece or for a short production. For long-lasting durability, however, or if you object to using animal products in your crafts, real feathers are not practical. With felt (wonderful felt) you can create lovely wings and feathers. Faux fur works well, too, especially for fuzzy baby bird puppets.

- Wing Base stencil (page 139) *or design your own*
- Wing Cap stencil (page 139) *or design your own*
- 9" × 12" (23 × 30.5 cm) sheet soft felt in color of choice
- 9" × 6" (23 × 15.2 cm) sheet soft felt in second color of choice (optional)
- 12 to 16 real feathers approximately 4½" (11.4 cm) long in color(s) of choice (for real feather wings only)
- pen or fine marker
- sharp craft scissors
- hot glue gun and glue sticks
- sewing materials
- stickpins

WINGS

Wings and feathers made from felt can be either glued or sewn, depending upon your preference. You can add zest and dimension to your design by using different colors for the wing base and the wing cap.

Directions

① Trace the Wing Base and Wing Cap stencils onto felt. Cut out the shapes.

② *Double* the base by gluing or sewing it to an unused portion of felt. Trim excess felt.

③ Align the cap on top of the base and glue or sew it down.

④ **If gluing:** In the base, make four parallel cuts beginning at the point and ending between the notches indicated in the cap **(A)**. Repeat for second wing. Put the puppet on your hand to determine wing placement. Mark the location with a straight pin **(B)**. Place a line of glue on the back of the base around the top curve only. Glue wings and hold while glue dries **(C)**.

If sewing: Sew four parallel seams from the point of the base to the top of the cap, passing over the notches in the cap **(D)**. Repeat for second wing. Put the puppet on your hand to determine wing placement. Pin in place **(E)**. To attach the wings, sew around the top curve. Tack stitches at both ends by sewing back and forth over the same area **(F)**.

> **TIP**
>
> Before attaching the wing to your puppet, be sure to have the face completed. Adding the wing should be one of the last things you do. This will help ensure proper placement. Once the wing is glued on, it cannot be removed.

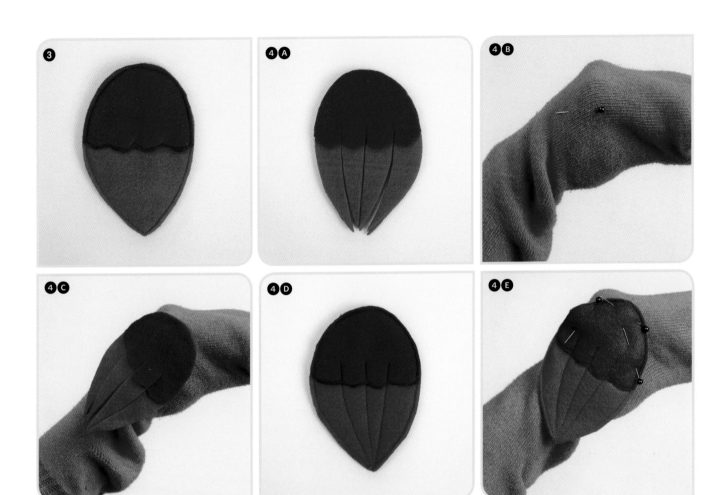

REAL FEATHER WINGS

Real feathers can be applied with hot glue or by sewing. The best way to utilize real feathers is to first attach them to a felt backing. This can serve as the wing base.

Directions

❶ Trace the Wing Base and Wing Cap stencils onto felt, twice.

❷ Cut out the shapes.

❸ With the stems of the feathers pointing toward the top of the wing base, create two layers (three or four feathers each) by gluing or sewing them on, one at a time, to the felt base (if gluing, add glue under each stem and lay feathers flat but slightly overlapping). Trim any part of the stem that extends above the base. The fluffy tops of the feathers should extend to *just below* the base.

❹ Align the cap on top of the base, sandwiching feathers in between. Glue or sew around the perimeter of the cap to secure.

❺ Repeat steps 1 through 4 for the second wing.

❻ **If gluing:** Put the puppet on your hand to determine where the wings will go. Mark places with straight pins **(A)**. Place a line of glue on the back of the base around the top curve only. Glue wings on and hold while the glue dries **(B)**.

If sewing: Put the puppet on your hand to determine wing placement. Pin in place **(C)**. To attach wings, sew around the top curve. Tack stitches at both ends by sewing back and forth over the same area **(D)**.

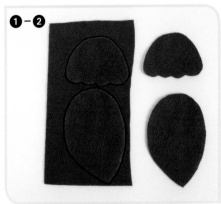

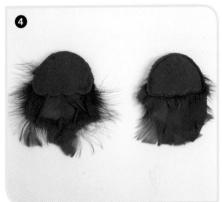

TIP

To create matching tail feathers,

1. Use the Tail Feather Base and Cap stencils (page 140).

2. Follow the directions for the Real Feather Wings or Felt Wings technique and attach to the rear of your bird.

LARGE FELT FEATHER

Felt feathers can be used individually or in groups to create full tail plumage such as on a rooster, turkey, or peacock.

- Large Feather stencil (page 140) *or create your own*
- Button stencil (page 135) *or create your own*
- 1 or 2 sheets 9" × 12" (23 × 30.5 cm) felt in color(s) of choice
- chalk, pen, or fine marker
- sharp craft scissors
- hot glue gun and glue sticks
- sewing materials

Directions

❶ Trace the feather stencil onto felt. Cut out the shape(s).

❷ **If gluing:** *Double* your feather by placing a line of hot glue down the center and adhering it to an unused portion of felt. Trim excess **(A)**. Add more glue between the two layers, but don't go all the way to the edges **(B)**. Make multiple diagonal cuts, fringing the edges. This will enhance the feathered look. **(C)** For multiple feathers, repeat steps as many times as needed.

If sewing: *Double* the feather by sewing around outer edge, attaching it to an unused portion of felt. Trim excess. Sew one long seam down the center of the feather. Tack at both ends. Sew multiple diagonal seams from the outer edge of the feather to the center seam, mimicking the veins in a real feather. Tack at both ends **(D)**.

❸ Attach feathers to the puppet using a felt *button* (page 41). For a tail plume, make multiple feathers and attach to your puppet using a large button.

TIP

For a little pizzazz, try using a different color of felt for each layer.

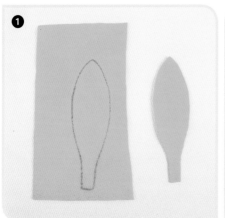

FLIPPERS AND FINS

If you are making a fish, shark, dolphin, or sea lion, the most outstanding features are their flippers and fins. This means that adding them is essential to your design. Felt is a great material with which to form fins and flippers. If you are primarily gluing your sock puppet together, stiff felt and craft foam can also be used.

First, determine the shape and size of the animal's fins or flippers and create a stencil(s). More than one may be required as many fish and marine animals have side (pectoral), back (dorsal), and tail (fluke, caudal) fins. Techniques for attachment will vary depending upon the shape of the appendage and where it is being secured.

- Fin stencils (pages 141 and 142) *or make your own*
- 1 to 3 sheets 9" × 12" (23 × 30.5 cm) soft felt
- 1 or 2 sheets 9" × 6" (23 × 15.2 cm) decorative soft felt in color(s) of choice (optional)
- chalk, pen, or fine marker
- sharp craft scissors
- hot glue gun and glue sticks
- sewing materials
- stickpins

SMALL PECTORAL FINS USING THE BUTTON TECHNIQUE

Directions

1. Using a Small Fin Stencil, follow directions for "Making a Layered or Appliquéd Appendages" on page 38.

2. Add any decorative accouterment desired.

3. Use the *button* technique to attach to puppet (page 41).

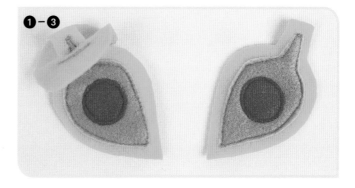

❶–❸

DORSAL AND LARGE PECTORAL FINS USING THE SPLIT TECHNIQUE

Directions

❶ Trace the Dorsal Fin stencil onto felt. Flip the stencil and trace again.

❷ Cut out both shapes.

❸ **If gluing:** Line up the fin shapes. Place a line of glue all the way around the edge of one shape, leaving ¼" (6 mm) at the bottom unglued. Adhere the shapes together **(A)**. *Optional:* Add decorative accouterment, if desired **(B)**. Put the puppet on your hand to determine placement. Mark with a straight pin **(C)**. *Split* (page 54) the unglued edge of the fin and add glue to both sides. Adhere to the puppet **(D)**. *Use caution: Once glued, it cannot be unglued!*

If sewing: *Optional*: Sew on decorative accouterment, if desired. Line up the fin shapes and pin together, leaving ¼" (6 mm) at the bottom unpinned **(E)**. Sew the shapes together, leaving ¼" (6 mm) at the bottom unsewn **(F)**. *Split* (page 54) the unsewn edge and pin both sides to the puppet **(G)**. Sew down on both sides. Tack stitches at each end **(H)**.

❹ Repeat steps 1 through 3 for the Pectoral Fins, as needed.

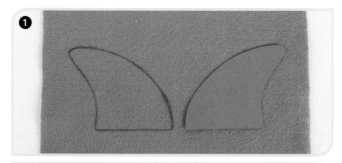

TIP

To glue pectoral and dorsal fins made from stiff felt or craft foam,

1. Trace a stencil onto your preferred material.

2. Cut out the shape.

3. With the sock on your hand, determine and mark placement.

4. Add glue to the flat, bottom edge of the fin and adhere it to the puppet.

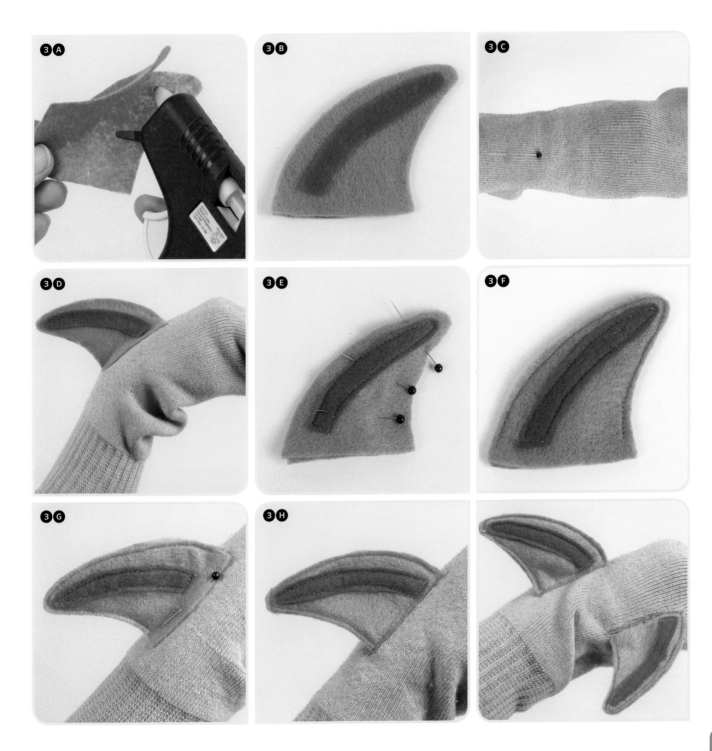

TAIL FINS AND FLIPPERS

Directions

1. Using a Tail Fin stencil, follow directions for Doubled Appendages or Appliquéd Appendages (page 38).

2. With the sock stretched flat on the work surface, align the tail fin so that the end just overlaps the opening of the sock. Pin in place.

3. **If gluing:** Add a line of glue along the flat edge of the tail fin and adhere it to the sock **(A)**.

   If sewing: Sew a seam along the flat edge of the tail fin, securing it to the sock **(B)**. *Use caution: Do not sew the sock together.* To prevent flopping, sew a second seam parallel to the first approximately ½" to 1" (1.3 to 2.5 cm) down **(C)**.

4. Add decorative accouterment, if desired.

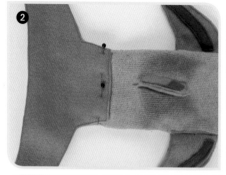

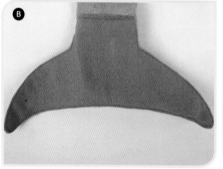

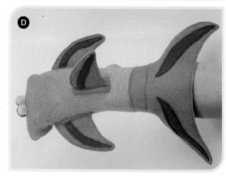

DOME SHELL

A basic dome-shaped shell for a turtle or a bug is relatively easy to make by either gluing or sewing soft felt to your sock. Changing the color and other decorative elements will effectively alter this single method to fit a number of different animals and insects.

- Dome Shell stencil (page 142)
- 2 sheets 9" × 12" (23 × 30.5 cm) felt in color of choice for shell
- 1 to 3 sheets 9" × 12" (23 × 30.5 cm) felt for decorative elements (optional)
- chalk, pen, or fine marker
- sharp craft scissors
- hot glue gun and glue sticks
- sewing materials
- straight pins

Directions

1 Trace the shell stencil onto both sheets of felt. Cut out the shells.

2 On one shell only, draw the cut lines indicated on the stencil. Cut slits in the shell. This will be the top shell.

3 Overlap the slits approximately ¼" (6 mm) and pin them together. Secure by sewing or with a thin line of glue.

4 *Optional:* Cut out your decorative elements and glue or sew them to the top shell.

5 *Optional:* If adding feet and/or tail, *double* the appendages (page 38) and glue or sew them to the underside of the top shell.

6 Place the top shell upside down on the work surface. Place the bottom shell, right side up, on top. Align the shells and carefully pin the edges together, leaving the spaces where your arm passes through unpinned, approximately 5½" (14 cm) at either end.

7 Before gluing or sewing the edges together, put the sock on your arm and slide it into the shell to make sure it fits well. Adjust pins if necessary.

8 Remove your arm and carefully glue or sew the edges together, removing pins as you go. If gluing, stay close to the edges so as not to lose room inside the shell. If sewing, remember to close your seams at both ends.

9 Slip your arm with the sock back into the shell. If making a turtle, secure the top shell to the sock with a little glue or a short seam at the back center point where the shell meets the middle of the forearm. This will enable the turtle to pull his head into his shell. For other shelled creatures, secure at the *front* most center point where the shell meets the wrist.

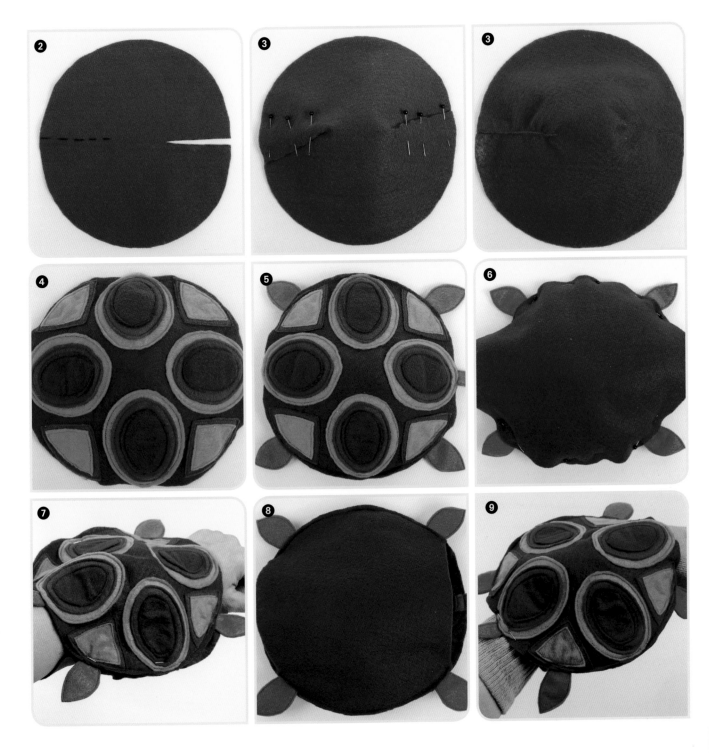

LIMBS

Traditionally, on a sock puppet the majority of detail is added to the head and face because this is what is most visible during performance and play. Additionally, a sock puppet is relatively small with limited space for decorating, so you want to choose your features carefully. The best time to add appendages such as legs, feet, or claws is when the addition is needed to help visually reinforce what type of animal you are making. For example, if you are constructing a frog that doesn't have much detail on its head or body, adding its distinctively springy legs will help make your puppet look that much more like a frog. Many birds share similar attributes, but their feet are often different. For example, adding webbed feet to a duck or claws to a chicken will help distinguish these birds from one another.

JOINTED LIMBS

We are demonstrating this method with a frog leg; however, you can make many different types of animal legs by creating a stencil that suits your needs. This method also utilizes the doubled appendage and *button* techniques (pages 38 and 42).

M A T E R I A L S

- Frog Leg stencil (page 141) or Duck Leg stencil (page 143) *or create your own*
- 2 sheets 9" × 12" (23 × 30.5 cm) soft felt in color(s) of choice
- chalk, pen, or fine marker
- sharp craft scissors
- hot glue gun and glue sticks
- sewing materials
- stickpins

Directions

❶ Trace the stencil onto felt twice. Flip and trace again twice so you have four separate pieces. Cut out all four pieces.

❷ *Double* the legs by placing them ink side down and gluing or sewing them to an unused portion of felt (feel free to use different color felt for this second layer, if desired). Trim excess.

(Continued)

❸ If gluing: Locate the ankle and place a thin line of glue horizontally across the front **(A)**. Fold the leg forward at the ankle, creating a horizontal crease. Hold in place while the glue dries. Repeat this step for the remaining legs **(B)**. Locate the knee and place a thin line of glue diagonally on the *back* **(C)**. Fold the leg backward, creating a diagonal crease at the knee. Hold in place while the glue dries **(D)**. Repeat this step for the remaining legs.

If sewing: Fold the leg forward at the ankle, creating a horizontal crease. Pin in place **(E)**. Sew a seam along the crease **(F)**. Repeat this step for the remaining legs. Fold the leg *backward* at the knee, creating a diagonal crease. Pin in place **(G)**. Sew a diagonal seam along the crease **(H)**. Repeat this step for the remaining legs.

❹ Put the sock on your hand and determine placement locations. Mark with stickpins.

❺ Use the *button* technique (page 41) to attach the legs to the puppet.

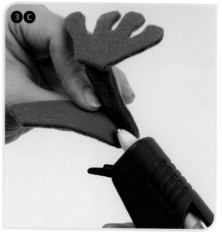

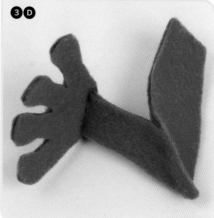

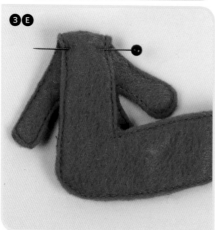

3G

3H

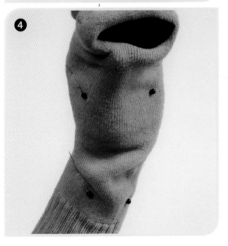

4

UNJOINTED LIMBS

Limbs made using this technique do not have joints; however; their hollow, or folded, nature gives them a distinctly three-dimensional appearance. This method works particularly well for making a variety of bird legs.

Directions

- -

❶ Trace the stencil onto felt. Flip the stencil and trace a second time so you have two legs. Cut out both legs.

❷ *Double* the legs by placing them ink side down and gluing or sewing them to an unused portion of felt. Trim excess.

❸ **If gluing:** Fold the legs in half lengthwise **(A)**. Beginning just above the foot, slowly add glue to a folded leg, holding it closed as the glue dries. Continue adding glue until the leg is completely glued together **(B)**. Repeat with the other leg. Once dry, use sharp scissors to carefully trim any excess glue.

If sewing: Fold the legs in half lengthwise. Pin in place **(C)**. Sew a seam from the top of one leg to where the leg meets the foot. Tack stitches at both ends **(D)**. Repeat for the other leg.

❹ Put the sock on your hand to determine placement. Mark with stickpins.

❺ Use the *button* technique (page 41) to attach the legs to the puppet.

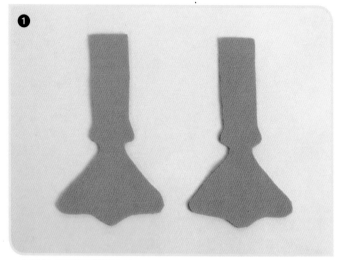

❶

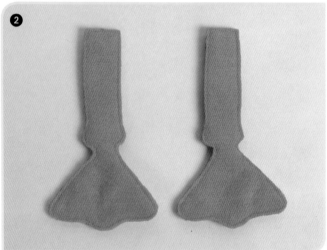

❷

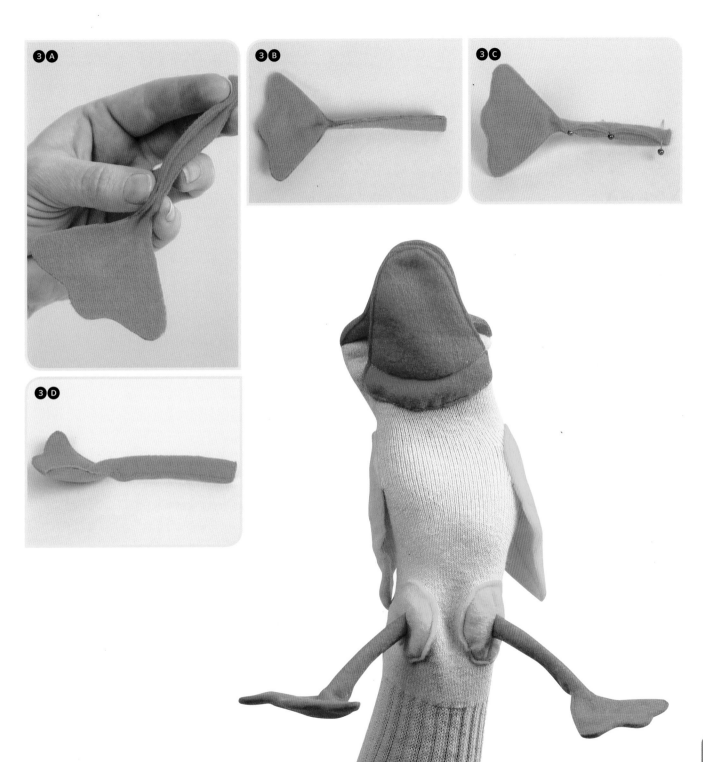

Gallery

AFTER LEARNING THE METHODS presented in the preceding chapters, you will have all the tools necessary to create any sock puppet animal design you can conceive. The *doubled* and *appliqué* techniques will serve nicely as the foundation on which to build all manner of body parts, appendages, and accessories. The varied attachment methods will secure them nicely to your sock puppet. Take stock in your new collection of stencils. Don't be afraid to modify them, and definitely add to them. They will take you anywhere you want to go in the universe of sock puppet design!

Initially, you were encouraged to explore the basic, most defining characteristics of your subject, to capture its essential elements for translation. As you become more confident in your abilities, you can begin to play with bigger and bolder ideas. Add more details, experiment with color, and seek out interesting materials, always keeping in perspective the need to retain the functionality of the puppet and the "essence" of the sock.

Look for subjects that lend themselves to sock puppet design, and then play with making them your own. Push the limits of your imagination by spontaneously combining features. Wildlife photography and records of extinct animals can be fabulous hunting grounds for subjects to turn into sock puppets.

To successfully achieve more elaborate designs, you will need to use a combination of techniques and delve more deeply into the use of decorative elements. The best feature additions will do both, by adding detail while also serving a practical purpose in the puppet's construction.

Shaggy Terrier

The extra use of shaggy fur gives this pup a look distinctive from many other sock puppets. Sewing around the perimeter of the fur only and avoiding glue helps maintain the sock puppet's flexibility. The intense terrier personality comes through button ears standing at attention, while the natural folds add a bit of playfulness. Accents include a long felt tongue and a medium-length faux fur tail that serves to reinforce the shagginess of this dog.

Zebra

Purple and white tie-dye in asymmetrical stripes gives this puppet a unique pattern with fantasy flair. A soulful personality is indicated through the use of eyes with heavy lids with lashes. The lush, two-tone mane is achieved by alternating colors of small faux fur rectangles. A simple, braided-yarn tail attached with a button completes the purple and white camouflage effect.

Bumblebee

The distinctive coloration is achieved with black on yellow tie-dye in a symmetrical, striped pattern. A photograph serves as the example from which to render the specific wing shape. The appearance of veins on the wings is achieved by stitching seams in white-on-white doubled felt, and the bouncy antennae are thin strips of craft foam hot glued to the back of small pop-up eyes.

Monkey

Split ears placed on either side of the head, rounded features, and hands are descriptive of this funny animal's distinctively humanoid appearance. The arms are made using a doubled limb, modified by inserting a chenille stem between the felt layers. A chenille stem has also been added to lend curve and flexibility to the long tail that utilizes the stuffed felt technique. The whole design is brought to completion with a fluffy, faux fur mane that wraps around the monkey's head.

Triceratops

The felt head frill is made using the *doubled* technique. The appliquéd stripes add strength, depth, and definition. These techniques, combined with added seams, give the frill its curve as well as the ability to stand up, away from the head. Using the *button* technique, the larger horns are stuffed and pulled through a single rectangular piece of felt made in the same color as the frill, creating the illusion of one continuous appendage. The tail is a modified, extra-long version of the *stuffed tail* technique. The beak is made using an altered duckbill stencil. It serves a dual purpose in that it is also supporting the horn in place of a button. The use of large, overstuffed parts creates the illusion of a very heavy, massive animal without taking away from the sock or the flexibility of the puppet.

Bat

The wings are made using the *doubled* technique with an appliqué design. This not only adds color but also serves to strengthen the wing and helps it remain outstretched, giving the appearance of flight. The extra seams lend a gentle curve, so they can also fold inward to appear at rest. The pop-up eyes are modified, using a smaller ⁵/₈" (1.6 cm) felt circle and a ¼" (7 mm) acrylic pompom. The whole design is coordinated by appliquéing the tiny button ears with blue felt to match the wing stripes.

Stencils

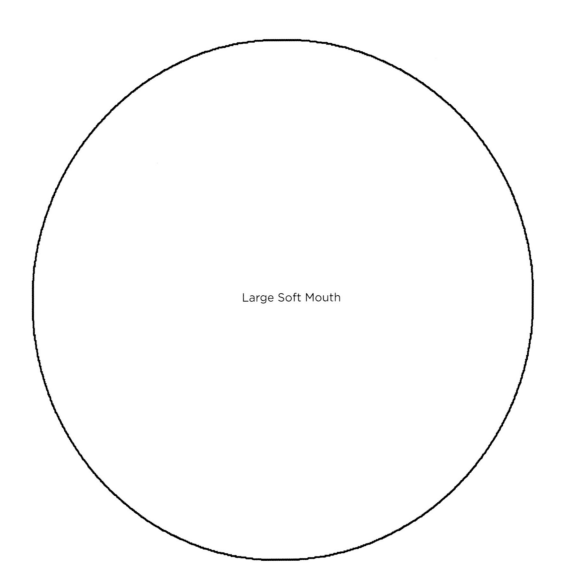

Large Soft Mouth

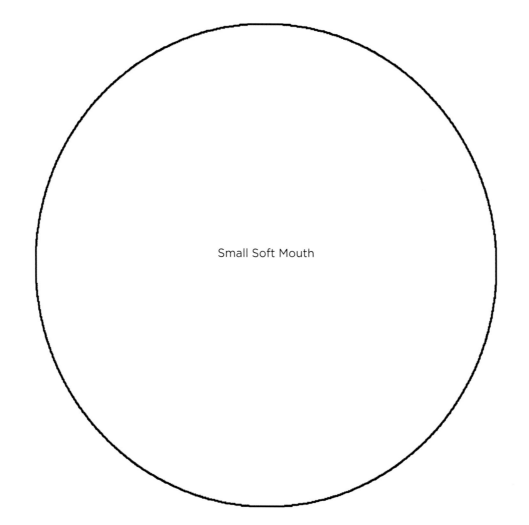

Small Soft Mouth

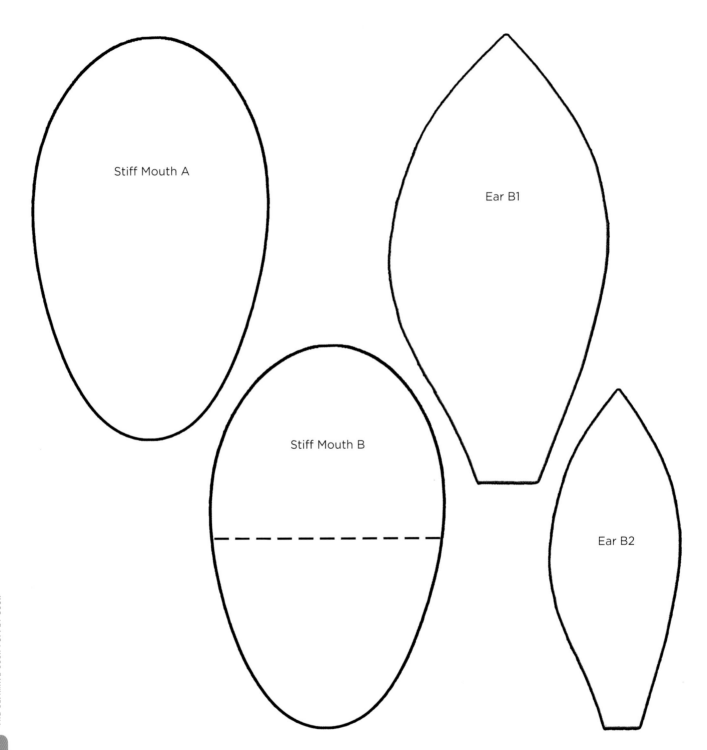

Stiff Mouth A

Ear B1

Stiff Mouth B

Ear B2

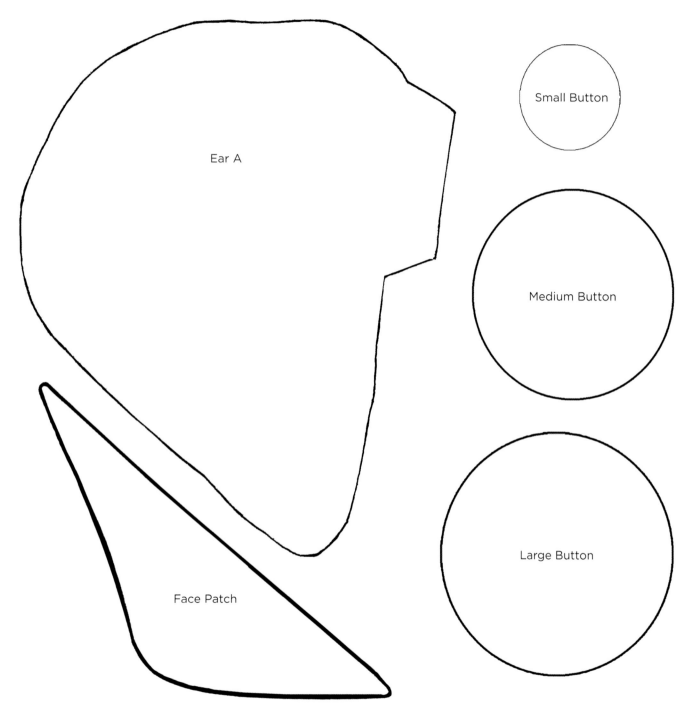

Ear A

Small Button

Medium Button

Large Button

Face Patch

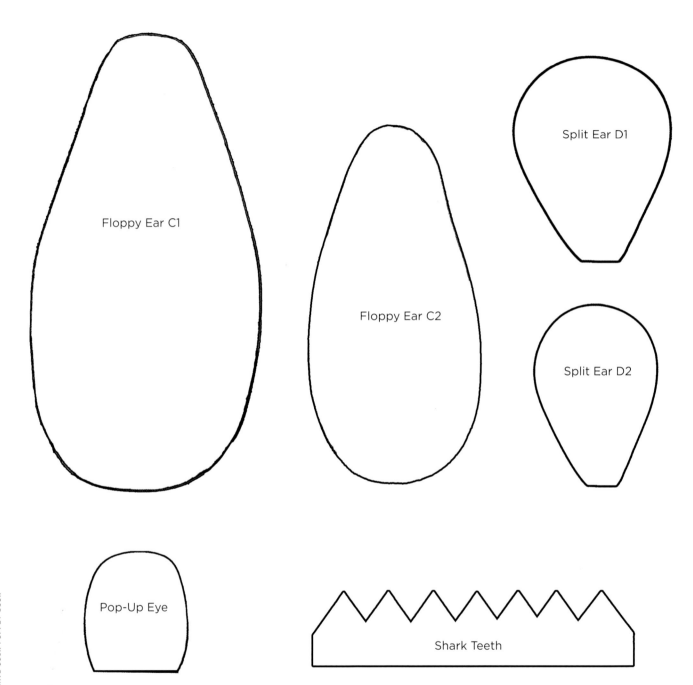

Floppy Ear C1

Floppy Ear C2

Split Ear D1

Split Ear D2

Pop-Up Eye

Shark Teeth

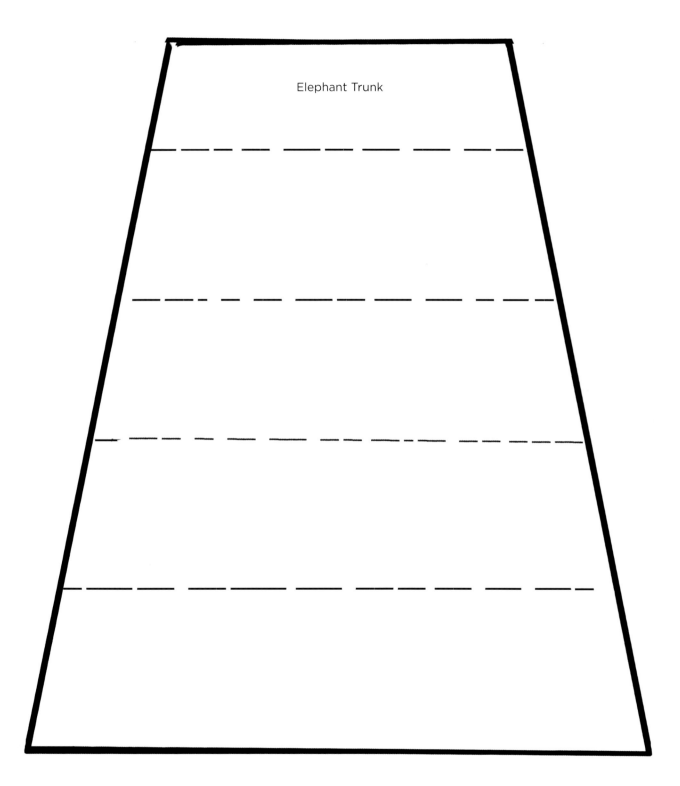

Elephant Trunk

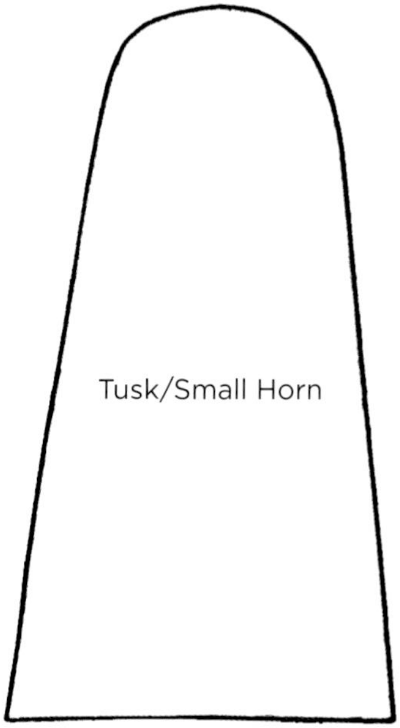

Tusk/Small Horn

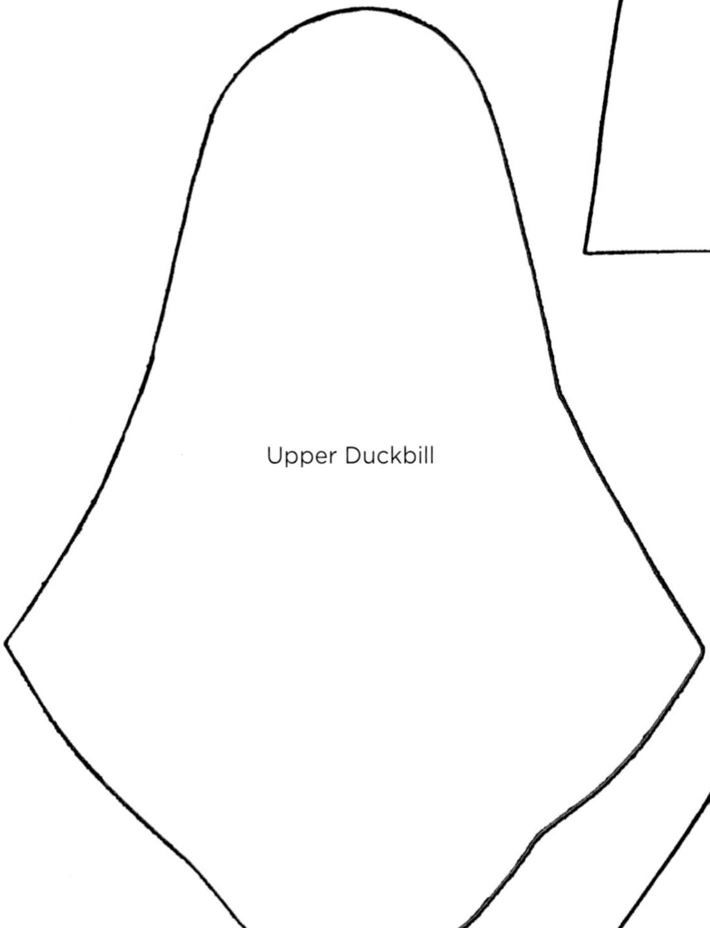

Upper Duckbill

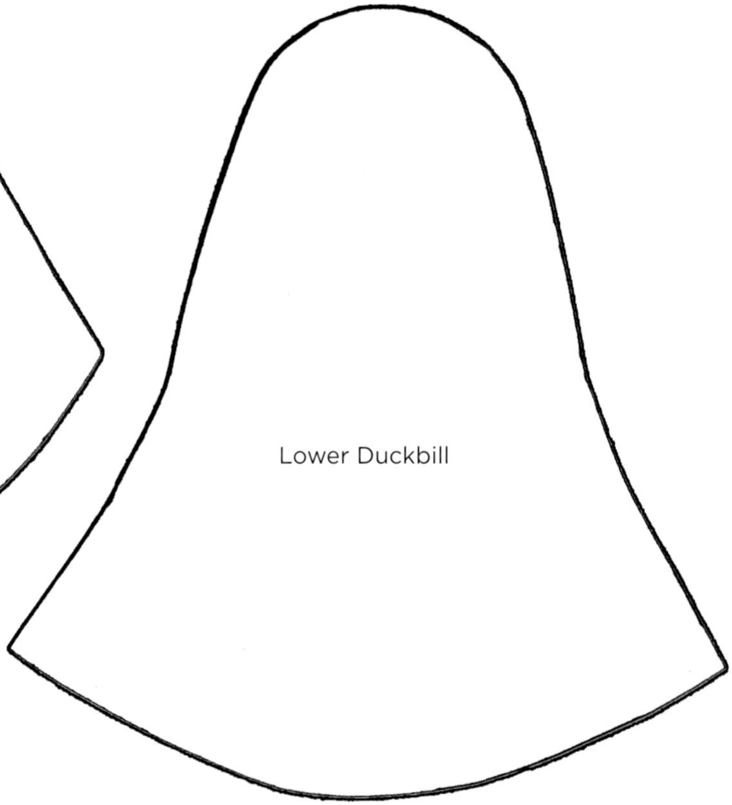

Lower Duckbill

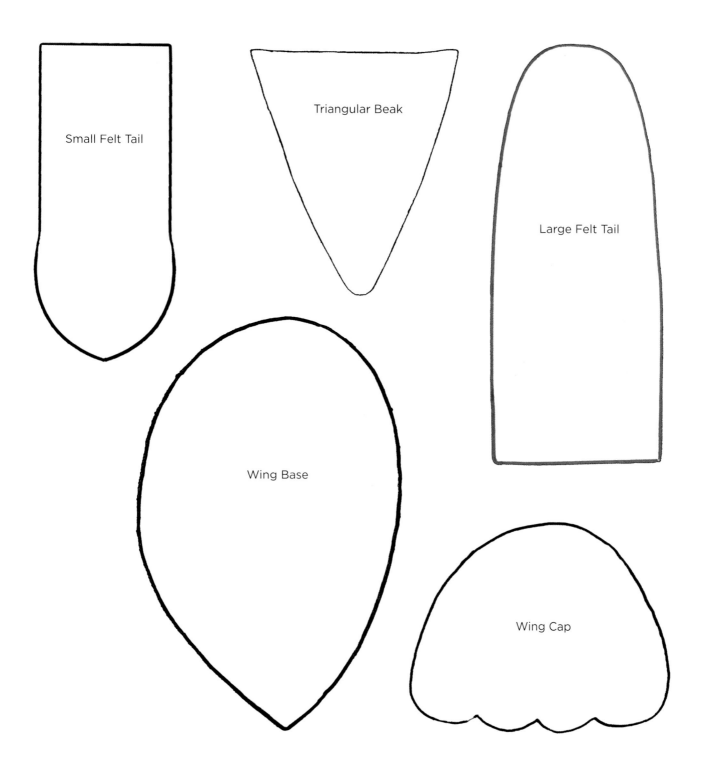

Small Felt Tail

Triangular Beak

Large Felt Tail

Wing Base

Wing Cap

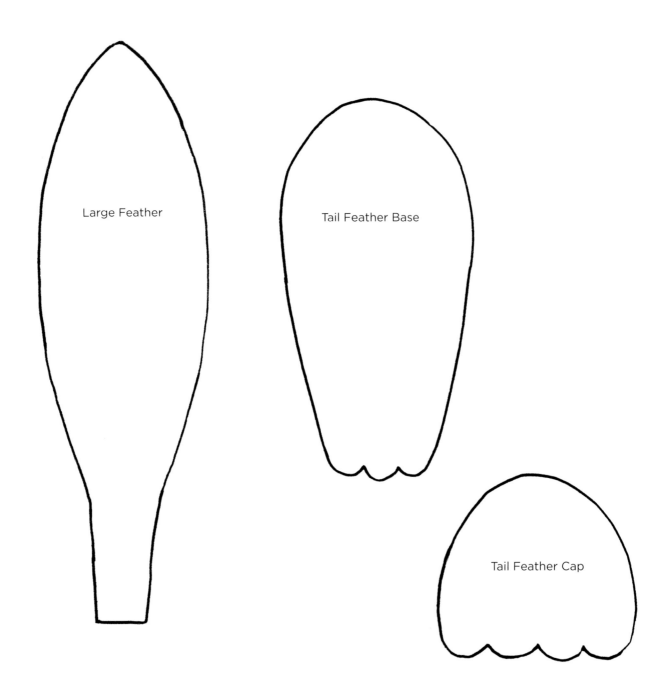

Large Feather

Tail Feather Base

Tail Feather Cap

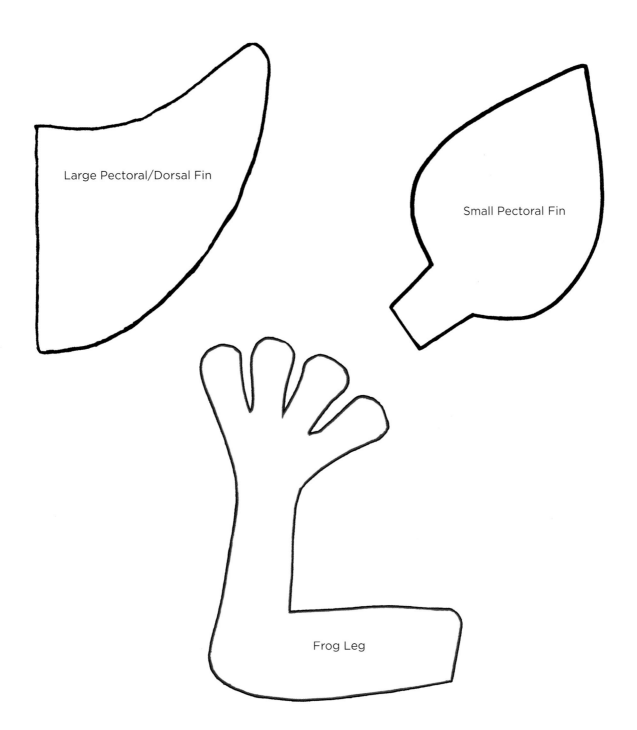

Large Pectoral/Dorsal Fin

Small Pectoral Fin

Frog Leg

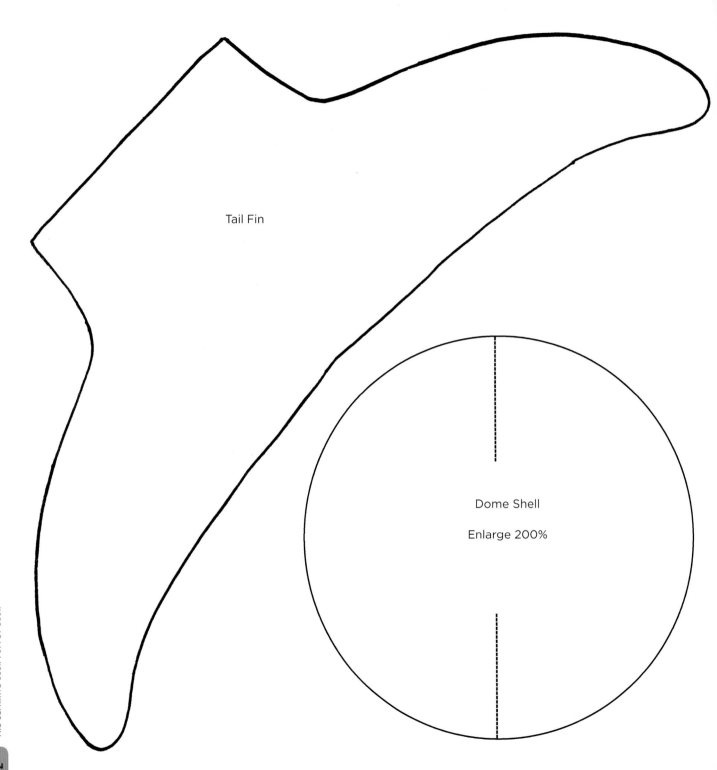

Tail Fin

Dome Shell

Enlarge 200%

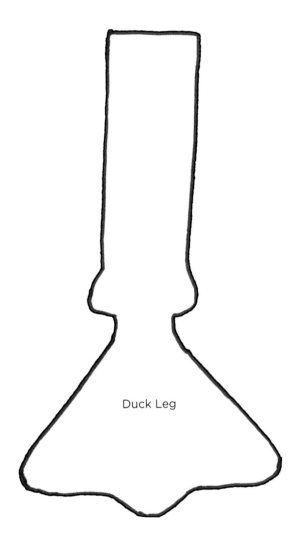

Duck Leg

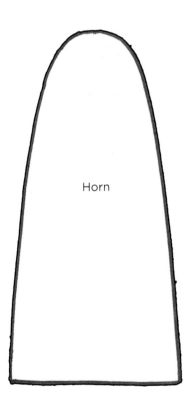

Horn

About the Authors

TIGER KANDEL is a multi-media artist and educator. She has an MS in art therapy and a BA in art history and child development. Tiger has designed and implemented numerous art workshops and puppet-making techniques for educational, recreational, and therapeutic venues. At times, she conducts professional development workshops educating others in her original methods of teaching puppet making and three-dimensional art to regular and special needs populations.

HEATHER SCHLOSS has an MS in art therapy and a BA in costume and theater design. A multimedia artist and designer, Heather is well versed in folk art, costuming, mask making, and puppet design and has incorporated her experiences in the theater and her knowledge of design history to create the highly detailed and fanciful look of Socketts®. She began developing educational art activities for preschool and kindergarten children while working in early childhood centers in Vermont and New York.